THE
MAMLUKS

THE
MAMLUKS
SLAVE WARRIORS
OF MEDIEVAL ISLAM

JOHN BRUNTON

AMBERLEY

First published 2023

Amberley Publishing
The Hill, Stroud
Gloucestershire, GL5 4EP

www.amberley-books.com

Copyright © John Brunton, 2023

The right of John Brunton to be identified as
the Author of this work has been asserted in
accordance with the Copyright, Designs and
Patents Act 1988.

ISBN 978 1 3981 0734 2 (hardback)
ISBN 978 1 3981 0735 9 (ebook)

British Library Cataloguing in Publication Data.
A catalogue record for this book is available
from the British Library.

1 2 3 4 5 6 7 8 9 10

Typesetting by SJmagic DESIGN SERVICES, India.
Printed in the UK.

CONTENTS

AUTHOR'S NOTE

So that this book may be easier to read for those unfamiliar with Islamic history, there will be no attempt at Arabic phonetics. All names are written in the form in which they can be most easily understood. Similarly, Christian chronology will be used throughout. For the curious, the appendices offer some guidance concerning both.

As is common practice, there is a need to distinguish between 'Mamluk' and 'mamluk'. When spelled with a capital letter, 'Mamluk' refers to the military ruling class, and to the regime controlling Egypt and Syria in the period covered. A 'mamluk' is an individual freed slave soldier. This convention will be used throughout the book.

INTRODUCTION

In the centuries between the collapse of the Crusader states of the Levant and the rise of the Ottoman sultanate, one powerful and illustrious state dominated the Islamic Near East. The entire civilisation of medieval Islam came close to the edge of destruction when the Mongols sacked Baghdad. But the Mamluks, a cadre of freed slave-soldiers, seized control in Egypt and ruled that land and Syria, fighting off attacks first from the west and then the east. Under their rule the region first flourished and then sank into a long decline, marked by the Ottoman conquest of 1517. Even then, the Mamluks survived as vassals of the new empire, lasting long enough to oppose Napoleon's invasion of Egypt in 1798 and only meeting their ultimate end through treachery.

Usually taken as slaves from the Turkish or Circassian homelands, these men were not only trained as soldiers but depended fully on those who owned them and would serve them long after they were freed; this bond made them more trustworthy than relatives. Throughout the Mamluk period most of those who served as senior *amirs* (officers), and most sultans, began their lives in Egypt as someone else's personal property.

It was a harsh regime, with treachery and usurpation rife, and the native populations suffered heavily from high taxation and oppressive treatment. Colourful as the history of the Mamluks was, the deepest stain was blood red. The majority of its sultans came to the throne by usurpation; treason and rebellion were commonplace, and carnage part of daily life. But in this cruel period the Mamluks saved Islam from devastation by the Mongols, brought the Crusader states to an end and built a powerful empire of their own. Mamluk patronage of religion and the arts brought significant progress, and the buildings they commissioned rank among the world's most impressive architectural achievements.

This book illustrates an underrated episode in history, and its importance both at the time and since. The gap between the Crusades and the Ottoman threat to Europe requires further understanding and debate.

I

BEFORE THE MAMLUKS

For most of its recorded history, from the most ancient times to the July Revolution of 1952, the rulers of Egypt were always foreigners, or the descendants of foreigners. In this context the Mamluks appear as yet another dynasty of outlanders, if perhaps the most outlandish of all. Throughout the same period, Syria was often linked with Egypt. Rather than the modern state of that name, this term describes the region between the Levantine coast and the Euphrates, often called 'Greater Syria'. The history of Syria often ran closely with that of Egypt, and so it was in the time of the Mamluks.

As early as 4500 BC there was a form of settlement on the banks of the Nile, with the Ancient Egyptian civilisation rising on the union of Upper and Lower Egypt more than a thousand years later. The empire of the Pharaohs fell into a long decline over the next two millennia, being conquered by the Ethiopians in 715 BC and the Assyrian empire a century later. The Egyptians, however, regained their independence after a short time, and held it until 525 BC when Egypt became a province of the Persian empire.

Until the twentieth century, no Egyptian of native stock would rule their people.

Persian hegemony came to an end in 331 BC when Alexander the Great wrested both Egypt and Syria from them, later adding Persia itself to his conquests. For Alexander, Egypt was a prized possession: he had himself crowned pharaoh and built his great city at the edge of the Nile Delta, and Alexandria would be the administrative capital of Egypt for almost a thousand years. After Alexander's death in 323 BC his general Ptolemy became pharaoh, as did his descendants in turn. Over the next two centuries the Ptolemaic kingdom itself was eclipsed by the growing influence of Rome. In the first century BC, Rome arrived in strength in the person of Julius Caesar. Finally, in 30 BC, on the death of Cleopatra, Caesar's successor Augustus turned Egypt into a Roman province.

The Mediterranean having become a Roman lake, the Roman empire continued to grow. Over the following five centuries Rome rose to its peak, embraced Christianity, fell into decline and finally came apart as Germanic tribes settled its western lands in the fifth century AD. Despite the collapse of the western half, however, the Eastern Roman empire survived for another millennium, mutating into the Greek-speaking cultural entity centred on Constantinople which historians now call the Byzantine empire. Early in this period, both Egypt and Syria were lost to the Byzantines. When the Byzantines were busy fighting off a brief Persian occupation of eastern territories including Egypt and Syria, a new challenger emerged. In Mecca and Medina, the Prophet Muhammad was preaching of the One God and His revelations. Shortly after Muhammad's death in 632, his Arab armies entered both the lands the Byzantines and those of the Persians. Through conquest the Muslims were able to create the conditions necessary for their new faith to spread.

Soon after defeating the Byzantines at the Battle of the Yarmuk in 638, the Arabs took control of Syria. The cities of Palestine would follow during the next few years, some surrendering after long sieges. With the way into Egypt clear, there was little time lost in its conquest; the commander Amr ibn al-As, who led the Egyptian expedition, met little resistance. Under the Byzantine officials, taxes had been high and the native Coptic churches had been persecuted for maintaining the Monophysite doctrine of the single (and human) nature of Christ, which the Church in Constantinople had condemned as heresy. As in Syria, Monophysites and Jews had been accused of collaborating during the recent Persian occupation and had suffered reprisals when the Byzantines returned. The Egyptians therefore had little reason to be loyal to the emperor, and Amr took Egypt by 642 with very little blood spilled in its defence. He set up his base on the right bank of the Nile, a little upriver of the division of the delta. This settlement, known as Fustat ('the Camp' or 'the Ditch'), became the first Arab capital of Egypt.

The Egyptian people accepted their new masters with little dissent. The Muslims brought an atmosphere of religious tolerance in this early period, which was a welcome relief from the dogmatic conflicts of the Byzantine world. The *jizya*, a poll tax for non-Muslims, was lower than any the Greeks levied. Many Copts even volunteered in 645 to assist in the defence of Egypt against a Byzantine naval invasion which sought to regain the lost province. Egypt settled into life as a Muslim country, and Muslims grew in number both through Arab settlement and native conversion.

For over a century, Arab expansion continued – westward across North Africa and into Spain, eastward through Persia and into central Asia – but at the same time Islam was divided by quarrels over who should be Caliph, or successor to the Prophet as leader of the Muslim community. In 644, after the murder of Umar, the second Caliph, who had launched the early conquests, the succession was disputed and dubiously resolved by appointing Uthman in his place. When Uthman was in turn assassinated in 656, there was a civil war between his supporters and those of the fourth Caliph, Ali, and this continued until

660 when the Umayyads, Uthman's family, defeated their enemies and established a hereditary caliphate at Damascus. The followers of Ali, who later adopted different religious views, formed the Shi'ite branch of Islam. After the Umayyads had been caliphs for almost a century, a revolt in 749, supported by non-Arab Muslims, brought the Abbasid clan to power. Descending from an uncle of the Prophet, the Abbasid caliphs exercised a far more authoritarian regime than the Umayyads from their capital of Baghdad, which they built on the Tigris. They held the titles of Caliph and Commander of the Faithful for many centuries.

Egypt played no large part in these events. A governor appointed by the Caliph resided at Fustat, sending an annual tribute to the capital. But in the ninth century, from the time of Caliph Harun-ar-Raschid, the authority of the Caliphate over all Islam was obviously weakening and independent Muslim princes established hereditary states throughout the Islamic lands. The Caliph of Baghdad still commanded respect as the supreme authority, but that was all.

In 868 Egypt became virtually independent in this manner when its governor, Ahmad ibn Tulun, son of a Turkish ex-slave soldier, ceased to report to Baghdad. He ended the annual tribute, instead using the revenues to finance grandiose building projects. He built a new city, known as *al-Qitai* ('the Wards' or 'Concessions'), to the north of Fustat. The mosque he also built in Fustat survives as a distinctive example of early Islamic architecture. With his large army of slaves, Ibn Tulun went on to become a serious military contender; he added most of Syria to his domain, and proved powerful enough to intervene at one point in a dispute for the succession to the Caliphate. Ibn Tulun's death in 884 was followed by a hereditary dynasty, but neither his son nor his two grandsons proved successful rulers and the Tulunids only lasted the three generations. In 905, shortly after the last of the line was murdered, an Abbasid army invaded Egypt and restored rule from Baghdad.

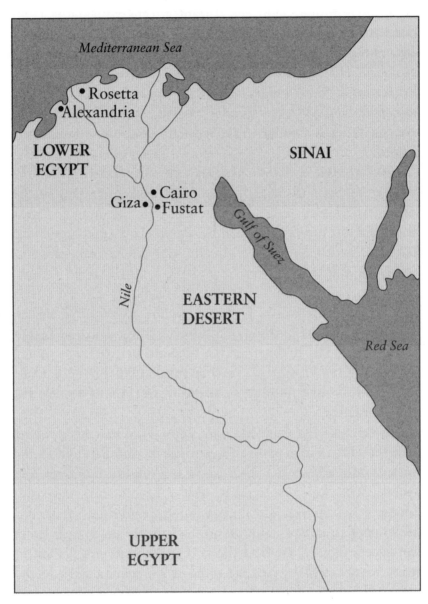

Egypt from the seventh century.

Having regained Egypt, Baghdad was soon forced to allow its new governors virtual autonomy, with the Caliphate still weakening. Muhammad ibn Tughj, an energetic amir from Transoxiana, took control in 933 and with the Caliph's blessing took the title of *ikhshid*, or prince, after which his dynasty is named. His two sons followed him in this dignity, as next did Kafur, a Nubian slave who had dominated the Ikhshidid administration after its founder's death. When Kafur himself died in 968 and famine weakened defences, a new conqueror arrived.

The Fatimids, a Shi'ite dynasty claiming descent from the Prophet through the marriage of his daughter Fatima to the Caliph Ali, carved out an empire in north Africa to the west of the Libyan desert from 909. Once secure in this region the Fatimids raided Egypt periodically, the Ikhshidids failing to supply an effective counter. In 969 the fourth Fatimid Caliph, al-Mu'izz, sent his general Jawhar, whose army entered Fustat with very little resistance. Preparing for the arrival of al-Mu'izz, Jawhar ordered the building of a new city to the north of Fustat. Mars being in the ascendant at the time, the new city was named *al-qahirah* ('The Victorious'), or Cairo as the West knows it. Once the Fatimid Caliph took up residence in 973, Cairo became the capital of Egypt.

The Fatimids too extended their dominance over Syria, along with the Holy Cities of Arabia, plus Sicily and Sardinia in the western Mediterranean. Once again magnificent buildings and majestic state occasions could be seen in Egypt, while trade with Europe was reopened. The regime was largely benign; there was no attempt to compel subjects to become Shi'ite, and at times Sunni, or orthodox, Muslims featured prominently in government service. An exception was the reign of the sixth Caliph of the line, al-Hakim, a psychopath whose harsh treatment of Jews and Christians, along with many meaningless atrocities, has seen him dubbed 'the Caligula of Islam'. Al-Hakim disappeared in 1021 while riding in the hills, probably murdered.

Al-Hakim's successors mostly came to the throne as minors and grew up into weak and effete rulers, often manipulated by corrupt, scheming Wazirs, or chief ministers. Economic reverses also took their toll. The native Egyptians, most of whom remained Sunni, had little affection for their Shi'ite masters. The Fatimids had by now suspended their push toward Baghdad, making the Nile region their centre of concern while the Seljuk Turks, now self-styled champions of Muslim orthodoxy, captured Syria. The North African lands, once the Fatimid heartland, declared themselves independent from Cairo and Sunni in their religious persuasion while the Mediterranean islands were also lost. Towards the end of the eleventh century there was a brief Fatimid revival, chiefly due to the efforts of a capable wazir and a son who succeeded him, which coincided with the fragmentation of the Seljuk sultanate after the death in 1092 of Sultan Malik Shah. The Fatimids regained Palestine for a short time before a new enemy appeared from an unexpected quarter and turned Palestine into a Christian kingdom.

The First Crusade was far from expected. The Franks, as the Muslims called all European Christians, arrived in the closing years of the eleventh century and found Syria divided into petty amirates. Having embarked on a mission to liberate the biblical lands from the Muslim infidels, they advanced haphazardly down the Levantine seaboard and finally captured Jerusalem in 1099. Europeans ruled in this region for the next two centuries, expanding their territory over the entire Syrian littoral region and through the Negev Desert to the Gulf of Aqaba. They created four states, known collectively as Outremer ('beyond the sea'): the Kingdom of Jerusalem, the Principality of Antioch and the counties of Tripoli and Edessa.

The Europeans imported their style of feudalism along with many other institutions. Edessa was lost early in this period when the Turkish amir of Mosul, Imad-ad-Din Zangi, captured nearly all of the region in 1146. The Second Crusade came from Europe in response, but failed to regain any territory and only increased

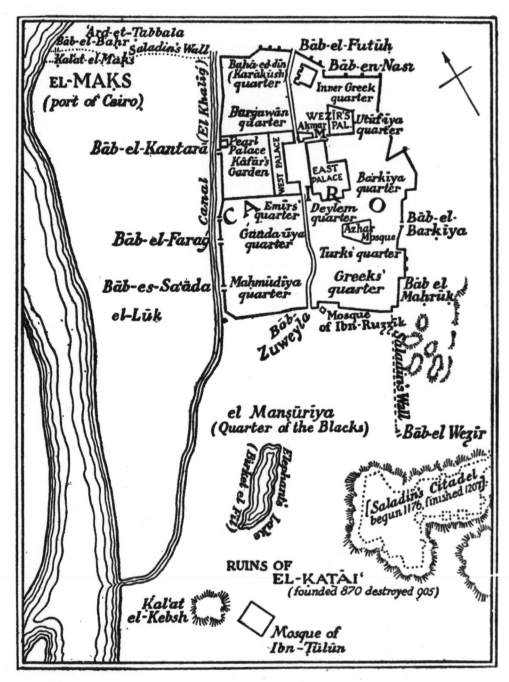

After Stanley Lane-Poole,. Plan of Cairo before 1200.

Muslim support for the Zangids by threatening Damascus. Zangi had died by this time, but his son Nur-ad-Din Mahmud added Damascus to his possessions in 1152. Nur-ad-Din continued his war on the Christians, reuniting all of Muslim Syria under his leadership in the process.

In Egypt, the decline of the Fatimids resumed. The Fatimids gave up the *imamate*, the divine leadership of Islam, thus losing what little credence they had. Violent coups on both the caliphate and the wazirate – eight in number between 1149 and 1163 – caused serious political instability and further loss of confidence. In Palestine, meanwhile, the Franks continued consolidating their territories. As the Zangid menace from the east persisted, they succeeded in reducing the remaining Fatimid coastal possessions to the south. In 1153, Ascalon, the last Fatimid stronghold in southern Palestine, finally fell. By the 1160s the Franks threatened Egypt itself, but by this time the situation had forced the three military powers to seek some compromise. Shi'ite Egypt was confronted by both Sunni Syria and Christian Outremer, and each of the three sought an alliance with one of the others against the third.

Although the Franks invaded Egypt several times, once even threatening Cairo, they eventually came to the conclusion that Nur-ad-Din was the more serious enemy. In Cairo successive wazirs intrigued with both Syrian powers, although the Caliph finally made an alliance with the Franks in 1167. But King Amalric I of Jerusalem betrayed this treaty. It may have been the wealth of Egypt that prompted him to attempt a major invasion of Cairo in 1168, but this proved disastrous in the long term when the Fatimid wazir appealed to Nur-ad-Din for help. The amir sent his Kurdish general Shirkuh at the head of a large army to intervene. Both Shirkuh and Amalric eventually agreed to withdraw, but Shirkuh and his army returned early the following year. The 1168 invasions proved crucial, for Nur-ad-Din was now seen by Egyptians as their protector against the infidel, and so demanded that Shirkuh be made wazir in Cairo. Al-Adid, the Fatimid Caliph, had no choice but to agree.

Three months later, in March 1169, there was a new development. Shirkuh, now virtually in control of Egypt, suddenly died. Command of the occupying army, and consequently the wazirs, now passed to Shirkuh's nephew and lieutenant, Salah-ad-Din Yusuf ibn Ayyub, or Saladin as the West knows him today. This Kurdish amir would stand out in Islamic history as a man of honour and attainment, showing himself to be a formidable soldier and an able administrator. Now in command of the vast resources of Egypt, he set himself three weighty tasks: suppress Shi'ism in Egypt, unite Egypt and Syria under a single ruler, and drive the Franks out of Syria.

In most of this he succeeded. As Caliph al-Adid lay dying in 1171, Saladin ordered that the *khutba*, the Friday prayers in the mosques of Egypt, be recited in the name of the orthodox Abbasid Caliph, and he then had it proclaimed that the Fatimid Caliphate had ended. The dying Caliph was never informed.

Saladin then set about several ambitious projects in Egypt. He vigorously persecuted Shi'ites, promoting Sunni religious teaching. He encouraged learning and the arts. He also had Cairo, Fustat and the Abbasid and Tulunid settlements between them enclosed by a great wall, and as part of this defence built a large citadel on an outcrop of the Muqattam Hills. This fortress, covering the eastern approach to Cairo, served as both a military and administrative headquarters and would also be the residence of Egypt's ruler from that time onwards.

Having set these schemes under way, Saladin soon left Egypt forever. In 1174 both Amalric and Nur-ad-Din died, each leaving his throne to a minor, and the new ruler was alive to the opportunity. Saladin spent the following years taking possession of the Zangid empire, with occasional battles against the Franks. By 1185 he had become undisputed ruler of all Muslim Syria and overlord of northern Iraq, Nubia, the Yemen and the Hijaz. The Abbasid Caliph in Baghdad sent him a robe of honour and endorsed him as sultan of all Islam. Saladin now prepared to renew the *jihad*, or holy war, against the Franks of Outremer. By this time certain Frankish lords were breaking truces in their irresponsible and aggressive activities, and this gave Saladin the pretext he needed. Soon he could set off for a complete conquest.

In July 1187, Saladin defeated Guy of Lusignan, King of Jerusalem, at the Horns of Hattin. The entire army of Jerusalem was either killed or captured at that battle and few had been left to defend the cities. The Muslims regained Jerusalem within days, and most of Outremer quickly followed. A few Frankish strongholds persevered: most of the northern cities including Antioch, Tripoli and Tyre, the fortresses of Krak des Chevaliers, Safad and Tortosa, and a few others. Saladin was unable to complete his conquest, and although he continued to besiege these pockets of resistance, some remained intact until help came from Europe.

In 1191 the Third Crusade finally landed, distinguished by the size of its following and its three famous leaders, at least at the outset. The German Emperor Frederick Barbarossa drowned in a river in Asia Minor on the way, and King Philip Augustus returned to France early in the campaign; it was King Richard the Lionheart of England who commanded the crusade most of the time as the crusaders dwindled in number. Richard led the reconquest over some of the lost coastal territory but was unable to retake Jerusalem itself, and the crusade ended in September 1192 when Richard and Saladin agreed on peace at Ramleh. The Christians kept nearly all the Mediterranean coastline, the hinterland mostly remaining in Muslim hands. Frankish Syria thus survived in a much-reduced form for almost another century, into the Mamluk period.

Saladin died in Damascus a few months after Ramleh, bequeathing his empire to his family; thus the Ayyubid dynasty, named after Saladin's father, ruled over Egypt, Syria, northern Mesopotamia and the Yemen for nearly sixty years. In doing so they laid the foundations for the rise of the Mamluks. Saladin's sons and brother each took possession of a large region. One son, al-Aziz, inherited the title of sultan, but the Ayyubid sultanate was never again unified as in Saladin's time. At best it was a confederation of petty amirates, and at times its princes plotted and warred against each other. One branch of the family became dominant but none ever succeeded in regaining Saladin's empire in its entirety. As soon as Saladin's brother al-Adil, known to the Franks as Saphardin, installed himself in his inherited lands in northern Iraq he set about overthrowing his nephews. By expert intriguing he played them off one another, eliminating them in turn. By 1200, al-Adil had gained Egypt and most of Syria. Only in Aleppo did the direct line of Saladin continue.

Al-Adil brought some stability to the region, making more truces with the Franks than campaigns against them. He also promoted trade with Venice and Pisa, encouraging economic growth. But when he died in 1218 the lands were divided again between his sons. The eldest, al-Kamil, became sultan shortly before the Fifth Crusade landed in the Nile Delta and seized the port of Damietta (the Fourth had been redirected to Constantinople in 1204, dismembering the Byzantine empire). Even with the help of his brother al-Muazzam, who ruled in Damascus, al-Kamil failed to drive out the crusaders, although the crusade later collapsed when its leaders disagreed over terms and eventually withdrew from Egypt. Afterwards al-Kamil quarrelled with al-Muazzam and other Syrian Ayyubids. Such enmity among Muslim rulers reduced their threat to the Franks, who took advantage of this by regaining Ascalon, Safad, Beirut and other territories which Saladin had captured. In 1229 al-Kamil ceded Jerusalem to the German Emperor Frederick II, who claimed the crown of the kingdom in return for his aid against his Muslim relatives.

Al-Kamil's reign was mostly auspicious for his subjects. He too sought improved relations with the west and set about many building and irrigation schemes. There was some material prosperity, but at times famine and civil war wrought misery. Al-Kamil died in 1238 and his relatives fought another war for supremacy. Al-Adil Abu Bakr II, the designated heir, came under attack from an-Nasir Ismail, Amir of Damascus, and at the same time there appeared from exile al-Kamil's eldest son, as-Salih Najm-ad-Din Ayyub.

Although as-Salih met with a serious defeat in Palestine in 1239, where most of his army deserted and left him to be taken prisoner, he later returned to the fight. By 1240 as-Salih had won both Egypt and Damascus, laying claim to the sultanate and reigning for ten years as the last effective Ayyubid sultan. Many of his relatives refused to accept him as overlord and he was always in a state of conflict with the Ayyubid princes of Syria. The amir of Aleppo, an-Nasir Salah-ad-Din Yusuf, named after his illustrious forefather, considered himself the rightful heir to the empire; he was known as the 'little Saladin'. In 1244 as-Salih retook Jerusalem after Khwarezmian tribesmen, who had been his allies during the civil war, had occupied part of Palestine before As-Salih drove them out, grabbing Jerusalem from the Franks on the same campaign. Jerusalem remained a Muslim city until the twentieth century.

Apart from Syrian Ayyubids, Khwarezmian tribesmen and Franks, there was serious concern that the Mongols were moving closer. Although their progress was slow at this time, they had spread westward over the plain of Iran and reduced the Seljuk Turks of Anatolia to vassalage. It was felt that, sooner or later, Syria and Egypt would know the Mongols' exacting policy of unconditional surrender or total annihilation.

As-Salih built an elite military corps that proved the source of his strength. He had attempted to dispense with the feudal military system which had existed under his predecessors, and created a regular army, thus becoming less dependent on feudal amirates. His troops were freed slave-soldiers, or *mamluks*, highly trained and personally loyal to as-Salih. The practice of Muslim princes having mamluks in their retinues was already long established, their traditional role to provide a personal bodyguard. As-Salih's innovation was to raise a large contingent and to use them as his elite troops. The sultan's mamluks served him as a permanent military force on his campaigns, and sometimes as the nucleus of a larger army. Some were promoted to the senior grades of amir and became prominent in his government.

When as-Salih died, it was his mamluks who finally succeeded him. These were the men who would save Islam from the menace of the Franks and grant their master's wish to halt the Mongol conquests.

2

TURKS, SLAVES AND SOLDIERS

By the time as-Salih Ayyub began his project of raising a corps of mamluks there had already been an established mamluk system in the Islamic lands for several centuries. His significant innovations were the size of the corps he created and, to an extent, how he deployed it.

Although not all mamluks were Turks, there were more of this race than any other among them, at least in the early period. The Turks set the standards by which later mamluks developed, and long after Turks ceased to be in the majority the Mamluk sultanate was still known to its neighbours as *mulk-al-atrak*, the Kingdom of the Turks. The Turks came originally from Central Asia, close to the Mongol homelands near Lake Baikal, and closely resembled the Mongols in race, language and culture; they were a hardy, pugnacious people whose survival depended on their herds and the grazing grounds over which they often fought. Leadership among Turkish tribes was never clearly defined, and they appointed temporary leaders called *hans* to lead military campaigns and mediate in disputes over grazing rights.

Despite their unwillingness to form a nation, the Turks retained a similarity in language and culture; the language spoken in present-day Istanbul can be regarded as a dialect of those spoken by the Turkic peoples in Outer Mongolia and eastern Siberia.

In the second century BC, the Turkish migrations began. Having formed part of a short-lived Mongol empire in the sixth century AD, many moved westwards onto the Eurasian steppes when it fragmented. A number settled in the region known as Transoxiana, between the Oxus and Jaxartes rivers, which flow into the Aral Sea, to the north and east of what was then the Persian Sassanid empire. In Transoxiana there was created in AD 522 the first large Turkish nation. The Göktürk Khanate, as it was called, never developed further than a confederation of tribes paying nominal allegiance to a supreme chief. Within a generation this large khanate fragmented, although a remnant continued until 744. When the Arabs conquered Persia in the seventh century, Turks came increasingly into contact with the Islamic peoples, initially as enemies and trading partners. Once the Göktürk state collapsed, the Muslims advanced beyond the Oxus. For centuries afterwards, the Transoxiana region was the eastern frontier zone for Islam.

Turks were often seen in the Islamic lands from the ninth century onwards, both as slaves and free. Many served as mercenaries, and their reputation as ferocious warriors made them ideal recruits. The sources describe them as spending long hours on horseback, fighting furiously, showing expertise with the bow, and often sustaining all this over long periods with very little to eat. Some rose to senior ranks and gained important governorates.

In the mid-tenth century, a number of Turkish tribes withdrew from the Ghuzz confederacy in the lands north of Transoxiana and, having converted to Islam about that time, moved southwards. Taking advantage of the disunity of the Abbasid Caliphate, the Seljuk Turks carved out their own territory between the conflicting amirates of Persia and Khorasan. Once their leader Seljuk had organised them into an effective military force they set about conquest. A century later a successor of Seljuk had become ruler over lands from the Oxus to the Euphrates, and had even forced the powerless Caliph in Baghdad to grant him the title of sultan or `executive power' in return for his protection. As champions of Sunni Islam the Seljuks reconquered Syria, driving out the Fatimid heretics. In 1071 they defeated the Byzantine Emperor at Manzikert, beginning the extension of Islam into Anatolia and the spread of their own empire almost to the Bosporus.

When the Seljuk Sultan Malik Shah died in 1092, this empire fell apart as his sons contested the succession and saw the empire split into petty amirates centred on cities like Damascus, Aleppo or Mosul, each ruled by a Seljuk amir jealous and suspicious of his neighbours. Such a state of affairs made it easier for the Franks to progress through Syria during the First Crusade and eventually take possession of Jerusalem itself. Some of these petty principalities survived into the Mamluk period.

In the following centuries, the Ghuzz also migrated as they expanded their territories. Taking a westward movement across the steppes to the north of the Black and Caspian seas, they settled lands now in the Ukraine and Kazakhstan. In 1093 they besieged Kiev, making their way among the southern Russian principalities. They were known as Polovtsi to the Russians, and to the Byzantines as Cumans. Among these Turkish tribes of the steppes, one became known for its warlike qualities. The Kipchak (or Qipchaq) Turks, who lived by herding cattle in the lower Volga region, gained a reputation for their aggressive nature, even among their Turkish neighbours, and it was from the Kipchaks that many of the early Mamluks were recruited.

When Genghis Khan brought the Mongols westwards early in the thirteenth century, many steppe tribes were driven west before him. With the western steppes more crowded, fighting over grazing grounds broke out far more often than before. As a result, many Turkish prisoners of war came into the hands of Muslim slavers. The *ribats*, strongholds the Arabs had built on the frontiers and where slaves were often bought, saw unprecedented volumes of human merchandise. As time went on, and the Turks came to hear of the rich and plentiful land of Egypt and the prospects a Turkish slave could find there, parents in the Kipchak lands would often willingly sell their children into slavery. Children could be a liability in this harsh nomadic lifestyle, and enslavement promised far more than the steppes ever could.

The Prophet himself had sanctioned slavery but had emphasised that a Muslim must treat his slaves with compassion and kindness; it was the act of a pious Muslim to grant his slaves their freedom, an act that signified their adoption as his sons and daughters. Freed slaves could also rise to the highest positions: Tulun, whose son Ahmad became independent ruler of Egypt, and the Ikhshidid Kafur are two examples. The Slave Dynasty in India from 1206 to 1336 is also significant, overlapping chronologically with the Mamluks in Egypt, and their succession also often passed from master to ex-slave. Their first sultan was also called Aibak. There was always slavery in Islam; even in the present day, fundamentalist Islamic organisations such as ISIS and Boko Haram see fit to perpetuate the institution. For that matter, many Christian states also engaged in slavery in varying forms until the nineteenth century.

Using slaves as soldiers was only practised in Islamic societies, however, and began at the time of the early conquests. When questions arose as to what to do with the prisoners taken during Arab campaigns in Khorasan in the seventh century, Caliph Umar, mindful of the limits of military resources, ordered that they be enslaved and made to serve in the armies. The practice established, the Arabs used Khorasanians as slave soldiers and as they advanced eastwards tended to absorb Turks into their armies in the same way. As time went on, the armies of Islam were increasingly composed of non-Arab races, and Turks, both slave and free, were usually considered the best warriors.

As a further development, the Abbasid Caliphs became interested in the institution of *mawali* or freed slaves.

They observed that freedmen could be far more willing and trustworthy than most others, as gratitude towards whoever freed them made the mawali willing to give good service to their former masters. Once the bond of slavery was removed, another link – partially of gratitude, but also of dependence and the emotional tie of loyalty to one's redeemer – was substituted. In practice, a ruler could not always depend on his amirs or even family members to remain loyal, and might see them changing allegiance when it suited them, but at least in theory his *mawla* was far more dependable. With this in mind, when the Caliph al-Mu'tasim succeeded in 833 he developed this institution by building a corps of Turkish ex-slave soldiers to serve as his bodyguard. In doing so he began the mamluk system.

The word *mamluk* literally means 'one who is owned' and emphasises the relationship between slave and master. Al-Mu'tasim had slaves purchased as young boys, trained rigorously in the arts of war and instructed in the Muslim religion. On reaching early manhood, 'as soon as their beards were grown', they would be released. Al-Mu'tasim ensured that all his mamluks were first-generation slaves from Turkish and other races known for their prowess in warfare. He prevented his mamluks' sons from diluting the corps. Many of his men could not speak Arabic, and some never converted to Islam, but they were loyal to him alone.

In 838 they formed the core of al-Mu'tasim's army when he invaded Byzantine territory, but when not on campaign the mamluks terrorised the people of Baghdad. Their unruly and often violent behaviour eventually forced the Caliph to move his capital, and his mamluks, upriver to Samarra. Having promoted many of them to senior ranks and to high offices, al-Mu'tasim ruled through their willing service and when he died in 842 the mamluks continued to dominate the government. The caliphs who followed became their puppets, and the mamluks made and unmade caliphs as it suited them. Such events had striking parallels in Egypt centuries later.

In the centuries to follow, many Muslim princes emulated al-Mu'tasim's mamluk system. In the twelfth century both the Fatimids and the Zangids used mamluks, the latter with a wider military role than simply as bodyguards. When Shirkuh invaded Egypt in 1168 he brought large numbers of mamluks with him. Saladin had a force of 500 such soldiers, which he used for such tasks as scouting and ambushes as much as for elite combat. Also in 1168, his son al-Afdal invaded Frankish territory at the head of an army which included over 7,000 mamluks. At Hattin the only Muslim soldiers mentioned by the chroniclers as doing outstanding service were mamluks. Throughout the Ayyubid period, Turks, both free and freed, figured highly in military and government service. Al-Kamil's time saw an increase in their importance, often at the expense of the Kurds. The practice of raising mamluks became commonplace, and they were often involved in the intrigues between Ayyubid princes in this period. In view of such developments it was not as much an innovation when as-Salih Ayyub set about building his private regiment of mamluks.

As early as 1229, as-Salih, then al-Kamil's heir and deputy in Cairo, became interested in raising this mamluk army. Although such a practice was established at the time, the Ayyubid armies were mostly composed of levied troops commanded by Kurdish amirs who might change sides during intrigues. As-Salih was attracted to the idea of a regiment using the mamluk system that would produce not only highly trained soldiers but those who would remain loyal to him personally. It has been suggested that he was not only thinking of his own ambitions: the Mongols were shown to be gradually moving westwards again, which was a horrifying prospect. At some point in the future, it was reasoned, the Mongols would threaten the Ayyubid sultanate and a strong military force would be much in need. As-Salih chose mainly Kipchak Turks, as they were considered the most pugnacious and the hardiest of soldiers, and Kipchaks were available in large numbers in the Egyptian slave markets at that time.

As-Salih's activities came to a halt in 1234 when his stepmother, seeking to advance her own son by al-Kamil, persuaded the sultan that as-Salih's actions were made in preparation to overthrow him. Al-Kamil had as-Salih exiled to a fortress in northern Iraq, his half-brother replacing him as heir. Without the resources, as-Salih was unable to go on building his mamluk army; by the time his father died in 1238 he had only eighty mamluks. Yet these eighty stayed with him; even during the 1239 campaign, when all others deserted him, the mamluks willingly went into captivity with as-Salih. When he Salih finally became sultan in 1240, he renewed his efforts to build his following of mamluks, now further convinced of their worth. His wealth as sultan made it possible to buy hundreds of boy slaves every year, and as amirs died or forfeited property in disgrace as-Salih also took possession of their un-freed mamluks. Three future sultans, Aibak, Baibars and Qalawun, came into his possession as forfeits. As-Salih gradually placed his mamluks in senior military and government positions, raising several to the ranks of the foremost amirs, and displacing Kurdish amirs in the process. One of the most prominent at this time was Baibars the Elder, his title distinguishing him from the sultan Baibars al-Bunduqdari. This Baibars proved an able military commander, until he traitorously allied with the Khwarezmians in 1244. He was later arrested and died in prison.

At first the sultan's followers were known as the *Salihi* mamluks, as was customary, but a short while later they gained another name by which they were more often known. Due to the Salihis terrorising the people of Cairo with their violence, robbery and other brutal excesses, the sultan built a complex on Roda, an island in the Nile, at that time some distance from the city. It included a barracks and a palace, and as-Salih lived there with his mamluks, preferring this to the Citadel. As the Egyptians often speak of the Nile as a sea, calling it *Bahr-an-Nil*, the men based on Roda became known as the *Bahri* ('sea' or 'river') mamluks. The name remained with them, especially after the creation much later of the *Burji* ('tower' or 'citadel') mamluks.

The Bahri regiment continued to recruit using the same methods, only in a slightly modified form after their benefactor's death. From that time nearly all those who ruled Egypt (apart from the sons of the sultans) or rose to powerful office had first arrived as captives and had served a long apprenticeship as slaves. Power and wealth usually passed from one generation of freed slaves to the next, a mamluk often marrying his patron's widow, this practice continuing until the nineteenth century. In fact, as-Salih began an unbroken line of mamluk recruitment that lasted six centuries.

The boys, usually sold into slavery in their homelands, would be transported by a slave trader, often a Persian, to the slave markets of Cairo or sometimes to a Syrian town. Buyers might look for one with the makings of a soldier and one such would usually bring a good price, roughly 800 dinars in the early period, although the Mamluk sultan Qalawun took pride in having fetched a thousand when he was a boy. In later times their values were much lower; the sultan Qait Bey was originally bought for just 80 dinars.

In Cairo the sultan's slave buyer had the first choice on all for sale, and as-Salih and his successors snapped up the best boys on offer. Once purchased for the sultan the slaves would be placed in the *tibaq*, or training schools. The tibaq may have appeared in the time of Baibars I, and there is no information on how as-Salih trained his mamluks. In Baibars' time there were twelve tibaq, each designed for 1,000 trainees. The boys slept on rush mats in dormitories of twenty-five each under the supervision of an educated and trusted eunuch. They were often given new names on enslavement, although there were some exceptions. They might also be entrusted individually to an older mamluk who acted as their counsel and friend, a relationship which sometimes lasted long after their release. In the first few years their training consisted of religious teaching and some elementary education. They were taught the Quran, the Shari'a, prayers and Arabic script, together with a little Arabic language. Discipline was severe. The boys seldom left the *tabaqa*, and always returned by nightfall. All transgressions were severely punished.

Having gained a thorough religious education, and approaching adulthood, the boy would begin training as a *faris* or trooper. In the military school at Cairo he would first learn the arts of horsemanship. Many Turkish boys may have ridden before. Each mamluk would be trained in all forms of equitation, riding horseback without harness, leaping onto a galloping horse, and complicated movements in formation where several horsemen would move as a well-coordinated team. Once all this was mastered the aspiring faris would next be taught the use of the lance, to wield it with pinpoint accuracy. Afterwards he was trained in the use of the bow, and then the sword. A faris would be expected to use all three weapons on horseback while remaining in full control of his steed. Only after such a long and rigorous training had produced a high degree of proficiency could a mamluk, now approaching manhood, be granted his freedom and enlisted as a faris of the sultan's army.

On receiving his *'itaqa*, or certificate of release from slavery, the young mamluk's situation changed dramatically. Having owned nothing for so many years, he was now given a horse, armour and weapons and was put on the sultan's payroll. He was also granted a feudal holding, at this stage usually the income from half an Egyptian village. He received food and fodder rations and occasional gifts of horses or camels, and would return to the tabaqa every month to be paid.

After almost a decade of such a process, the result was not only a well-trained soldier, a light cavalryman skilled at arms and tactics, but one whose mind had been indelibly conditioned with Muslim religious values but retaining the traits typical of their homelands: hardness, self-sufficiency, ruthlessness, and above all else loyalty to the sultan. Their eventual release was the most important event in this entire process. Their gratitude towards whoever freed them was calculated to instil in them unquestioning loyalty. A mamluk would gladly serve his former master in war and peace. His loyalties could not be diverted. There was also a bond among *khushdashin*, or barrack comrades, who had been slaves, trainees and soldiers together, though it was not as strong as that between masters and former slaves, and it was often broken when power struggles emerged. It was nonetheless important, especially where political groupings are concerned; to a lesser extent than his own mamluks, an amir could rely on his own khushdashin. The bonds formed in the barracks often dictated relationships and alignments for a lifetime.

Yet, with a note of cynicism, one could question whether such bonds of gratitude would maintain the complete loyalty of an ex-slave once he had been released. After all, every faris would wonder what good it would do him to remain his master's loyal follower now that he was his own man again. However, the mamluk system proved very effective in practice. To be a mamluk of the sultan, or at least of a senior amir, was desirable and carried material advantages and a measure of power. He would depend on his lord for rewards, which meant increased material means and positions of authority if he served well. To be without such patronage was to his disadvantage and there were few alternative openings, and this would leave him with no means of his own. To serve his former owner was therefore in a mamluk's interest. He could of course make the journey back to his homeland, but this was not very appealing when so much was possible in Egypt and Syria.

As one major paradox of this system, a mamluk could become very rebellious if he stood to lose something. There are isolated instances of mamluks turning on their patrons, in some cases even killing them. Such incidents were regarded with horror at the time but were by no means impossible. The bond could thus be broken by mismanagement and cruelty on the patron's side, or in a few cases by the sheer ingratitude of his mamluks. 'Even his own mamluks deserted him' became a phrase used to suggest a man was in a truly sorry state.

Even after his lord's death, when a mamluk was free to seek service elsewhere, loyalty to his memory often continued. As one noted example, the Bahri sultan Qalawun continued to style himself *as-Salihi*, over thirty years after as-Salih's death. Many mamluks upheld the cause of their patron's heirs, although in many cases they supplanted them afterwards.

The mamluks of amirs had fewer opportunities than those of the sultan. There was no provision for their military training. Some might enter the royal service but find themselves considered inferior to those raised in the tibaq. There were exceptions to this rule: Aibak, Baibars and others became sultan having previously belonged to Ayyubid amirs. It was often a severe punishment for a sultan's un-freed mamluk to be given to an amir. At least in the later period an amir's mamluk would have a vested interest in their patron becoming sultan, which would place him in line for advancement.

Life for the common faris was usually harsh and obscure, with few rewards, and many never advanced beyond this point. Promotion could only come after he had proved himself many times over. Those who attained the rank of amir needed to have shown special ability and prowess. If a mamluk gained the sultan's personal interest at an early stage he may be taken into the royal household, to serve as a page or other familiar. The *khassikiya*, or corps of pages, effectively became an officer training school, and whoever completed a term of such service was automatically created an amir. In the later Mamluk period the sultan's household was the usual route of advancement to amir, and the ranks increasingly less so. Too often a mamluk then served as a sultan's familiar before taking up a senior command without any real military experience. Many prominent amirs throughout this time continued to be known by their former household positions. Baibars al-Jashnakir and Yalbugha al-Khassiki were always, as their titles show, remembered as having been respectively a taster and a page in their sultans' intimate service.

If a mamluk became an officer, he would usually be created an Amir of Ten, or of the first class as it was known. He would have certain responsibilities including commanding troops on campaign, would gain a larger feudal holding, and would be eligible for a number of positions in government. He was also expected to raise and maintain at his own expense ten mamluks, who would ride with him in combat. At the next stage the rank of Amir of Forty, or of the second class, could be attained where the amir's income and responsibilities were further increased. This class was also known as that of Amir of Drums, for this was the lowest rank at which an amir was allowed to have a contingent of drummers, and possibly other musicians, in his following who went into battle with him and played outside his house in the evenings. The senior Mamluk amirs would have large military bands, according to their standing, and it would often be a status symbol for one to have a larger band than another.

The highest class of amir was that of One Hundred, although the same rank is often referred to as Amir of One Thousand. This was because on a major campaign an Amir of One Hundred would be expected to command 900 *halaqa*, or auxiliary troops, together with his own hundred mamluks. It was often known as *amir mi'a muqaddam alf*, indicating both numbers.

Of this senior class there were never more than two dozen at any one time. They would serve as viceroys, army commanders and regents and after 1250 they could regard themselves as contenders for the sultanate. Such amirs were rich and powerful: they could, by a system of alliances and intrigues, control the government. Each had a private army of loyal mamluks, and some could raise vast military resources for either war or rebellion.

There also existed the grade of Amir of Five. This was in fact an honorary rank, awarded to veteran mamluk soldiers after long service, or to relatives of the sultan or of the most powerful amirs.

Although Turks have mostly been discussed up to this point, it must again be emphasised that the corps of Mamluks was by no means entirely composed of Turks. In the earlier period the

Kipchaks were considered the best for this purpose, and their character and prowess set the standards that other mamluks were expected to meet. But from the time of the original Salihi mamluks onwards there were other races. The Circassians, a pastoral people from the Caucasus mountains, formed the second-largest ethnic group and in the late fourteenth century, when Turks were not so easily found in the slave markets, the Circassians replaced the Turks almost entirely. As a race they were different in character from the Turks, but from that time the Mamluks were mostly Circassians. There were also many Mongols and Anatolians. The sultan Kitbugha and the regent Salar were both Mongols, the sultan Lajin was described as a 'Greek' and was probably an Anatolian, and the later sultan Timurbugha was said to have been an Albanian. Fifteenth-century European travellers to Egypt claimed to have spoken to mamluks of Italian, German and Hungarian origin. After the Ottoman conquest, Bosnian and Armenian mamluks are mentioned in the sources.

Whatever their origins the mamluks all had Turkish names, either original or given, and spoke Turkish in the Kipchak dialect throughout the period. There are cases on record of men from the central Islamic lands adopting Turkish names and bribing traders to sell them in Egypt, so that they may rise through the opportunities of Turkish mamluks. The practice of men voluntarily entering slavery in Egypt is not unusual. When Qusun came as ambassador to Cairo from the Mongol Khan of the Golden Horde, he persuaded Sultan an-Nasir Muhammad to buy him, and his price was sent to his nearest relative. Qusun later became an important Mamluk amir in an-Nasir's service.

Mamluks wore a distinctive dress that comprised a kind of military uniform. Over a shirt and trousers they wore a kind of surcoat with a diagonal stripe of hemline running from the left shoulder to the right hip. This was known as a Tatar coat, as distinct from a Turkish coat which had a stripe running from the opposite shoulder. They wore boots of yellow leather in the winter, and of white leather in summer. Over these they wore a kind of overshoe. They also sported a variety of hats. In the early period they wore the *kalauta*, a triangular hat trimmed with fur, either yellow (the heraldic colour of the regime as a whole) or yellow and red, and this was then the badge of the Mamluk military class. At other times turbans were worn, as was a conical hat with an upturned brim called a *saraqui*. Drawings of Mamluks made by European visitors in the early sixteenth century show them wearing a kind of tall busby. Ceremonial dress was much more elaborate. A sultan would wear the black robe of the Abbasids on his investiture, and new positions and honours conferred were symbolised by clothing with a robe of honour. There were many variations in regalia in the public ceremonies.

The Mamluks had a distinctive form of heraldry. This was by no means unique in Islam – it is suggested that the Franks first learned heraldry from the Muslims – but it played an important part in public life. It was a primitive system in which insignia was either derived from office or personally chosen. It never developed along the lines of complicated rules and royal control as it did in Europe. Amirs who had served in the sultan's household simply used the badge of their former office. The armourbearer would take the symbol of the sword, the secretary the pen-box, the marshal a horseshoe, the cupbearer the cup, and so on. On one occasion at least the sultan himself invested them with their device: when as-Salih made Aibak at-Turkmanni his taster, he presented him with the device of a table. All other evidence suggests that heraldry was an informal affair. There were individual exceptions; for instance, heraldic animals are in evidence. Baibars al-Bunduqdari used the lion, or panther. There are feline figures on everything he built, and on his coins. Qalawun used the duck. These could have been chosen as 'canting arms' in reference to their names (Baibars means 'Lord Panther' and 'Qalawun' is similar in sound to the Turkish word for duck). Generally, however, Mamluk heraldry was based on badges of royal offices. In the later period political factions used these motifs for group identification, and such symbols appear everywhere in the art and architecture of the period.

Even though it was the language of the native population and the administration, few Mamluks could speak much Arabic and so they relied heavily on a small pool of Turkish interpreters. Fewer still, at least in the early period, were literate, with most only able to sign their own names in Arabic script. The later sultan Inal could not even do this; his secretary had to write it down for him to trace. Yet there are many exceptions. The Bahri Amir Baisari was noted for his devotion to literature and his great library. Some of the Circassians of the later period gained a good education, and a few studied for diplomas in Islamic law and theology.

When not on active service, mamluks were expected to practice their military skills daily and to take up related sports such as polo or archery. Many would aspire to be awarded the coveted status of *mu'allim*, master of one of the four military arts. Mamluk training was a popular spectator sport for many Egyptians. However, as we have seen, off-duty Mamluks were often unruly and predatory, terrorising the native population, pillaging and raping women and young boys. Although alcohol is forbidden in Islam many mamluks showed a fondness for drink, particularly *kumiz*, fermented mare's milk. In the fifteenth century, as discipline deteriorated, it was quite common to see Mamluk troopers rioting on the least pretext, often inebriated. Given the boisterous nature of most mamluks, a wise sultan would send them on campaign or other military activities whenever possible, although others sought to appease the troops with indulgence.

In matters of religion, many Mamluks showed a zeal typical of new converts. Particularly after rising to wealth and power they gave much in effort and money towards the benefit of Islam. The medieval city of Cairo is full of religious buildings commissioned by Mamluks, with mosques and foundations both educational and charitable much in evidence, including some of the most beautiful buildings in the world. Many amirs and sultans made large donations to charitable causes, and at times distributed money to the poor. Despite the harsh and predatory nature of the Mamluk regime, there were many sultans and amirs much loved by the people for their piety and generosity. In their later years some Mamluks gave up their military and political careers to become dervishes and holy men.

Mamluks were not allowed to intermarry with the Egyptians, although sultans sometimes married daughters of *qadis* (judges) or wazirs. Some took former slave girls as wives, although many preferred the barracks for a home and saw marriage as upsetting their lifestyle. Homosexual acts were commonplace, often between amirs and their mamluks. Many of the sultans' pages probably gained their advancement in this way. One of the duties of the eunuchs of the tibaq was to keep the boys isolated from adult mamluks. They produced comparatively few children, fewer still of whom survived to adulthood – children born to foreigners in Egypt seldom lived long.

The sons of mamluks were barred from entering the Mamluk corps itself. They were known as the *awlad-an-nas* ('the sons of the people') but were still considered part of the military class and usually formed the elite corps of the halaqa. Some became scholars, as many Mamluk amirs had their sons thoroughly educated. A few sons of amirs became amirs themselves, but this was by no means a common practice. The exception was always the son of the sultan, who would become sultan himself, at least theoretically. The awlad-an-nas formed a link between the Mamluks and the native population. They had Arabic names and lived like Egyptians. They were a class in an awkward position, disinherited from their fathers' possibilities. Those of the awlad-an-nas who rose to prominence often did so in the sphere of learning. The best example is Ibn Taghri Birdi, son of a prominent Anatolian Mamluk amir, who distinguished himself as a historian having served in his younger days as a halaqa officer and an Amir of Five. Ibn Taghri Birdi's writings are an important historical source on the Circassian period.

The Mamluk institution was essentially one of relationship and conditioning. An adult mamluk was not a slave in the sense usually understood, and not strictly a free man either, but a legally freed man, whose psychology had been moulded by his adolescence in slavery. The mamluks could have left for their homelands any time after release; there was a certain amount of free will involved in their roles. It would be simplistic to see the relationship between mamluk and former master as motivated by gratitude over being freed. Whoever freed the slave was essentially a patron on whom the mamluk depended for sustenance and further advancement once freed, and the same patron knew that his mamluks followed him in part out of self-interest, for who trusted any mamluk other than his own? The story of the Mamluks explores many a variation on this theme.

By creating the Bahri regiment, as-Salih gained what he wanted. His mamluks served him loyally as the most effective soldiers and governors, and although revolt was not unknown he could trust them far more than Kurdish amirs and his own relatives. His governance was effective and he feared less from intriguing and rebellion, while his military successes against his Syrian relatives were encouraging. The Bahris remained close to their sultan, loyal to him and to each other, and reaped the benefits for as long as he lived.

But as in all mortal endeavours, this could not last forever. When their patron died or fell from power, a mamluk's fortune radically changed. Whoever succeeded him could only rely on the loyalty of his own mamluks and would seek to put them in the place of the existing cadre. At such a juncture, the struggle between the *status quo* and the interlopers dictated the political developments of such times. When as-Salih died in 1250, it would have implications for the entire Islamic world.

3

FROM AL-MANSURA TO AIN JALUT

The transformation of the Salihi Mamluks from the sultan's loyal followers to the rulers of the most powerful state in Islam owed more to circumstances than to design. In the decade spanning 1250 and 1260, they would fight off two serious attacks on Islamic civilisation, one from the West and one from the East, and bring down the fragmented Ayyubid empire. It was this moment that brought about the Mamluk sultanate.

In the twelfth and thirteenth centuries the practice of crusading, of furthering the cause of Christianity by force of arms, was lauded in Europe. The First Crusade had gained Jerusalem and much other territory by 1099, founding four states that were effectively colonies of European Christendom as the Seljuk state fragmented. The Second and Third were called when the Muslims took back land from the Franks, and after 1192 only a remnant of the Frankish states remained. There were several subsequent crusades, and many knights and soldiers undertook to go east and fight the good fight over the next century, but with little lasting result.

In June 1249 the Seventh Crusade landed in the Nile Delta, quickly seizing Damietta, the port at the mouth of the largest eastern branch of the river, and the Christian army then marched south. At the head of this host rode King Louis IX of France, a prince whose piety was already proverbial and who would be canonised after his death. Having recovered from a serious illness, the future Saint Louis had vowed to give thanks by taking the Cross; Jerusalem had been wrested from the Christians once again, and Louis was determined to regain it.

Over five years Louis raised a large army. Most were French knights, including the young Jean de Joinville who later wrote an account of the expedition. There was also a large English contingent, and members of the monastic military orders of the Temple and of the Hospital, but despite all his efforts support for the crusade was muted at best. The kings of England, Norway and Hungary were canvassed but were otherwise occupied, as was the Holy Roman Emperor. The initial intention was to follow the strategy laid out by Richard the Lionheart and previously attempted during the Fifth Crusade: occupy the Nile Delta, the centre of wealth and supply for the Ayyubid sultanate, and thereby regain Jerusalem by terms of surrender. It is likely that the early successes of the campaign caused the crusaders to rethink their objectives and Louis may have then decided that an outright conquest of Egypt was possible; he certainly treated Damietta like a conquered city. He actually came very close to capturing Cairo for Christendom, and could have seriously damaged Islamic civilization given the situation of the time.

Sultan as-Salih Ayyub had been aware of the planned invasion for a long time, but he was busy campaigning in Syria against his relative an-Nasir Yusuf, who ruled in Aleppo, when he heard that the crusader fleet was under sail. He hurried back to Egypt but was too late to prevent the capture of Damietta, instead making camp at Ashmar-Tanna in the Delta, and offering to come to terms with the Franks. He was prepared to hand over Jerusalem for the return of Damietta, but Louis, confident through his

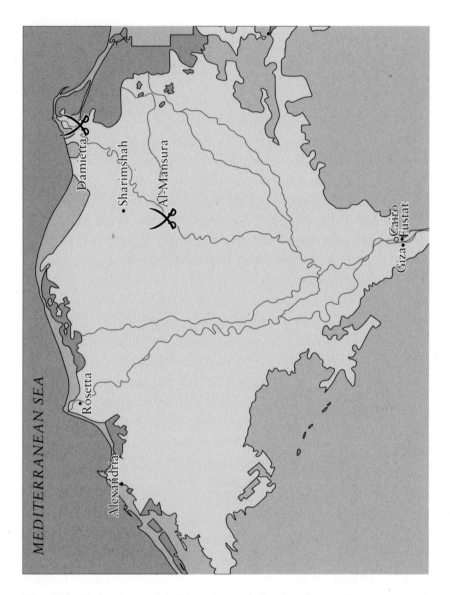

The Nile Delta in 1250. The sites of the battles at Damietta and Al-Mansura are marked..

progress to date, flatly refused to negotiate with the infidel and pressed on for outright conquest.

As-Salih was now a very sick man, terminally ill with tuberculosis and cancer, and visibly lame from a leg ulcer. His army was in disarray; even his Bahri amirs were in a rebellious mood, having been held in disgrace by the sultan for not preventing the invasion. Though he tried to project the image of a determined defender, on 22 November 1249, as the crusaders approached his camp, as-Salih died.

Resistance to the crusade might have collapsed just then, leaving the road to Cairo wide open to the Franks and changing the entire course of events in the Islamic world. But those closest to the dead sultan acted swiftly to reverse the situation. It was as-Salih's queen, Shajar-ad-Durr ('Tree of Pearls'), in alliance with the senior Bahri amirs, who saved the day. Shajar-ad-Durr was herself of Turkish slave origin, once sent as a slave girl from the harem of the Caliph in Baghdad as a gift for the Ayyubid sultan, but having borne as-Salih a son he made her his sultana. As far as a female mamluk was conceivable, she was such.

On her husband's death Shajar-ad-Durr immediately stepped into command. She announced that the sultan was ill and could see no one while the Bahris smuggled their master's body out of the camp and hid it in their barracks at Roda. Amir Faris-ad-Din Aqtai, who commanded the Bahri regiment, set out for Mesopotamia to fetch Turan Shah, as-Salih's young heir. In the meantime the sultana appointed Fakr-ad-Din Yusuf, the aged wazir, as commander of the army. The officers received their orders in writing from Shajar-ad-Durr, one of the palace eunuchs forging the dead sultan's signature. News of as-Salih's death would eventually leak, but by then the crisis had passed and Fakr-ad-Din was in firm control.

During its advance, the crusading army had marched alongside the Damietta branch of the river and had needed to cross many channels and streams diverging from the main course. Now only the Bahr-as-Saghir, a narrow watercourse, separated them from the Muslim army camped at al-Mansura. Early in 1250 there were a series of skirmishes on both sides of this channel but no decisive gains on either side. On 8 February, Louis' brother Robert of Artois led a party of knights across the Bahr-as-Saghir in a surprise attack on the Muslims. During the short fight, Fakr-ad-Din was killed, although a troop of Bahris soon cut down the Franks. The main body of the crusading army attempted to take advantage and attacked at this point, but nothing was gained; further weeks of indecisive fighting followed at the same spot.

The death of Fakr-ad-Din was a serious blow to the defenders, but his role as commander fell to the young Bahri amir Rukn-ad-Din Baibars al-Bunduqdari. From this first command, Baibars would prove the most successful of the Bahri Mamluks, and eventually one of Islam's most acclaimed sultans. According to Ibn Taghri Birdi, writing two centuries later, Baibars was born into the Barali tribe of Kipchak Turks around 1228, at the time of the Mongol incursions. In 1242, fearing a renewed Mongol attack, the Baralis placed themselves under the protection of a local khan. This prince treacherously attacked his vassal people, killing thousands and selling the rest into slavery, the fourteen-year-old Baibars included. It is not certain how true this story was, or even whether Baibars was a Kipchak at all. He had blue eyes, which hint at a mixed ethnic origin at least. It has also been suggested that he had once fought in the Mongol armies, which would explain his detailed knowledge of Mongol institutions.

Baibars was taken to Syria along with Baisari, who also became a Bahri amir, and was first sold in the slave market in Damascus. His first owner quickly returned him to the slave trader when persuaded that a white speck in the captive's eye was a sign of evil. The trader then took Baibars and Baisari to Aleppo, where he was bought by one of as-Salih's amirs, Rukn-ad-Din Aidakin al-Bunduqdari. The amir's title *al-bunduqdari* ('The Crossbowman') referred to the office he once held in the sultan's service and the title was consequently attached to Baibars. While Baibars was in Aidakin's service, his master fell out of favour with the Sultan as-Salih and was sent into exile, his property and his mamluks being seized. It was as-Salih who eventually released Baibars, and after a time in the khassikiya Baibars advanced quickly through the officer corps of the Bahri regiment.

Now, at twenty-two, Baibars showed his ability as a general. Dissatisfied with the stalemate at the Bahr-as-Saghir, Baibars sent a small force in boats down another outlet of the Delta, from which they carried their craft overland to the Damietta branch and attacked the enemy's supply lines. Soon most of the Franks' supply ships were being intercepted. There was already plague and dysentery in the Christian camp. Heat, flies and Bedouin tribes stirred up by Baibars harried the Franks as well, and the loss of supplies added hunger to these privations.

Louis waited too long before ordering the retreat, which he finally did on 5 April. After the Franks forgot to destroy the bridge over the Bahr-as-Saghir, the Muslim army followed and the next day they caught up with the retreating enemy at Sharimshah. Louis was ill at the time, and would not have surrendered, but during the battle a French sergeant named Marcel announced that he had done so without any such command from Louis. Marcel was later accused of working for the Muslims.

Having taken prisoner the entire crusading army, the Muslims first slaughtered the badly wounded and interned the rest. They treated King Louis well in captivity; he was kept in the house of a certain Ibn Luqman, given new clothes and Arab physicians to attend him. They even presented him with an elephant to take home. Negotiations then went on for a ransom. The two sides soon agreed that Louis and his army would be released for a million bezants and the return of Damietta.

The Bahris had a new problem soon after this victory, and while negotiations for the ransom were in progress there was a disturbing development within the Muslim camp. The new

Ayyubid sultan Turan Shah had arrived, and his behaviour was causing ill-feeling. While on the way he had sent letters to Shajar-ad-Durr demanding his father's money and jewels, and he proceeded to treat his stepmother and his father's amirs in an offhand manner. With his own mamluks, mostly young men from Iraq, Turan Shah spent his nights in drunken revelry. Dismissing the Bahri amirs from the council, he promoted his own entourage to ranks senior to them, conferring particular favour on a eunuch named Sabih.

Shajar-ad-Durr appealed to the Bahri amirs. It was obvious to them that as soon as Turan Shah had secured his position and after the Franks had gone, they would all be arrested and probably executed. The young sultan had even been seen, while in a state of drunkenness, cutting off the tops of candles with his sword and boasting that he would do the same to the Bahris. Although the amirs agreed that some speedy action must be taken, there was no clear consensus as to what. On 12 May, a few days before Louis was to be released, a number of Bahri amirs burst into Turan Shah's tent on the spur of the moment. At this point the amirs were not fully in agreement but Baibars as usual took the initiative, stabbing at Turan Shah with his sword. The sultan ran out screaming that the Bahris were trying to kill him. At this moment, apparently prearranged, other amirs gave orders for the army to march immediately to Damietta, leaving Turan Shah without protection. Now the waverers were convinced that he must be killed, or there would be reprisals. The amirs pursued the wounded sultan.

They chased Tuan Shah for a distance. At one point he climbed a wooden siege tower, but they set it on fire and shot arrows at him. He somehow managed to escape, and when his pursuers caught up he had reached the bank of the Nile and was trying to swim to a boat. They caught him before he could do so and laid into him with their blades, Aqtai striking the final blow. The body lay on the bank for three days before it was collected for a modest burial.

Shajar-ad-Durr resumed command. Her own son Khalil was still a small child, but she ruled as sovereign in her own right, not as regent. She took the title *al-Musta'simiyya as-Salihiyya Malikat al-Muslimin Walidat al-Malik-al-Mansur Khalil.* Besides showing her relationship to both as-Salih and Khalil, this title blatantly declared her former connection to Caliph al-Musta'sim. To save time, she was usually known as *Umm-Khalil.* As soon as the freed crusaders departed she and the Bahris returned to Cairo, where she set about assuming government with noted acumen. She had coins struck in her name and the *khutba*, or Friday prayers, recited with her own name as sovereign. But her reign would last just eighty days.

The Bahris supported Shajar-ad-Durr enthusiastically. They even considered her their barracks comrade; in nomadic Turkish society women had equal status. Either out of loyalty to her husband, or because they had confidence in her ability, they worked with her wholeheartedly. But when an embassy went to Baghdad to ask the Caliph for his approval of Shajar-ad-Durr's accession, al-Musta'sim showed a decidedly hostile response to the matter. He was probably annoyed at the prospect of acknowledging his slave girl as a sovereign ruler. 'Woe to the nations ruled by women,' he declared, quoting the Quran, and then ominously remarked that if they could not find a man to rule over them he would send one. The Caliph's endorsement was very important, especially after the murder of a legitimate ruler followed by usurpation. A woman as sovereign was practically unprecedented in Islam. The Syrian Ayyubids were already showing their opposition to the new regime in Egypt, and whoever the Caliph chose to be sultan could demand the support of all Muslims against the upstarts. Rather than risk this, the Mamluks agreed to Shajar-ad-Durr's abdication and to seek a settlement that al-Musta'sim would approve.

Several amirs were invited to become sultan, but they refused. At one point King Louis was half-seriously considered. It was eventually agreed that Amir Izz ad-Din Aibak at-Turkmanni be appointed, and as a show of legitimate succession the six-year-old Ayyubid prince Musa was named co-sultan. Shajar-ad-Durr as a further measure married Aibak; she continued to control the civil government, whereas Aibak mostly contented himself with the command of the army. The queen would often sit in the hall of state, observing the proceedings while concealed by a curtain. Aibak, the first of the Egyptian Mamluks to become sultan, was not strictly considered a Salihi; he came into the dead sultan's service having once been an amir's mamluk. Several others, including Baibars and Qalawun, had arrived this way, but Aibak was probably not released by as-Salih, and appears not to have been accepted so readily by the others.

As the Bahris did not fully consider him their khushdashin, Aibak could not really count on their support and was always suspicious of their intentions. As usual it was necessary to keep them busy, at least to reduce the chance that restlessness would drive them to plotting. He first sent them on a 'pacification' campaign against Bedouin tribes who had revolted soon after his succession. They conducted themselves with noted ferocity and treachery, calling a parley with the Bedouin chiefs and massacring them as soon as they appeared. Soon afterwards the Bahris were needed in Syria.

An-Nasir Yusuf, as-Salih's old enemy, rose against the new regime soon after the murder of Turan Shah and seized Damascus. He then formed an alliance of all the Ayyubid princes of Syria and early in 1251 led a large army into Egypt. In February he fought Aibak and the Bahris at Abbasa but lost and withdrew. The Mamluks captured some of the other Ayyubids, executing one of their dead patron's old enemies and releasing the others. Hostilities did not cease with this, so Aibak attempted an alliance with King Louis, now campaigning in Palestine; it was agreed but came to nothing. In 1253, after the mediation of the Caliph, Aibak and the Ayyubids agreed that the Mamluks could keep Egypt while an-Nasir Yusuf retained Damascus. An-Nasir awaited a new opportunity to move against the Mamluks, but the Syria was quiet for a time.

Aibak then decided to destroy the strength of the Bahris. Apart from their excesses in and around Cairo, they also ignored the new sultan's commands. Their commander Aqtai held his own court, corresponding with the Syrian Ayyubids as if he were sultan. By virtue of his marriage to an Ayyubid princess of Hama, Aqtai was even claiming to be rightful sultan and using the royal insignia of the Ayyubids under his own name. Confrontation would come sooner or later, and Aibak decided to act. In 1254 he lured Aqtai to the Citadel, where he had him seized and beheaded. Then he ordered the arrest of all Bahris and had many executed. as soon as this began many swiftly left Egypt, including Baibars, Qalawun, Sunqur-al-Ashqar and Baisari, together with about 700 troops.

The Bahris then scattered about different courts in Syria and Anatolia. Baibars became the leader of a large contingent who pledged their services to an-Nasir in Damascus. From there they attempted an attack on Egypt, which Aibak fought off. Again on the instigation of the Caliph, Aibak and an-Nasir made peace, and Aibak used the opportunity to persuade the Ayyubid that Baibars was too dangerous to employ. Expecting that he would soon be arrested, Baibars and his following fled to Kerak, now to serve under al-Mugith Umar, another Ayyubid prince with designs on Saladin's empire. He made two more unsuccessful raids into Egypt, and several into an-Nasir's territory. A few years later he returned for a time into an-Nasir's service.

By 1256 Aibak could feel more secure on his throne. The Bahris were either dead or in exile, and he had raised his own mamluks to senior military and government positions. Now he could send his co-sultan Musa into exile in Constantinople and abandon the legal fiction of co-rulership. He could very easily have founded a new ruling dynasty to replace the Ayyubids, but now he planned to eliminate Shajar-ad-Durr. The two had drifted apart, almost certainly after Aibak had turned on the

Bahris, but she was still powerful enough to pose a threat to him. Aibak was preparing to divorce her while he opened negotiations with the Ayyubid princes of Mosul and Hama for his marriage to one of their daughters. The queen became understandably suspicious and early in 1257 tensions exploded when a young mamluk of the sultan's household who was then in disgrace tried to escape punishment by telling the queen that Aibak was planning to kill her. Shajar-ad-Durr reacted savagely. She wrote to an-Nasir offering to help him overthrow Aibak and marry him afterwards. The Ayyubid suspected a trap and warned Aibak.

Before long Egypt was close to civil war, as the sultan and sultana prepared to fight each other. In what seemed to be an attempt to avoid this, Shajar-ad-Durr invited Aibak to a meeting of reconciliation at a polo court near Cairo. There, as Aibak was taking a bath to prepare for the meeting, five hired assassins burst in and stabbed him with their swords. Shajar-ad-Durr had ordered the murder, and this fact could not be concealed from the sultan's amirs – his own mamluks – when they tortured the queen's slave girls to extract confirmation. Shajar-ad-Durr was arrested and thrown into prison in the Citadel. She spent her last hours spitefully grinding her jewellery to powder.

The amirs chose Ali, Aibak's son by a previous marriage, to succeed as sultan, apparently honouring the principle of hereditary succession. His first act was to hand Shajar-ad-Durr over to his mother, whom Aibak had divorced on the orders of the sultana. She had her slave girls beat Shajar-ad-Durr to death with their wooden clogs. The body was thrown over the Citadel wall to the jackals, and later collected for burial. But apart from deciding Shajar-ad-Durr's fate, the new sultan had little scope for exercising his authority. At only fifteen, Ali he had to defer to his father's amirs while Qutuz, his father's deputy, in alliance with Ali's mother, controlled the government on his behalf. Qutuz was said to have been a member of the ruling family of Khwarazm before he became Aibak's mamluk and was preparing to replace

Ali as soon as he could find a credible pretext. He did not have long to wait.

Disturbing reports from the lands east of Syria hinted at a new threat from a much-feared enemy. The Mongols were again moving westward with a large army of conquest, leaving a trail of destruction and carnage, confirming the worst fears of Muslims over the previous half-century. The empire of the Mongols (or the Tatars as Arab sources also call them) began in a small way late in the previous century near Lake Baikal in central Asia. A young outlaw named Temujin gathered to his following first individuals, then tribes, and later entire peoples. In his old age Temujin, now known as Genghis Khan, was supreme ruler over an expanse stretching from Korea to the Black Sea, including Khorasan and other eastern Islamic lands, and after his death in 1227 the Mongol advance continued, though with far less vigour than before, mostly in Russia. But a slow grind of conquest had proceeded all along, and by 1243 they had gradually crushed the Khwarezmians in Iran, advanced into Azerbaijan and reduced the Georgians, the Armenians and the Anatolian Seljuks to vassalage.

In 1251 Mangu, grandson of Genghis Khan, inherited this empire and raised three armies to conquer the rest of the world. To his brother Hulagu he gave command of one he sent west. By the late 1250s Hulagu was leading the horde into Iraq. Each city was given the customary choice: they could offer immediate and unconditional submission, leading to absorption into the Mongol empire and its armies, or their cities would be razed to the ground, their women raped, and every man, woman and child butchered, their entrails cut open in search of precious stones they may have swallowed. Terror was the Mongols' most effective weapon: Iraq and southern Iran soon became a near-wilderness of smoke-blackened ruins of cities, the heads of their inhabitants piled into 'towers of skulls'. By reputation, and in their own eyes, the Mongols were invincible, and to resist them was madness.

In February 1258 the Mongols appeared before the gates of Baghdad. The Caliph had decided to resist Hulagu, expecting help from the Muslim princes, but this was a tragic miscalculation. Baghdad, for five centuries the centre of Islamic civilisation and the seat of the Abbasid Caliphate, was completely devastated, its mosques, colleges and palaces all put to the torch. Sparing only the Christian community who had supported them, the Mongols slaughtered the million inhabitants in an orgy of plunder, rape and bloodshed. Rather than spill the blood of a ruling prince, they rolled Caliph al-Musta'sim up in a carpet and trampled him to death with their horses.

Some eighteen months later Hulagu was advancing northwards, preparing to cross the Euphrates into Syria. An-Nasir Yusuf planned to enlist the Mongols' help in his war with the Mamluks. He did not see the absurdity of such an idea until Hulagu sent him the customary demand for his unconditional submission. An-Nasir then made vague statements about resisting the Mongols, but vacillated for a while between belligerence and submission, so much that he undermined the morale of his soldiers. Baibars and his Bahris in particular grew restless and abandoned him to return to Egypt. As the Mongols crossed the river in December 1259, panic spread through Syria, thousands fleeing for Egypt. An-Nasir finally lost his nerve and left too. In Amman, probably on Qutuz's orders, his bodyguard overpowered him and took him in chains to Hulagu, who had him beheaded.

After a week-long siege, Aleppo fell, the Mongols destroying it in the usual horrific manner. The Ayyubid Amir of Homs surrendered to Hulagu, while his counterpart in Hama left for Egypt. For all of northern Syria, the only options were to bow before the invaders or face annihilation, and most chose the former. Hulagu had already received the submission of the Christian King Hethoum I of Armenian Cilicia and by early 1260 he had also gained the homage of Hethoum's vassal and son-in-law Bohemund VI, the Frankish Prince of Antioch and Count of Tripoli. Co-operation between Christians and Mongols had become commonplace where both had common cause against the Muslims. Bohemund took advantage of the disruption and seized the city of Lattakieh and the coastal strip which separated his two domains. He also rode side-by-side with Hethoum and the Mongol commander Kitbugha to take possession of Damascus in March 1260, when the city unconditionally surrendered to the Mongols. Such an image of cooperation was the best course at a time when the world seemed to be falling under the Mongol yoke with no effective resistance in sight.

In Egypt, Qutuz used the emergency to replace Ali as sultan. Mongol raiding parties were already seen as far south as Hebron and Gaza, and he could expect an attack on Egypt at any time. When the Mongol envoys arrived in Cairo to confront Qutuz with their customary demand for immediate submission, he decided to stand and fight.

As soon as he was assured of the support of the amirs, Qutuz ordered that the four Mongol ambassadors be put to death. Each was taken to a separate quarter of Cairo to be publicly cut in half at the waist. Their heads were displayed on the Zuwaila Gate, where those of condemned criminals were usually placed. Now there was no question of any peaceful arrangement; an amir of northern Iraq who had crucified a Mongol envoy had recently been captured by Hulagu and forced to eat his own flesh until death released him. Suicidal as it appeared to challenge the Mongols in this manner, Qutuz had decided to stake all on a complete victory. The sultan was after all the executive power of Islam, with a fundamental obligation to defend it against whatever would destroy it. Its enemy was a teeming horde, terrible in its nature and convinced of its own victory, and Qutuz was now the commander of the Muslim defence. To rally support, he treated the campaign as the *jihad*, a holy war to defend Islam. Rather than wait for the invaders to reach Egypt and fight a defensive campaign there he decided to march into Syria and meet them head-on. The amirs at first refused to comply, but he told them he was going to Syria with those would march with him and appealed to them as Muslims. 'The guilt of the fate of the women of Islam will rest on those who refuse to fight,' he said. They assented.

Qutuz raised an army of over 100,000 men. He created new taxes and put all his resources towards this end. He enlisted Turcomans, Bedouins, Kurds, even peasants; anyone who could fight was welcomed. Many of the survivors of the Bahri regiment returned to Egypt, and Qutuz made them welcome, all past differences forgotten. In particular the sultan was glad to see Baibars al-Bunduqdari return with his following, and made him his general. Baibars lost no time and first sent advance parties to set fire to the woodlands of Syria, preventing the Mongols from using the wood to build machines of war. Then he set about training a small force, including the Bahris, in Mongol methods of warfare. As soon as preparations were complete, the great army set off for Syria.

About that time, disturbing news from the Mongol homelands reached Hulagu: the Great Khan Mangu had died and his brothers Kubilai and Arik Buka were disputing the succession. Hulagu decided to withdraw the greater part of his troops to Azerbaijan, leaving a small screening force in Syria under his generals Kitbugha and Baidera. Hulagu himself was on the way to Karakorum, the Mongol capital, to contest the election himself. Baibars, leading the vanguard of the Egyptian army, had captured some Mongol scouts at Gaza and learned of Hulagu's absence. He sent to Qutuz to bring the main body of the army on to attack the Mongols without delay.

While the Franks of the northern principalities had taken to ride with the Mongols, those of the Kingdom of Jerusalem were not so willing once the pope forbade any submission. With Kitbugha coming south from his base at Baalbek and the Muslim army passing through Frankish territory, the Europeans opted to provide the Muslims with supplies. They offered military aid as well, but this Baibars declined.

On 3 September 1260 the Muslims met the Mongols at Ain Jalut ('Goliath's Spring'), on the route to Damascus near the

Mountains of Gilboa. With only the small force Hulagu had left him, Kitbugha's army was outnumbered by at least three to one. The Mongols also attacked uphill. Even so, they made easy advances in the opening stage of the battle and cut down line after line of Muslim troops. The Muslim hit-and-run tactics initially did little to slow the invaders, but then Baibars hit them with his trained force. He used traditional Mongol tactics, based on the co-ordination of light and heavy cavalry, against the Mongols. While Kitbugha's men thought they were pursuing retreating Mamluks, they were taken by surprise when concealed troops appeared, loosing their arrows and surrounding the Mongols.

The Mongols fought their way out of the ambush and still might have succeeded, but Qutuz appeared on the field. Tasing off his helmet to show himself, he called out to his troops, 'O Muslims', exhorting them to defend Islam from its would-be destroyers. He then led a massive charge, which by its timing and its superior numbers overwhelmed the Mongols. Soon the invading army was falling apart. Kitbugha's horse was killed under him and he was captured by Baibars and beheaded in Qutuz's presence. The Mongols retreated east in panic. Eight miles on, at Baisan, they tried to regroup but the pursuing Muslims fell on them. Although the Mongols briefly turned the battle once more, their troops were soon running for their lives or being cut down where they stood.

As soon as the news of the invaders' defeat was heard, the Damascenes turned on the Mongol occupying force and drove them out of the city. They also enacted reprisals against collaborators, in particular Christians and Jews. Qutuz and Baibars spent the weeks following the battle overcoming the remaining pockets of Mongol troops in Syria. At one point a campaign was considered to retake Baghdad, but this obviously required military resources they did not have. For some time to come, the Euphrates would mark the frontier between the Mongols and the Muslims.

Ain Jalut could not really be described as a major military achievement for the Mamluks; it was in fact a victory of superior numbers at a time when most of the Mongol army had been withdrawn. It was not strictly the first time the Mongols had been defeated in battle, nor was it by any means the end of the Mongol threat to Syria. Had Hulagu not turned away it could have been the definitive showdown between the massed Mongol forces and the entire muster of the Islamic near east, and it might easily have been a Mongol victory. Instead, the greater number of the Mongols were still waiting beyond the Euphrates. Hulagu should not have put his personal ambition before this campaign, as the defeat deprived the Mongols of their most important psychological weapon by showing that they could be bested. The victory was also to the credit of Baibars, whose major contribution was recognised.

The victory also extended the Mamluk dominions throughout Syria. Qutuz now held by right of reconquest the regions of Aleppo and Damascus, which an-Nasir Yusuf previously held. The Ayyubid princes of Hama, Homs and Kerak agreed to his overlordship, and only the Frankish territories lay outside his control. Syria, although not fully subdued at this point, would be an important component of the Mamluk empire throughout most of its existence.

But once Syria was pacified, relations between the sultan and his general began to deteriorate. Qutuz was growing suspicious of Baibars' intentions, probably with some justification, and for this reason he snubbed the general when granting provincial governorships in Syria. It is not certain that Qutuz had promised him the governorship of Aleppo, but Baibars apparently expected it, and was angered when it went to Sinjar Ala-ad-Din Ali, the dispossessed Amir of Mosul. For all his service Baibars gained no reward at all. As a frontier lordship, an amir of the calibre of Baibars was needed to defend Aleppo against any renewed Mongol attack, but it would also have provided him with the means to rebel against Qutuz.

Baibars now felt sure that as soon as Qutuz was safely back in Cairo he himself would be arrested. As the army set out for Egypt in October, Baibars was planning his second regicide. He enlisted the aid of three Bahri amirs, Bektut, Anis and Bahadur. On 24 October 1260, he had his chance. A few miles from Cairo Qutuz halted the march and declared a day of hunting, planning to enter the city in triumph the following day. Baibars and his accomplices contrived to be alone with the sultan during that day.

Baibars approached the mounted sultan and asked for the gift of a slave girl, which Qutuz granted. As a gesture of thanks Baibars grabbed his hand to kiss. At this pre-arranged signal the other three amirs pulled the sultan from his horse and stabbed him with their weapons. In a version later told by Ibn Abd-az-Zahir, his secretary, Baibars did the deed on his own. In another, Anis was the sole killer. In any case, Baibars took full responsibility for the murder.

Qutuz's amirs apparently offered no resistance to the Bahris' reasserting themselves. The seniors of the regiment at first discussed elevating the oldest of their number, Balaban ar-Raschidi, to the sultanate. But one of the most senior, Aqtai al-Musta'rib, gave his voice for Baibars. According to Turkish tribal custom, whoever killed the leader took his place, even though according to some accounts Baibars had not killed Qutuz personally. It was decided that Baibars was the best candidate, given his achievements to date; he was, after all, the architect of the victory at Ain Jalut. Certain concessions were probably made to gain the assent of some amirs: promises of land and position, and payment of debts. On 25 October, the day after his predecessor's assassination, the amirs acclaimed al-Malik-az-Zahir Rukn-ad-Din Baibars al-Bunduqdari as their sultan.

The politics of the previous ten years had been dominated by the strength of the Bahris and their resistance to being marginalised, and attempts to produce an alternative sultan found the corps to be a serious obstruction. At the same time, the Bahris take much of the credit for defending Islam against its would-be destroyers; this was a time when the civilisation was in more serious danger than ever and the need for decisive leadership was paramount. Since the death of as-Salih, the Ayyubids had ceased to fill this role. Aibak and Qutuz were competent enough but neither had the support of the Bahris. Baibars would prove one of the most successful Mamluk sultans, but he also had the support of his barrack comrades. The sultanate was in uncharted waters, but Baibars was the best candidate to steer it at this time.

4

SULTAN BAIBARS

Baibars al-Bunduqdari may have been the fourth of his line, but he is considered the true founder of the Mamluk sultanate. He took control over what was then a disjointed and haphazard state of affairs which in the course of his reign he turned into a powerful and efficient empire. In doing so, he saved what was left of Islamic civilisation.

Having gained Syria, Baibars knew there were serious problems. Most immediate was the threat of a new Mongol invasion. At Ain Jalut the Mamluks had defeated the much-reduced screening force, and the Mongols, far from crushed, had established their frontier on the right bank of the Euphrates in preparation to invade Syria again, with vengeance as much in mind as reconquest. Syria was far from conquered in 1260 when the Mamluks had Damascus and Aleppo, both with governors appointed from Cairo, and two Ayyubid vassal states, and it was difficult to control these territories so far from Egypt. Many strategically important areas were held by the Franks, the Armenians and the Ayyubid al-Mugith Umar, all independent of the sultan, and some were likely to side with the Mongols. There was even the possibility of a new crusade from Europe in alliance with the Mongols.

There was opposition to the new sultan in Egypt itself with resentment over the coup. Baibars' claim to be rightful ruler was far from indisputable when in October 1260 there was no clearly defined procedure by which a sultan could be chosen. He had come to the throne by assassinating his predecessor and had gained control by slipping into the Citadel at night a few days later. Only after he had seized the fortress and the treasury was the death of Qutuz and his own accession proclaimed. In previous times the Ayyubid sultans would receive the endorsement of the Caliph in Baghdad on taking the throne, which would thus legitimise the accession; the Caliph had recognised Aibak as sultan in 1250, for example. But the Caliphate had ended with al-Musta'sim's murder when the Mongols took Baghdad in 1258 and now there was a dangerous political vacuum in which sultans could be made and unmade by force or treachery. Qutuz himself had been a *de facto* sultan of this kind. Baibars risked deposition by a conspiracy of amirs whenever he left Cairo.

In hardly any time after his accession Baibars was forced to subdue rebellious factions in Syria. The amir Sanjar al-Halabi, whom Qutuz had made governor of Damascus, immediately threw off allegiance to Baibars and proclaimed himself sultan. Baibars acted quickly, driving Sanjar out of Damascus with his troops. Sanjar was later arrested and imprisoned, although Baibars would pardon him and make him governor of Aleppo. No sooner had Damascus been retaken than Aleppo rose in revolt. The mamluks of the late an-Nasir Yusuf and those of his father now declared their defiance. They tried to raise all Syria against the Mamluk regime in Egypt, but no revolt came about on this scale and Baibars subdued Aleppo with swift punitive action.

There was another threat from al-Mugith Umar, Amir of Kerak and the last independent Ayyubid prince in Syria. His domain lay in a strategically critical position, between Egypt and northern Syria and close to the Frankish states. Baibars, who had briefly been in his service, bore an old grudge over the way al-Mugith had treated his wife while at Kerak and decided to remove him. In 1263 Baibars lured al-Mugith to Cairo and had him seized on accusations of conspiring with the Mongols and beheaded. The amir's deputy in Kerak refused to submit to Baibars, but the city was taken by force soon afterwards. From that time a Mamluk governor resided there.

The remaining Syrian Ayyubids, the princes of Hama and Homs, had pledged their allegiance to Qutuz after Ain Jalut, and Baibars confirmed them in their petty amirates on receipt of their submission to him. When the Amir of Homs died in 1262 he was replaced by a Mamluk sub-governor under the jurisdiction of the Viceroy of Damascus. The other Ayyubid amirate continued until 1341 as a Mamluk vassal state.

As an attempt to legitimise his rule Baibars at first gained the endorsement of the Hafsid Caliph, a claimant to this title in the Maghreb. This arrangement was far from adequate, as few Muslims to the east of Egypt recognised this caliphate. While Baibars was still campaigning against the Syrian rebels a more viable solution appeared. Ahmad ibn az-Zahir, a young Abbasid prince who had escaped the Baghdad massacre with his cousin, had since been hiding in the desert and now contacted Baibars. The sultan had the *ulema* (a body of religious scholars) verify the young man's genealogy and they declared him to be the uncle of the late Caliph. Baibars invited Ahmad to Cairo.

There was staged an elaborate and colourful ceremony, beginning with the Abbasid's entry into Cairo in style. He was proclaimed Caliph, taking the regnal name al-Mustansir Billah, and invested with the black robes and other trappings of the Abbasids. The new Caliph then formally conferred the sultanate on Baibars, making a lengthy pronouncement of his sultan's powers and duties. There was to be no doubt now: Sultan al-Malik-az-Zahir Rukn-ad-Din Baibars al-Bunduqdari was the executive power in all Islam, leader of the jihad, and destroyer of all enemies of the faith.

Al-Mustansir then expected his sultan to restore to him Baghdad, the city of the Abbasid Caliphs, and this Baibars seemed to set out to do, but his actions hint at a hidden agenda. Shortly after the double investiture, the Caliph and the sultan both set out on campaign. Baibars only went as far as Damascus, and al-Mustansir continued, with an army largely composed of Bedouin and Turcoman irregulars and 800 regular cavalry, mostly provincial Mamluks. Such an army could not expect much success. The young Caliph led it across the Euphrates, to meet a large Mongol force near Anbar. Most of the Muslim troops fled, leaving those who remained, including al-Mustansir, to die on the battlefield.

It is believed that Baibars deliberately sent the Caliph into a suicidal position. Perhaps he realised that the Caliph would not be as grateful once his domain had been restored to him and might soon become his rival. This view has more recently been challenged. It may have been al-Mustansir's incompetence that caused the debacle; he was expected to have joined with an Egyptian army already in the area before crossing the river, and he did not. Yet it is obvious that Baibars did not treat the expedition as a serious venture. Baghdad would not have been an easy conquest, and holding it would be more difficult still; Baibars and Qutuz had conceded that in 1260. Baibars made no real attempt to raise an adequate army, nor to lead the campaign personally. It seems much more likely that he planned the young Caliph's death. Then again, as the restored Caliph had given him the all-important endorsement as sultan he had performed his required act, but what would have happened if Baibars required support for a dynasty he expected to establish? He might have kept the Caliph's cousin out of the fight if he planned it that way, but that young man was also at the battle.

Baibars' treatment of al-Mustansir's successor shows that he was more interested in the Caliphs' service to him than in restoring the Abbasids to power. The other Abbasid prince, al-Mustansir's cousin, had escaped from Anbar and now filled the office as al-Hakim Billah. But as soon as he began to assert himself, Baibars placed the young man under house arrest in the Citadel, where he remained for nearly thirty years, apart from appearances in state ceremonies. The restored Abbasid Caliphate was a travesty, the Caliphs puppets of the Mamluk sultans who used them as a legalistic and ceremonial device to endorse whoever became sultan by inheritance or coup.

Having been formally invested by the dead Caliph, Baibars' prestige increased, beginning when the Sharif of the Hijaz, ruler of the Red Sea coastal region of Arabia centring on Mecca and Medina, pledged his allegiance to the Mamluk sultan. The Hijaz kept its autonomy, but the Mamluk sultans enjoyed the prestige of defenders of the Holy Cities of Islam and leaders of the annual pilgrimage. Baibars added to his titles *Khadim al-Haramayn*, Servant of the Two Holy Places, a title which Saladin had once held.

By 1263 Baibars was expecting a new Mongol attack. Hulagu had reached the Mongol capital of Karakorum in 1260 only to find that his brother Kubilai had been elected as Great Khan. Having been invested by Kubilai with the title of *ilkhan*, or subordinate ruler, of Persia, he returned to the west and set about consolidating his territories. He added Mosul and southern Iran to his possessions and planned to renew the conquest of Syria. Geographically speaking the Ilkhanate covered a vast area: not only Iran as we know it, but modern Iraq too and with influence spreading far into Anatolia. Hulagu ordered the extension of Mongol rule into southern Iran and set about raising an army of conquest for Syria and then Egypt.

The Muslims also sensed the genuine threat of an alliance of the Christians of Europe with the Mongols. Some European princes had long favoured this idea, including Louis IX. Nestorian Christianity was not uncommon among influential Mongols, in particular in Hulagu's entourage; his wife Dokuz

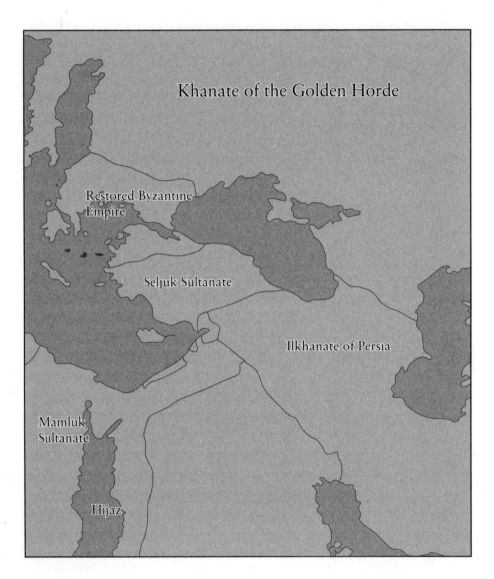

The Middle East c.1265.

Khatun was a Nestorian, as were many influential elements. Ignoring important doctrinal differences, the prospect of persuading the Great Khan to accept baptism in the Roman rite was attractive. Not only would it bring all Asia to Catholicism, they reasoned, but it could crush Islam from both sides. Louis had in 1254 sent the Franciscan William of Ruybroek to Mangu's court for this purpose, and he attempted the Great Khan's conversion.

After a time, many Europeans concluded that such an alliance was not a sensible proposition. The Mongols would never accept the concept of co-operation; they expected to dominate all Europe as they did Asia. They were interested in hearing about Europe but debated the merits of conquering it. Mangu had dismissed William with the message that if all the princes of Europe would come to Karakorum and bow down to him he would then consider Christianity. Nevertheless, there had already been some Christian collaboration with the Mongols in 1260, by the Armenians, the northern Franks and the Syrian Christians. At Baghdad the Christians there had given the Mongols assistance; a mutual enemy prompted them into some collusion. A Mongol counter-attack at the same time as a new crusade from Europe would have been disastrous.

With this in mind Baibars sent out some effective diplomatic missions, knowing that some Westerners were more interested in commercial and political advantage than crusading; the Venetian, Pisan and Genoese city-states in particular gained favourable trade concessions. Charles of Anjou, King Louis' brother, who was then building his own empire in the Mediterranean, entered into a good relationship with Egypt and was unwilling to break it when the crusade did come about. Baibars' undertook a mission to Michael VIII Palaeologus, the newly restored Byzantine Emperor, who had good cause to be suspicious of Frankish intentions. The Fourth Crusade of 1204 had been diverted to dismember the Christian Byzantine empire, and Michael had only in 1261 regained Constantinople. Baibars undertook to divert the

Franks' attention from the Byzantines by harrying Frankish Syria and Michael closed the land route from Europe to Syria.

Baibars' most important diplomatic achievement was setting the two western Mongol khanates against each other in arms. Bereke, Khan of the Golden Horde, in the region north of the Black Sea and the Caspian, had become a Muslim. Baibars wrote to him in his own hand, reminding him of his duty as a Muslim to protect the lands of the faithful from its enemies. Bereke had already clashed with his cousin over a territorial dispute, and his conversion gave him further cause to oppose Hulagu, who had murdered the Caliph, and as a result of Baibars' urging he attacked the Ilkhanate. When Hulagu was at last ready to lead his army across the Euphrates he was therefore forced to turn and defend his northern frontier from the Mongols of the Golden Horde. Bereke died in 1265 and his successor remained a pagan, but Baibars continued the good relationship with the Golden Horde, working mainly through the Muslim court officials. This khanate remained an important ally of the Mamluks for as long as it existed. Egyptian architects were responsible for several majestic buildings in Sarai, the khanate's capital.

Hulagu also died in 1265, and his son Abagha succeeded as Ilkhan. Abagha had too many enemies to attempt a full-scale invasion of the Mamluk sultanate at this time. The empire of Genghis Khan was fragmenting: Kubilai Khan, who had moved his capital to Peking, was less powerful than his predecessors and his relatives still disputed his succession. Kubilai was the last of the Great Khans to be acknowledged as overlord by the other Mongol rulers, and even then he could not prevent them from fighting amongst themselves. Conversion to Islam was progressing in the Ilkhanate and some had misgivings over making war on fellow Muslims. Opposing alignments kept Abagha busy resisting the Mongols to his east. Baibars also stirred the Amir of Shiraz and the Bedouin tribes of Iraq to revolt against the Ilkhan. In Baibars' time the Mongols never invaded Syria in strength. There were a number of short, inconclusive raids; in 1268 the Mongols besieged Bira, and in 1271 and 1272 they came again, but each time it was a small force which retreated when Baibars advanced to meet it. The Mongols were still a threat throughout Baibars' reign, but their vast army of conquest never materialised.

As the immediate danger of a Mongol invasion subsided, Baibars began dealing with other hostile elements on the fringes of his empire. The most significant of these was the Kingdom of Cilicia, or Lesser Armenia. King Hethoum I had proved the most ardent Mongol supporter in this region, and an advocate of Christian co-operation with the Mongols. He had ridden with Kitbugha in 1260, and in 1263 a combined Cilician and Seljuk army had laid siege to Ain Tab, a Mamluk border fortress. The little kingdom's strategic position, on the near side of the Euphrates and commanding the only practicable route into Anatolia, gave further cause for concern. As soon as Baibars had pacified Syria, he began on a series of campaigns against Cilicia. Each time the kingdom suffered: the Mamluks destroyed, slaughtered and looted wherever they went. In 1266 Cilician territory from Adana to Tarsus was reduced to a smouldering wasteland, and later campaigns repeated the treatment. In 1275 the Mamluk army even occupied the capital, Sis, for a short time, and the same year they destroyed the port of Ayas, for the first of many times. The Mamluk sultan eventually agreed to grant peace to Hethoum, and then only after the king had ceded most of his border fortresses to the Mamluks. The Cilicians nevertheless continued to aid the enemies of the Mamluks in the times of Baibars' successors and the Mamluks would periodically wage war against them for the following century.

The Frankish states of the Syrian sea coast now came into focus. For nearly two centuries these petty states of Latin Syria, or Outremer, had been a source of bitter resentment to many Muslims, but they were also treated as a permanent fixture where trade and cooperation would go on. They had first been formidable states in the twelfth century, but by this time little remained of what they had then controlled; there was only the strip of coastal territory salvaged by the Third Crusade and a few later additions. The titular king of Jerusalem, an absentee, reigned through a proxy in Acre, the Holy City itself long lost to the Muslims. The northern Franks were ruled by Bohemund VI, Prince of Antioch and Count of Tripoli, vassal and son-in-law of Hethoum. The coastal towns were dominated by rival Venetian and Genoese merchants, who had recently fought a war. The two large orders of warrior monks, the Knights Templar and the Knights of the Hospital of St John, controlled most of the remaining hinterland from their fortresses and were also at loggerheads. After Saladin had failed to destroy Outremer completely, this remnant had survived due to lack of decisive Ayyubid leadership.

Baibars was mindful of the support that some of them gave to the Mongols in 1260. He bore a grudge from his younger days when they joined with the Syrian Ayyubids against as-Salih Ayyub, and alongside some economic rivalry in trade with Europe there were serious considerations involved. If the European alliance with the Mongols had come about, they would use Outremer as the landing stage for a new crusade. It is uncertain whether Baibars made a conscious decision to destroy the Frankish states; it would have been a serious military operation to do so when he still had the Euphrates frontier to watch, and it might provoke a crusade. If this was his plan, his campaigns were designed to chip away at the Frankish territories and make a final conquest easier in due course. It is also likely that Baibars was treating them the same way as he did the other potential allies of the Mongols, destroying their defences and terrorising them into submission.

Using the pretext of a dispute with the military orders over their reluctance to release Muslim prisoners, Baibars embarked on a series of short raids on Christian territory. In 1263 he sacked Nazareth and destroyed the Church of the Virgin. From 1265 his efforts became more intense. He besieged and captured towns on the coast and had them razed to the ground, their citizens butchered or taken as slaves. Beginning with Caesarea, then Haifa, Toron and Arsuf, each was rendered uninhabitable. Safad, the stronghold of the Templars in Galilee, which dominated the road to Damascus, came under siege in 1266. When Baibars heard that Bohemund was besieging Hama as a reprisal, he took his army to drive them back and afterwards laid siege to Safad. After three weeks, Baibars took the fortress by promising the Templars safe conduct if they surrendered and beheading them when they emerged, after which the Mamluks conquered Galilee with little difficulty. Baibars then ordered that the fortress at Safad be repaired and used as a base for further attacks on the Franks. It later became a provincial capital in Mamluk Syria.

The following year Baibars broke through the line of defence along the Litani River, menacing the northern principalities. In 1271 it was the turn of Krak des Chevaliers, the Hospitallers' great castle, the central point of defence on the plain of Tripoli, and which had proved impregnable even to Saladin. The Hospitallers were finally forced to surrender, although this time Baibars kept his word when he allowed the brethren safe passage to the coast. He was even said to have felt sorrow at seeing the old Grand Master forced to leave his home. Chastel Blanc and Akkar, also on the line of castles defending Tripoli, were taken the same year. At one point Baibars attempted a naval attack on Cyprus, the main routing point of supply and military aid for the Syrian Franks. In 1270 he despatched a large invasion force in seventeen galleys to the island only to hear that all but six ships had been wrecked off Limassol. Baibars may have abandoned this plan, but the Mamluks would come to Cyprus much later.

This piecemeal destruction of Frankish towns and castles continued. Three times the Muslims besieged Acre, but each siege ended without result. Antioch was not so fortunate when Baibars suddenly appeared before its gates in 1268. He took the city, massacred thousands, enslaved many more and had the buildings torn down stone by stone. Antioch had been the first gain of the

First Crusade, and its loss was a terrible omen to the Christians in Europe.

By this time the Europeans had realised that not even the pitiful remnant that was Outremer would last much longer unless they acted, and by 1268 the Eighth Crusade was finally in preparation. St Louis, now ageing and weakened by illness, again took the Cross and exhorted all Christians to embark for the Holy Land. But by this time even the prospect of losing all the Frankish territories could not raise crusading fervour so easily in Europe, and political ambitions often trumped religious zeal. His army when it mustered was much smaller than in 1249. Charles of Anjou, together with the Genoese, skilfully diverted the crusade to Tunis; both parties had political designs there and neither wished to offend Baibars. In August 1270 the crusaders besieged the north African city, but plague soon struck down most of their army, King Louis included. In November Charles declared an end to the crusade, his own ambitions satisfied.

Latecomers to the crusade went straight on to the Holy Land, but not in groups large enough to make a substantial difference. One exception was the English contingent led by Prince Edward of Cornwall, later King Edward I. Edward's small force succeeded in frustrating Baibars' plans a little, and the Mongols made a token invasion in support of it. The prince was forced to return to England after eighteen months as his father Henry III was dying. Only a larger crusading army could have stopped the sultan at this time, and fewer knights in Europe were now willing to take the Cross than in the previous century.

Baibars made several truces during this time, usually with strategic considerations. Some, such as those made with John of Montford, Lord of Tyre and with the ruler of Tortosa, involved the Franks ceding territory and renouncing revenues levied from Muslims. When local lords made peace without their king's permission, Baibars succeeded in neutralising some quarters while campaigning against others. It appears that Prince Edward's little crusade forced the sultan to make more truces than he would

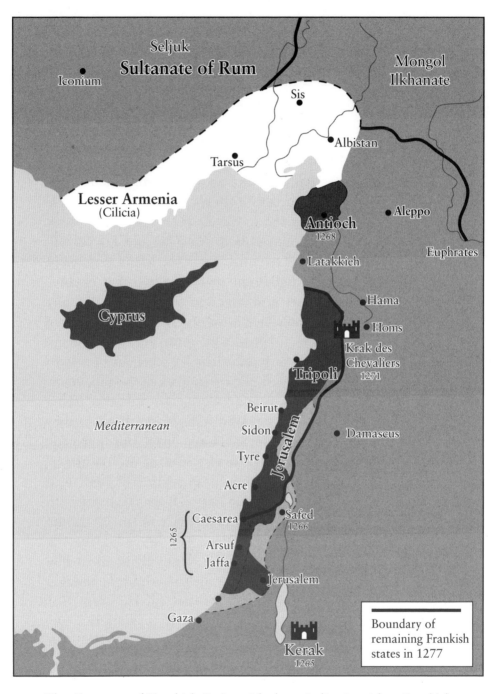

The Conquest of Frankish Syria, with dates indicating when Frankish territories were lost to the Mamluks.

have liked, though he still broke the treaties whenever it suited him. In 1272 he finally made peace with King Hugh III of Jerusalem, promising no hostilities for ten years, ten months, ten days and ten hours, and afterwards gave the Franks little trouble. The final destruction of Outremer would come about in his successors' time, but Baibars had reduced Latin Syria to a narrow coastal strip from Acre to Tortosa with an isolated Lattakieh, and most of the eastward defences destroyed.

At the same time that Baibars was campaigning against the Christians he was dealing with dissident Muslims in Syria. He spent some time curbing the power of the Assassins, a secret Shi'ite order. For two centuries both Muslims and Franks had lived in fear of this sect's terrorist activities. Many prominent men of both religions had been murdered when a devotee appeared, seemingly from nowhere, and struck with alarming precision and often a poisoned weapon. The Assassins acted without fear of their own subsequent fates. In 1256 Hulagu had destroyed the Assassins' headquarters at Alamaut in eastern Iran, but a colony remained in their fortresses in the mountains of northern Syria. Besides their opposition to orthodox Islam, Baibars saw the sect as a potential ally of the Franks; they were after all paying tribute to the Hospitallers. The systematic reduction of the Frankish territories changed the Assassins' domain from a border principality to an enclave in lands held by the Mamluks, and as these Shi'ites were in no position to resist Baibars by 1265, he could order an end to the tribute the Assassins levied from other rulers. The following year he demanded that their payments to the Hospitallers go to him instead. For a few years he acted as their overlord, appointing and dismissing their chieftains as he desired. He used their services, either as soldiers or as hitmen. It is likely that the murder of Philip de Montford in 1270 and the attempt on Prince Edward's life in 1272, when his wife Eleanor is said to have sucked the poison from his wound, were both carried out by Assassins on Baibars' orders.

The Assassins thus subjugated, he gradually wore down their military strength. Their fortresses were captured one by one, Baibars imprisoning their leaders at appropriate times. There was an unsuccessful attempt to assassinate Baibars in 1273, and the sect's resistance faded away shortly afterwards. In that year the last of the Assassins' strongholds fell to the Mamluks, and Baibars enjoyed prestige throughout the region for ending the cult's long reign of terror.

The Druzes and Nusairis, other heretical sects in the Lebanon, who at times sided with the sultan's enemies, received equally harsh treatment. The Bedouin Arabs of both Egypt and Syria, who never fully accepted Mamluk overlordship, also had rough handling. In 1266 the Christian village of Kara, to the north of Damascus, whose men often waylaid Muslim pilgrims, felt his wrath. Mamluk troops harried the villagers, tore down the monastery and dismembered the monks. Many men were taken as slaves and some eventually became senior Mamluk amirs.

Baibars also ordered the Mamluk governors of Cyrenaica and Qus to conduct campaigns which extended his authority in the Libyan desert and in Upper Egypt. There were several expeditions into the Upper Nile region against the independent Christian kingdoms there. The kingdom of Nubatia was annexed to the Mamluk empire, and that of Makuria reduced to vassalage by 1275. The third kingdom, Alwa, remained outside of the Mamluk orbit, too far away to be of any significance. Baibars once sent a punitive campaign to Suakin on the Red Sea coast, whose ruler had shown indifference to harassment of merchants bound for Egypt. The Mamluk expeditions heralded the spread of Islam into the Upper Nile region. Baibars had offered the Sudanese the traditional three choices of conquered peoples: conversion to Islam, payment of a poll tax, or death. Most chose the second option and effectively became *dhimmis*, peoples under the protection of Islam. Security of trade routes also considered, Baibars had effectively played the part of a Muslim sultan once again, extending Islam into new territory.

In matters of civil government Baibars acted with the same acumen and energy that he had shown on campaign. He was still comparatively young – aged thirty-two on his accession – and led a remarkably active life. When in Cairo he spent his afternoons on the drill field, practising archery and horsemanship, and he often worked late into the night on affairs of state. When he ordered that the Frankish towns be demolished the sultan would often be seen wielding a pick alongside his men.

At any one time Baibars was busy on several projects at once. His public works included the Lion's Bridge, which links Cairo and Fustat over the Cairo Canal, the Piebald Palace at Damascus, the az-Zahir Mosque in Cairo, a road to Damietta with sixteen bridges, fortresses in Syria, several irrigation schemes, and dredging the Serdas and Alexandria canals . On many of these works Baibars' personal motif of the lion, or panther, can still be seen. He promoted religious charitable foundations, including one for the burial of poor Muslims. His charity breathed new life into the al-Azhar college-mosque, which had fallen into disuse under the later Ayyubids. As a result of Baibars' aid and encouragement al-Azhar became the important centre of Islamic learning it remains to this day.

Baibars' innovations to the Islamic legal system were a constant characteristic of the Mamluk regime. The *Shari'a*, or orthodox Muslim law code, had four distinct interpretations in Egypt by this time: the Shafite, Hanafite, Malikite and Hanbalite schools of thought. The Shafite persuasion was the most followed and the chief *qadi*, or judge, was invariably a Shafite, but discrepancies between the four produced difficulties in legal processes. In 1265 Baibars appointed not one but four chief qadis to his court in Cairo, representing each of the four schools. There was a similar arrangement for Damascus. This act gave all four equal status, although the Shafite chief qadi held a modest seniority over the other three. Baibars declared that it would give all people a choice between the four interpretations.

His real motives may have been linked with his own preference for the Hanifite school, but it is more likely that he wanted to weaken the *ulema*, which could be a powerful pressure group at times. This action was unpopular, especially when it caused even more confusion than before, and it is said that Baibars' campaigns against the Franks and Shi'ites soon afterwards were calculated to regain lost popularity. Yet this fourfold system of Islamic law continued throughout the Mamluk period. Baibars also introduced the Great *Yasa*, or Mongol legal tradition, to Egypt for the benefit of the Mongols who now lived in the sultanate. The sultan was an admirer of Mongol institutions, and encouraged the entry of Mongol refugees.

He had the army quadrupled in size and at one point had 1,600 regular troops under his command. To finance this and many other projects, he overhauled the existing systems of raising revenue. He first abolished some taxes, including the unpopular wheel tax, which Qutuz had imposed. Then he created new ones. In particular the *jizya*, the tax levied on non-Muslims, was doubled.

Baibars also improved the messenger service. Communications were important in this vast empire, especially between Cairo and the Euphrates frontier. A despatch rider service, with relay stations throughout the domains, was set up. At the same time he had the pigeon post, begun during Fatimid times, extended and improved. There were about 1,900 pigeons kept in the Cairo Citadel and many more at relay stations elsewhere. Some birds had special markings so that messages they carried would be for the sultan's eyes only. Baibars attended to all despatches as soon as they arrived. He ordered that he was to be woken if one arrived while he slept, and on one occasion even strode naked from his bath to receive a message. He would lose no time at all before he had a reply ready for despatch.

Baibars also developed a highly effective intelligence system. He had many enemies, both within and outside his domains. The sultan had an army of spies throughout his lands, and knew a surprising amount about almost everyone's activities. He also had agents at the Ilkhan's court. Travelling merchants and Khafaja tribesmen, who often crossed into Mongol territory, also aided him this way.

Baibars would inspect everything personally. He often appeared unannounced in all manner of places, and his officials lived in fear of an unexpected visit from the sultan. Baibars even visited brothels in disguise, once catching an amir engaged in illicit sexual activities. The sultan expected his orders to be enacted accurately and without delay; he brooked no insubordination and would severely punish all transgressors. Many of the most severe penalties – executions and mutilations – were carried out in front of his soldiers as stark examples.

Baibars took his religious convictions seriously. On pilgrimage to Mecca, he went in disguise, mingling with the crowds; few Mamluk sultans after him could feel secure enough on their thrones to go on pilgrimage. As a Muslim prince he did far more than provide the customary good works, such as building mosques and making religious endowments. He waged war on prostitution, wine and hashish. He imprisoned all prostitutes until they could be married off and closed the wine shops. Yet he and his closest associates drank alcohol in private.

He showed continued loyalty towards his old barrack comrades. This was a prudent policy, as they were still a powerful grouping, and saw that many of the old Bahri regiment had positions in his government. Aqtai al-Musta'rib, who had called for his election, served Baibars for some years as *atabak*, effectively chief minister at that time. Other Bahri amirs, such as Qalawun and Baisari, held senior posts too. At the same time Baibars advanced his own mamluks, the Zahiris, to the rank of amir and into positions of responsibility, but this he did not do so quickly as to arouse the opposition of the Bahris. Baibars also restored his former master Aidakin al-Bunduqdari to his previous state as a senior army officer, enjoying wealth and comfort again. Aidakin suffered persecution in the next reign, but afterwards lived again in comfortable circumstances until his death in 1285.

Despite his love for learning and scholarship, Baibars had no interest at all in music. No musician ever had any patronage from him. It was a mistake for the people of the last city he conquered to greet him with a band of musicians, for this aroused his annoyance.

For most of Baibars' reign Syria was his chief concern. This was necessary, for the region's integration into the Mamluk empire was no easy task. As it transpired, when Baibars incited the Golden Horde to attack the Ilkhanate he closed the one window the Mongols had on reconquering Syria, and the Ilkhanate seldom had the leadership to conquer thereafter. Towards the end of this time Baibars felt this threat neutralised and his frontier more secure, so he looked towards Anatolia, a region under the Ilkhan's vassalage.

Early in 1277 Baibars set out on his last campaign. Over the past year he had observed the affairs of the Seljuk sultanate of eastern Anatolia. Its sultan being a small child, its government was dominated by an official named Mu'in ad-Din Suleiman, usually known as *al-Parwana* ('The Chamberlain'). Al-Parwana had plans to revolt against the overlordship of the Ilkhan and began intriguing with the Mamluk Sultan. Although Baibars was interested in breaking Abagha's hold over Anatolia, he could not spare the troops when the Seljuk amirs rose in revolt against Abagha in the summer of 1276 and decided to leave the affair to run its own course. Abagha sent a large army to suppress the Seljuk revolt. Baibars then came to the conclusion that the Mongols would attack Aleppo afterwards, and decided to intervene. He set off with his army to Anatolia, to reverse the Seljuks' imminent defeat.

In April 1277 the Mamluks crushed the Ilkhan's army near Albistan. It was a hard-won battle, but the Mongols suffered heavy losses, including some of their commanders. Al-Parwana, who had skilfully changed sides during the rebellion, had fled with the child sultan to Tokat. He negotiated with Baibars for his protection, but the conditions that the Mamluk demanded, and the likelihood that his protection would not be effective, led al-Parwana to decide on remaining on the Mongols' side. Baibars then went to the Seljuk capital of Caesarea (or Kayseri), where the Muslims received him as their deliverer. He set himself on the throne, received the homage of the Seljuks, had his name recited in the khutba and had coins struck in his name. Al-Maqrizi later pointed out that whereas Caesarea in Outremer was Baibars' first conquest, Caesarea in Anatolia would be his last.

Soon afterwards Baibars decided that his new conquest was untenable. Abagha was on his way with a new army, and the Mamluks had gone too far from home ground and into unfamiliar mountainous territory, so he abandoned Anatolia and set out for Aleppo. As the Mamluks passed the scene of the battle at Albistan, the dead still lay there. Baibars had all but a few of the Mamluk corpses buried, so that it looked as if the Muslims had suffered few losses in defeating the Mongols, as was how Abagha would have seen it when he passed. The Anatolian expedition had brought still more prestige to the Mamluk sultanate, but little else. It was a long time before the Mamluks came again to eastern Anatolia, and then they came to stay. Whether Baibars wished to extend his influence into this region afterwards, thus impairing the leverage of the Ilkhan, is not certain, for he did not live much longer.

Baibars died in Damascus on 20 June 1277, shortly after celebrating his victory, at a feast where copious amounts of kumiz were drunk. He complained of extreme pains in his stomach, and died two days later. Legend speaks of poison; an astrologer had predicted that a king would die in Damascus that year, and Baibars decided that it would be a minor Ayyubid prince in his service, after the young man's popularity for his feats on the campaign aroused the sultan's jealousy. Baibars allegedly poured a potion in the amir's kumiz and later drank the poisoned cup himself by mistake. In reality, he may have simply drank too much kumiz, although the symptoms he complained of make the poison story convincing. He was fifty years old.

Baibars was a treacherous despot who often broke his word and could commit the most horrifying acts of cruelty. Yet the same could be said of many others: his amirs, his foreign enemies and many contemporaries in Europe. Baibars was simply the most successful player of such terrible games. Yet his achievement is indisputable. The Mamluk sultanate was a militarily strong and well-ordered state where the civilisation of medieval Islam survived and flourished, long after the Mongols had destroyed much of it. Baibars' reign was characterised by high taxes, harsh treatment, and much bloodshed on the sultan's command. Still, the alternative would not have fared well under the Mongol yoke.

Together with Saladin and Harun-ar-Raschid, Baibars al-Bunduqdari ranks with the most prominent figures of Muslim legend. Al-Maqrizi summed him up as the best of all the sultans. The Egyptians were still singing his praises long after the Mamluk sultanate itself ceased to exist.

5

QALAWUN AND HIS SONS

It is a distinctive feature in the history of the Mamluk sultanate that most of its sultans gained the throne through usurpation. However, almost a century after Baibars the sultanate was hereditary – not through the line of Baibars but that of Qalawun, who followed him as sultan a few years later.

Baibars left three sons – Baraka, Salamish and Khidr – two of whom in turn became sultan. Baraka had been designated his father's heir as early as 1264, and it is obvious that Baibars had every intention of establishing his dynasty. But Baraka showed himself an arrogant, overbearing young man who possessed none of his father's acumen, and he alienated the court very quickly. First he dismissed and later executed his regent and had several Zahiri amirs, his father's mamluks, imprisoned. His most astute piece of statecraft was to launch a new offensive on Cilicia, placing his father-in-law Qalawun and the other most senior Bahri amir, Baisari, in command, which was calculated simply to keep them far away from court. With friends of his own age Baraka led a life of indulgence, oblivious to the fact that he could not afford to offend the powerful amirs when his own supporters were not yet well placed. In August 1279 a palace conflict erupted between the Zahiris and the new sultan's household mamluks. The Bahris acted again, as Qalawun and Baisari returned to demand that the new mamluks be dismissed. During the rising Baraka's supporters, even his own mamluks, deserted him, and he was forced through the Caliph's mediation to abdicate. After this bloodless coup the deposed sultan was sent to exile in Kerak. He died there a year later, officially in an accident on the polo field.

Qalawun emerged as the most powerful from the coup, and as a senior amir with long service he was quickly in command. The other Bahri amirs then suggested that he become sultan, but Qalawun refused, saying that the family of Baibars should retain the succession, which was strange given the events as they unfolded. In reality Qalawun's position was not yet secure, and he was mindful of the Zahiris, Baibars' own mamluks who were still senior amirs, and who might remain loyal to Baibars' children. There was also Baisari, his equal in rank, who could become a serious challenger. The amirs then agreed to elevate Baraka's seven-year-old brother Salamish. Qalawun, having appointed himself atabak, became Salamish's regent.

Qalawun quickly set about removing the Zahiris. He had many seized and imprisoned, as he did other potential enemies. He replaced them in their offices with his Bahri barrack comrades, and a few of his own mamluks, the Mansuris were also created amirs and granted positions of responsibility. This was a potentially dangerous direction, but he could fully trust his own mamluks before all else. Qalawun made the Bahri Sunqur al-Ashqar viceroy of Damascus, and at the same time made his armour bearer Lajin al-Husami commander of its citadel and its garrison, displaying a pattern of governorship often used by the Mamluk sultans. Baisari by this time ceased to show interest in politics, having mostly abandoned himself to gambling and drink. After a hundred days as regent, Qalawun felt secure enough to make his bid for the throne. 'You know well that the empire cannot survive,' he told the amirs, 'if it is not governed by a man of mature age.' Having gained their unanimous assent he had Salamish, who had spent his short reign in the nursery, sent to Kerak to live with his brother.

On 27 November 1279 the amirs offered their homage to as-Sultan al-Malik-al-Mansur Sayf-ad-Din Qalawun al-Alfi as-Salihi al-Alai. The titles preceding his personal name mean 'the Sultan, the Victorious King, Sword of the Faith'. He was often known as al-Alfi ('The Thousander') for his prestige, having once been sold for such a high price. Throughout his life he identified as as-Salih's mamluk. The last title commemorates his first owner.

The name Qalawun (pronounced 'Qala'un') means 'duck' in Turkish, but it is more likely a corruption of the Persian *kilavun* ('Great Ransom'). Qalawun was a little older than Baibars, born about 1220 into the Burj-Oghli tribe of Kipchak Turks. He was not enslaved until his late twenties and was first bought by the amir Ala-ad-Din Aqsunqur. On this amir's death as-Salih acquired him and released him soon afterwards. Qalawun was known for his broad shoulders and powerful appearance and rose to become a senior Bahri amir. After escaping the purge of 1254 he first went to Anatolia and later joined Baibars at Kerak. During Baibars' reign he served in high office and married his daughter to the sultan's eldest son.

In ten years as sultan Qalawun built on Baibars' many successes. Like Baibars he was a capable soldier and administrator, but more often than Baibars he would make conciliatory gestures when he thought they would accomplish more than coercion. Having inherited so much from Baibars' efforts he developed it all further. He continued to cultivate the many diplomatic connections. The intelligence system his predecessor had built became very important, in particular when a plot among the Zahiris to assassinate him was discovered in 1280.

As expected, he soon had to contend with the Mongols. On hearing of the death of Baibars, Abagha had renewed the Ilkhanate's ambitions on Syria and was raising a large army. In 1281, when he was ready, the ideal opportunity arose. The Bahri Viceroy Sunqur-al-Ashqar proclaimed himself sultan in Damascus while the Zahiris' revolt was going on and attempted to seize all Syria. The revolt was quickly suppressed and Sunqur imprisoned, but while Qalawun's troops were still reasserting his supremacy on Syria, Abagha ordered the invasion. The Ilkhan sent 80,000 troops, including large Georgian and Cilician contingents, under the command of his brother Mangu Timur. By October 1281 the Mongols had occupied most of northern Syria as far as Hama and were advancing to meet Qalawun at Homs. Qalawun had raised over 50,000 men, including Turcomans, Bedouins, Egyptian and Syrian peasants, and any others he could find. He pardoned Sunqur-al-Ashqar once he had agreed to fight in his service and gave him an important command.

The two armies met on 31 October near Homs. It was a hard-fought battle, where at an early stage Qalawun was forced to take refuge on a nearby hill, expecting defeat, and Sunqur fled with the Damascene troops of the left flank he commanded. In the centre, however, the Bahris fought on. Even as they gradually wore down the enemy, Sunqur's troops were proclaiming as far away as Gaza that Qalawun's army had been defeated.

A young Mamluk amir, Azdemir al-Hajj, rode into the Mongols' camp, professing that he had deserted and requested an audience with the Mongol commander. This being granted, Azdemir immediately stabbed Mangu Timur. The Mongol survived, but had to be carried off the field and died soon afterwards. His guards quickly disposed of the amir. At this moment of confusion in the Mongol camp Qalawun ordered the charge. The Mongols panicked, their lines breaking as they took to flight. The Mamluks still had to deal with the Mongol right flank, which had returned from pursuing Sunqur, but the invasion had collapsed and the sultan's army quickly regained control of Syria.

The Battle of Homs was decisive for Qalawun's reign and the Mongols did not invade again for some time. Abagha died a few weeks after the defeat, allegedly of drink, and a coup followed. Arghun, his young son, was speedily ousted by his uncle Tequdar, and this usurper then announced his own conversion to Islam, repudiating his former Nestorian Christianity. Tequdar now styled himself Sultan Ahmad and set about persecuting the Christians in the Ilkhanate as a show of his new faith. He then sent to Qalawun an offer of an alliance as Muslims together. Qalawun was not convinced and refused to allow religion to interfere with political issues related to the Ilkhanate. The Golden Horde, still not committed to Islam, was a valuable ally to the Mamluks and an enemy of the Ilkhan, and Qalawun decided against changing sides for such an insecure alliance. He made the more prudent choice, for Sultan Ahmad lasted only two years. Having made too many powerful enemies he was finally overthrown and executed by Arghun, who returned with the support of Mongol religious traditionalists.

As Ilkhan once more, Arghun, himself inclining towards Buddhism, sought a new alliance with Christian Europe against the Muslims. He offered Jerusalem to King Philip the Fair of France in return for support. Unlike his predecessors he no longer spoke with as much faith in Mongol invincibility and now wrote, '*If*, with the authority of heaven, we conquer these people...' No action came of these plans, nor any new crusade and the Mongols did not fight Qalawun again.

The Mongol threat again subsiding, Qalawun could continue Baibars' policy of reducing the sultanate's lesser enemies and allies of the Ilkhan. Collaboration with the Ilkhanate was as real as ever; both Leo II of Armenia and the Knights Hospitallers had fought on the Mongol side at Homs. Qalawun attacked Cilicia, again doing the little kingdom serious damage. Afterwards he made a ten-year peace, in return for an annual tribute of a million dirhams, the release of Muslim prisoners, and the Armenians' agreeing not to build defensive castles. Without the Ilkhan's effective support, King Leo had no choice but to agree.

In Outremer the situation had changed a little since Baibars' campaigns, as the Franks had a new protector. Charles of Anjou was now King of Sicily and Albania and ruler over large areas in Greece, Italy and North Africa as well as his French possessions. He had in 1277 added the crown of Jerusalem to his titles and finally ousted his Cypriot rival Hugh III of Lusignan two years later. Charles was very popular with Muslims and Qalawun was reluctant to fight him, as the good relationship up to that point was not to be abandoned lightly.

In the spring of 1282, all this changed. The Revolt of the Sicilian Vespers brought down Charles' regime in Sicily and his Mediterranean empire, much of it more notional than real, soon evaporated, leaving Charles' deputy in Acre with no effective military support from the West. Charles lost interest in Palestine, and spent his remaining years campaigning to regain Sicily.

Qalawun had made a number of treaties with some of the Frankish cities and lordships during the Mongol invasion to ensure their neutrality. He made more afterwards, usually to keep some neutral while he attacked others, just as Baibars had done. Towards the end he disregarded them altogether. In 1285 he besieged the fortress of Marqab (or Belvoir) by surprise, the Hospitallers inside surrendering after a month. Many of the remaining towns fell in the next few years, each as in Baibars' time reduced to rubble as soon as it was taken. Late in Qalawun's reign the County of Tripoli ceased to exist. In 1287, although Latakkieh was included in a treaty made with the count, it was attacked and taken. An earthquake had breached the wall, and the sultan thought it too much of an opportunity to waste. Two years later the city of Tripoli itself fell, together with the rest of the northern Frankish principality. All that now remained of the Frankish Kingdom of Jerusalem was Acre and its hinterland. Qalawun was preparing a final onslaught in 1290, using as a pretext an alleged outrage of Muslim merchants to resume the jihad. He would have besieged Acre then had he not died on the way. The dream of Saladin and then Baibars had almost been fulfilled.

Late in his reign Qalawun sent an expedition to Nubia to install a puppet king. The original ruler returned as soon as the Mamluk troops left and killed his rival. Qalawun agreed to accept this king in return for tribute.

Qalawun was very popular with the people of Egypt as an able and clement ruler. He had begun his reign by abolishing severe taxes, although his treatment of Christians was harsh. He encouraged trade with both east and west. Making contacts with notable merchants of Yemen, Sind, India and China, he issued trade permits. He also attracted embassies from the Italian cities, the German empire, and other European states. Industry and commerce flourished and there developed the trade network that functioned throughout the Mamluk period.

Like other Mamluk sultans, Qalawun financed many ambitious building projects. His most celebrated was the Maristan, a religious, educational and social complex on Bayn al-Qasrayn in the centre of medieval Cairo. The building contained a mosque, an orphanage, a nursery, a public library, a children's religious school, a lecture hall where the four schools staged regular public lectures, a free public hospital, well-staffed and equipped laboratories and a mausoleum where Qalawun and his son an-Nasir Muhammad are interred. This complex was still in use in the 1850s and part still stands, a new building within its precinct now used as an eye hospital.

When the Sharif of the Hijaz paid homage to Qalawun, as he had to Baibars, he now granted the new sultan the *kiswa*, the honour of providing and draping the Kaaba each year with the traditional black-and-gold cloth. To the present day the Egyptian government continues to fulfil this privilege.

In Qalawun's time the Mamluk army attained its highest standard of discipline and organisation. Qalawun strengthened his hold over Syria by installing a permanent garrison of Bahris at Kerak. The Roda barracks was still a centre for political dissent and Qalawun began another, separate regiment in closer contact with him to offset Roda. This, roughly a third of his regular troops, was quartered in a new barracks in the Citadel. They were mostly Circassians rather than Turks, and became known as the *Burji* ('Tower' or 'Citadel') Mamluks. In the reigns of Qalawun's descendants, the Burjis would eventually become the dominant faction, and they were instrumental in the Circassians supplanting the Turks almost entirely.

Although the last of the original Salihi mamluks did not die until 1307, there were not many left by the end of Qalawun's reign; most, like the sultan, were old men by then. Qalawun founded a second Bahri regiment stationed at the Roda barracks to replace them, but this never approached the standards of the original Bahris and was classed with the third-rate troops often used for less demanding roles. By the end of his reign Qalawun had less cause to placate the Bahris, given their depleted numbers. He had also removed the Zahiris from their positions of power, and there was little chance of Baibars' family trying for the throne, the two surviving sons in exile at Constantinople. Qalawun now knew no restrictions on promoting his own mamluks to the most senior roles.

Like Baibars, Qalawun prepared to pass the sultanate onto his own son. Early in his reign he designated his eldest son Ali as his heir, and Ali's name often appears on his treaties with the Franks as a co-ruler – an important political device for such an insecure regime. But Ali suddenly fell ill and died in 1288, and his brother Khalil was then named successor. There is a story that Khalil had poisoned his brother, and also that Qalawun decided in the end to disinherit Khalil but did not live long enough to sign the decree, but there is no evidence to corroborate either allegation, and when Qalawun died in November 1290 it was Khalil who succeeded him.

At twenty-seven Khalil was energetic and belligerent, and he spent most of his short reign engaged in military campaigns.

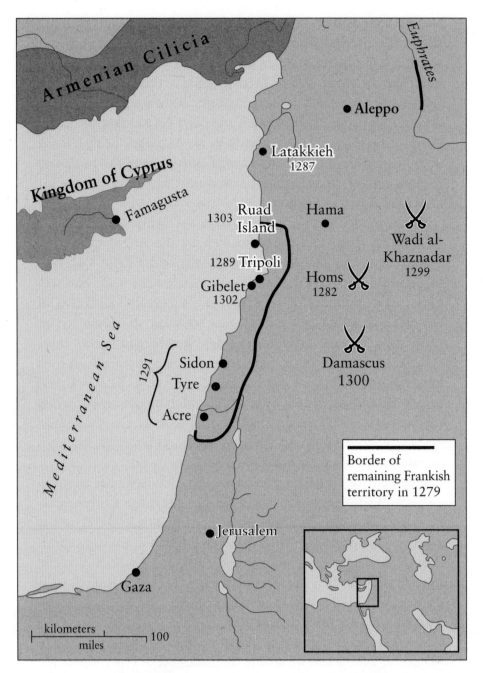

The Conquests of Qalawun and his sons. After Khalil took Acre the other coastal towns surrendered.

His first act was to carry out his father's campaign against Acre, a short but hard-fought siege. The Franks, who had learned too late the need for unity against the Muslims, fought valiantly both before and inside the city. Despite the arrival of King Henry II with reinforcements the defenders were hard pressed. On 17 June 1291 the Mamluk army broke through the defences and Acre fell. The city was looted, with all inside beheaded and the buildings razed. It was the end of the Frankish Syria that the First Crusade had begun; all the remaining towns, Tyre, Sidon, Beirut, Tortosa and the rest, surrendered without further resistance. Only two small pockets of hostile Franks remained: the town of Gibelet near Beirut until 1302, and the waterless island of Ruad off Tortosa, where a garrison of Templars maintained a token resistance until 1303. After Acre fell, all other Christians in the former Frankish territories submitted to the sultan and the European colonisation of the Levant finally ended.

Perhaps given the chronic shortage of military support from the West, the Frankish states were doomed to fall sooner or later. Even in the Ayyubid period however the lands had been established so long and their trade and connections so welcome that the Muslims had little enthusiasm for their conquest, and at the same time there was no real Muslim leadership after Saladin to pursue their destruction. It may be said that it was the presence of the Mongols in Syria and Iraq that gave impetus. Cooperation between Mongols and Franks was limited, but Muslims were uneasy about the prospect of a major Mongol invasion in conjunction with a full-blown crusade from Europe.

The end of the Kingdom of Jerusalem was much lamented in the West, although few admitted that little effort had been made to defend it in all that time. The Templars would be blamed for the loss but that was far from justified. The Europeans would seriously debate new crusades and the restoration of Jerusalem to Christendom from then until the sixteenth century, but this was mostly talk.

Khalil then led the jihad north again. The Ilkhanate was in a state of disarray following the death of Arghun in 1291. His brother Gaikhatu had usurped his son and had sunk the Ilkhanate into economic chaos by the introduction of paper money. Thus the Mamluks could attack the Armenians of Cilicia with little prospect of a Mongol intervention. The city and fortress of Hromlka, known to the Muslims as *Qilat-ar-Rum*, was a Cilician enclave and a patriarchal see on the right bank of the Euphrates. Khalil's troops captured it and renamed it *Qilat-al-Muslimin*, but did not try to hold it when Mongol troops reappeared. Khalil seriously considered a conquest for Islam of all Mongol Asia, but nothing came of his ideas; perhaps even he recognised them as too grandiose.

Khalil's arrogant and high-handed actions provoked opposition among the Mansuris. He had many amirs arrested and some executed. Sunqur al-Ashqar died in prison. Khalil had Turuntai, his father's wazir, killed in front of him. The amir Lajin-al-Husami, whom he had dismissed from the governorship of Damascus, he almost personally strangled with a bowstring. Khalil treated many others in a similarly humiliating manner, even a chief qadi. The new sultan continued his father's policy of recruiting Circassian mamluks to offset the strength of the Turks. He appointed the Turkish amir Baidera al-Mansuri as viceroy but confined his confidence to his wazir Ibn as-Salus, a Syrian Arab who had previously been a merchant. Once again the resentment of established amirs to the rise of new favourites triggered conspiracy, and a faction grew around Baidera and Lajin. The Mansuris once again disliked the presence of Khalil's mamluks.

In December 1293, when the sultan and his party were hunting in the Delta marshes, Khalil struck Baidera in a fit of rage. The amir and his associates decided to act. Later, as the sultan was riding out with a small escort, they set upon Khalil and killed him. The Mansuris proclaimed Baidera sultan. When news of this reached Cairo the Circassians rose against the plotters, together with many other Mansuri amirs who sided with them. Amir

Kitbugha finally killed Baidera and most of his faction, although two other ringleaders, Lajin and Qarasunqur, escaped into hiding.

As Khalil had only left a small daughter, Kitbugha's faction placed Qalawun's third son, the eight-year-old Muhammad, on the throne. An-Nasir Muhammad, as he was known, would reign the longest of all the Mamluk sultans, a total of forty-three years over three separate reigns. At his birth, it was said, a three-tailed comet was seen over Baghdad. Although it was only in the third reign that he ruled by his own will, he was one of the most capable and productive of all the sultans.

As expected, an-Nasir's first reign was little more than a vehicle for Kitbugha's ambitions. Kitbugha was a Mongol who was taken prisoner in 1260 when the Mamluks regained Hama, and had so impressed Qalawun that he had become his mamluk, rising through the ranks once Qalawun became sultan. As Viceroy of Egypt Kitbugha fought a short civil war with Sanajar ash-Shujai, Commander of the Cairo Citadel, who had the support of the Circassians, and whom he finally defeated and executed. Soon after this Khalil's mamluks, the Ashrafis, revolted. After putting them down Kitbugha used this as a pretext for his own usurpation. A mature, capable warrior must be sultan, he told the amirs in December 1294, and they agreed to his accession. The boy sultan an-Nasir was deposed and placed under house arrest in the Citadel nursery.

The pattern was thus repeated. An amir had used a minor as a puppet while he established his own position and usurped the throne once his position was secure enough. Kitbugha may have tried to establish his own dynasty in due course, but the practice showed every sign of continuing, and no hereditary line might have come about. But as soon as Kitbugha was enthroned his luck turned against him. It appears that he had moved too quickly to the throne. Too many of the Mansuris withheld their support, and he could not rely on Khalil's Circassian mamluks. He was forced to pardon Lajin and Qarasunqur and to make Lajin Viceroy of Egypt.

Kitbugha's two-year reign was fraught with disaster. The Nile failed to rise one year, bringing crop failure and famine, and plague killed over 17,000 people in one month. There was also an indecisive dispute with the King of Yemen over the suzerainty of the Holy Cities. Much more damaging to Kitbugha was his decision to allow the Uwairat to settle in Syria. These were Kitbugha's own tribe of Mongols, who had fled persecution from the new Muslim regime in the Ilkhanate. From Baibars' time such migrations were encouraged, and Kitbugha thought they would strengthen his position. But the Uwairat refused to accept conversion to Islam, or even to observe fundamental Muslim custom, and Kitbugha was despised for having admitted them. Kitbugha's popularity was not improved by his overbearing and tactless manner. His arbitrary dismissal of officials in favour of his own supporters once again aroused opposition. In 1296 the faction headed by Lajin decided to act again. When Kitbugha was returning from a visit to Damascus the amirs waylaid his party. Kitbugha escaped but the rebels declared him deposed in his absence. Now Lajin became sultan.

Lajin, a 'Greek' (probably an Anatolian) known for his red hair, had a distinguished career as a provincial governor behind him. He at first proved a diligent ruler, responsible for many buildings and charitable works. He pardoned Kitbugha, who then served as governor of Hama until his death in 1303. He also released the Caliph from the state of house arrest that Baibars had imposed upon him. Lajin declared war on drunkenness, even having offending amirs flogged.

But Lajin in his turn made too many enemies. He appeared to be under the influence of Mangu Timur, one of his own mamluks, and the Mansuris had agreed to his elevation on the condition that he did not promote his own mamluks to supplant them. Mangu Timur became a senior amir so quickly that the established amirs were soon wary. It was a mistake to blatantly threaten the position of an established corps of amirs, as many a Mamluk sultan would discover. Lajin carried on in a pious manner while Mangu Timur ran his government, often dismissing amirs from their positions and having others imprisoned on falsified charges. Even the old and popular Baisari was cast into the Citadel dungeon. Although Lajin had first said he was keeping the throne to hand to an-Nasir Muhammad when he was old enough, he later named Mangu Timur as his successor.

Lajin also conducted a *rawk*, or land survey and redistribution. Such reassessments happened at times, although this was the first since the one ordered by Saladin. As all feudal holdings in Egypt were returned to the sultan's hands and then reallotted, Lajin would have kept more lands than he had previously, possibly to raise more of his own mamluks. The redistribution never actually took place given subsequent events but the amirs, fearing their incomes would be drastically reduced, were understandably discontented.

In October 1298 a new conspiracy formed when Tughji and Kurji, two former supporters of Lajin, joined with Salar, a Mongol Mansuri amir. In January 1299 they heard that the sultan knew of their plot and decided to act. Kurji stabbed Lajin to death as he was playing chess (or at prayer, according to another account) and others murdered Mangu Timur shortly afterwards. Other amirs rose in outrage against the act and the amir Bektash killed Tughji and Kurji.

Afterwards the Turkish and Circassian Mamluks clashed over the succession, but neither side was powerful enough to oust the other. Deadlocked, both groupings agreed to restore an-Nasir Muhammad as sultan, and for each faction to appoint a representative as joint regent. At thirteen an-Nasir was still too young to rule by his own will and the two amirs controlled his government between them. The older amirs, the remainder of Qalawun's original following, nominated Salar. The Burji, mostly Circassian Mamluks, were represented by one Baibars, usually distinguished from his more illustrious namesake by his household title *al-Jashnakir* ('The Taster'). This Baibars, probably a Circassian himself, commanded the army, while Salar, the intriguer and manipulator, headed the civil government. The two often clashed and their rivalry damaged morale.

Elevating an-Nasir did not in itself solve the realm's problems. In 1301 an earthquake destroyed a large part of Cairo and the homes of many people. The Mongols also invaded. Ghazan, son of Arghun, had seized the Ilkhanate with the support of its Muslims, had ordered that all his subjects follow him in embracing Islam and then decided to extend his domain to the Mediterranean. In the autumn of 1299 Ghazan set out across the Euphrates with an army that included Cilicians and other vassal peoples and a number of renegade Mamluks such as the amir Kipchak al-Mansuri, who had with others defected after Lajin's murder. In December the Mongols met the Mamluk defenders at Wadi al-Khaznadar, between Hama and Homs.

Never before had the Mamluk army suffered a worse defeat. Hampered by bad weather, locusts and the Uwairat tribesmen who still campaigned for Kitbugha, the defenders' morale was low, the joint regents' behaviour being partially responsible. The Mongol archers did the Mamluk horses serious damage, and even the defenders' use of the new weapon, 'Greek Fire', or naphtha, made little impression on the invaders. Salar and the Burjis fled the field and the rest soon followed.

Ghazan halted the pursuit of the Mamluk army. He made Kipchak his governor of Damascus, appointed another Mamluk defector to Aleppo and considered Syria annexed to the Ilkhanate. After a few months he took his army away to fight another enemy to the east of his lands and the Mamluks repossessed Syria soon afterwards. They pardoned Kipchak, conducted reprisals on others who had collaborated with the Mongols, and prepared for Ghazan's promised return. Ghazan did come back late in 1300, and for over two years the fate of Syria remained undecided. There were two indecisive campaigns, and Ghazan sent embassies to Europe seeking another alliance with the Franks. Finally, in 1303, the Ilkhan once again invaded, to meet an enlarged Mamluk army near Damascus.

Damascus was a hard-fought battle, and it looked at first like the Mamluks would lose again. Their right wing fled the field, but the rest of the army stood firm despite heavy losses. The Mamluks finally drove back the Mongols, and a tenth of the original army returned to Tabriz. The Persian Mongols would invade Syria once more in 1312, but their threat to the Mamluks effectively ended on this campaign. For a few years after 1299 effective government in Syria ceased. The Bedouin tribes took heart from the first Mamluk defeat, jokingly named their two principal chiefs 'Salar' and 'Baibars', and ran unchecked throughout the region. The state of affairs in Cairo demoralised the provincial governors. The joint regency caused further problems and loss of morale. When a campaign was decided on to extract unpaid tribute from the King of Yemen, Salar placed himself in command in a blatant attempt to win greater prestige over his co-regent. Baibars quickly interposed and as a result of the ensuing quarrel this expedition never took place.

As this was happening an-Nasir Muhammad was growing up, and began to take an interest in affairs of state. On reaching his early twenties he was becoming frustrated at playing the ceremonial role without the power he could expect as sultan. Salar and Baibars kept him under virtual house arrest in the Citadel, unable to see ministers and without any resources of his own. By his own account, even what he ate was restricted. When Salar discovered that his wazir had advanced the sultan money to buy presents for his ladies, he had the official tortured to death on falsified charges of embezzlement. Although the civil government supported Salar, and the military favoured Baibars, the people as a whole very much loved an-Nasir. Many of his father's former mamluks, including some Syrian governors and other senior amirs, also supported him. The young puppet sultan was constantly trying to free himself from the control of his regents. In 1307 he conspired with the commander of the Citadel to have Salar and Baibars arrested but the plot was discovered and suppressed. Salar and Baibars wanted to have an-Nasir deposed after this, but popular support for the sultan made them abandon this plan.

In February 1308 an-Nasir announced his intention of making the *Hajj* (the pilgrimage to Mecca); he would be the first Mamluk sultan to do so since Baibars al-Bunduqdari. His joint-regents agreed to it, thinking it best he was out of Cairo for a while. But when he reached Kerak, an-Nasir went no further and announced his intention of taking up residence there. He had spent part of Lajin's reign in the city. Salar and Baibars sent demands that he return to Cairo if he were to remain sultan. It appears that an-Nasir abdicated, or at least his regents announced that the throne was vacant. By this time the Burji Mamluks had become the strongest faction present in Cairo and Salar prudently declared for Baibars during the succession debate, no doubt preparing further intrigue for later. Baibars al-Jashnakir thus became sultan, with Salar as Viceroy of Egypt. An-Nasir was confirmed as Baibars' governor of Kerak.

The reign of Baibars the Second was short, unstable and demoralising. As the Nile again refused to rise that year, food prices increased dramatically while Salar and his supporters still antagonised the new sultan. There was widespread popular support for the return of an-Nasir, and many of the sultan's mamluks were deserting to join him in Kerak. Baibars sent several letters to an-Nasir demanding the treasure he had brought with him, and that he send to him all but fifty of his royal mamluks, the rest belonging to the office of sultan. An-Nasir made submissive-sounding replies, but succeeded in delaying any act of restitution.

Within a year an-Nasir returned. Perhaps he realised that Baibars would not leave him alone, or perhaps he had come to Kerak in the first place because he could do little in Cairo and would find support there. He made contacts with several disaffected elements in Syria, including the Mansuri amirs Qarasunqur, now governor of Aleppo, Kipchak in Hama and Asendemir in Tarabulus, together with many other amirs in Syria.

Only the Viceroy of Damascus, a mamluk of Baibars, would not join the revolt. Many Bedouins also rallied to his cause.

In January 1310 an-Nasir marched on Cairo. As so many came over to the young man's side Baibars found his own position untenable, despite the Caliph's clear endorsement, and promptly abdicated. An-Nasir Muhammad then ascended the throne for the third time, to remain until his death in 1341. At twenty-four he was certainly old enough to rule on his own, and did so wisely and justly. This third reign would be considered the high point in peace and prosperity for the Mamluk sultanate.

His first acts were reprisals. He pardoned Salar and Baibars, giving each a minor governorate, but as soon as they thought themselves secure he had both arrested. Baibars was strangled, and Salar starved to death in prison, on each occasion the sultan reminding them of their past unwillingness to give him the food he had requested. He had Caliph al-Mustakfi, who had supported Baibars' accession, exiled to Qus, where he and his family lived like peasants for several years tilling the soil; he was known as the beggar caliph. An-Nasir later secured the succession of his own Abbasid nominee to the Caliphate. He also arrested twenty-two amirs within a month of his accession, replacing them in their positions with his own mamluks. All the victims had supported either Salar or Baibars. In doing this he had eliminated most of the established amirs. Not even those who had supported him lasted long. Kipchak died soon after and the other two were at first promoted to better Syrian governorates until the sultan realised they could not be trusted. Asendemir was imprisoned and Qarasunqur fled to the court of the Ilkhan before he could be arrested; he lived in Tabriz until his suicide some years later, after both he and an-Nasir had made several attempts to assassinate each other.

Thus by 1312 an-Nasir had disposed of his most powerful potential opponents. The sources say that he was a short man, with a lame foot and a squint. He had studied Islamic law and theology at a madrasa in Damascus, and had obtained a diploma.

He was the first Mamluk sultan to speak fluent Arabic; he was after all born in Egypt. His means were modest, and he wore no jewellery and lived without great show of riches. He worked long hours at his duties, attending to a large amount of business personally. He appointed no wazir, nor after 1326 a Viceroy of Egypt. The sultan held public court himself twice a week except in Ramadan where he heard petitions from his subjects. He was severe with amirs who treated the common people harshly. He abolished some onerous taxes, and limited the amounts his amirs could extract from the people.

He made some poor choices in appointing senior officials, or may have given them unjust treatment. Two scribes, both Christian converts to Islam, knew both the sultan's trust and his wrath. First was Karim-ad-Din al-Kabir, who became unpopular in 1322 when payments to the royal mamluks fell two months into arrears. The other, an-Nashu, used a form of compulsory purchase to extract money for himself out of the native Egyptians, until the sultan was urged by his Mamluks to put a stop to this in 1339. Al-Kabir was banished and later found strangled. An-Nashu was put to death and his wealth appropriated. An-Nasir also put much of his trust in the amir Tankiz al-Husami, a former mamluk of Lajin. For most of the third reign Tankiz was not only governor of Damascus but commanded all the other governors of Syria as subordinates. He and the sultan were of like mind in every issue, and each married the other's daughter. But in 1340 the two had a disagreement. An-Nasir, fearing that Tankiz would join with the Mongols, had the man arrested and later murdered. A sad end to a long and close friendship.

There were many plots and rebellions against the sultan, which he always punished with death or mutilation. The Druzes in particular rose in revolt against him. An-Nasir always succeeded in suppressing the revolts before they reached a serious stage. In 1331, his cupbearer Bektimur and his son were poisoned on the sultan's orders as it appears they were plotting against him. Despite all this turmoil, an-Nasir's rule was far more secure than those of his predecessors. Unlike them he was not forced to campaign in Syria frequently. He made the Hajj three times in his reign, a clear sign that he feared no coup while he was away.

An-Nasir tried to be even-handed towards the Christians and Jews. This was not easy while the tide of popular feeling was running high against non-Muslims. Many Christians were brought before the courts accused of arson and nearly always put to death; starting fires was believed to have been a major preoccupation among Christians at this time. The sultan could do little to protect dhimmis against this wave of fanaticism, except in a few cases, such as when a fanatical Sufi hacked a Christian scribe to pieces on seeing a Muslim kiss the Christian's hand; an-Nasir promptly had the Sufi hanged. A marked religious intolerance would recur throughout the time of the Mamluk sultanate.

In the tradition of his predecessors, an-Nasir conducted and supervised many public works. He built no fewer than thirty mosques and many public drinking fountains, baths and schools. To this were added roads, bridges and dams. His most spectacular public work was the dredging and widening of the canal joining Alexandria to Fuah in the Delta. Over fourteen years from 1311 this scheme employed over 100,000 workers. It was linked to an ambitious irrigation project which opened new land for cultivation on the western side of the Delta. An-Nasir even founded a new village, an-Nasiriyya, beside the canal. Cairo was linked by water to Alexandria all the year round, which improved communications, commerce and agriculture.

An-Nasir conducted his own land survey and redistribution, repeating the one Lajin had ordered. The *rawk-an-Nasiri*, conducted in Syria in 1313 and in Egypt two years later, made sweeping changes where the sultan kept nearly half the available land in Egypt, and most of the remaining fiefs were allotted to the sultan's mamluks and the amirs. No record on the Syrian rawk has survived. This redistribution increased the sultan's personal revenues and those of his own mamluks. Many amirs found their own incomes reduced drastically; it was said that an-Nasir deliberately gave poorer fiefs to the more popular amirs. It also downgraded the halaqa, for they had fewer fiefs distributed to them, and mostly those with lower incomes. Although it continued to exist in a reduced form, the halaqa lost most of its prestige and saw less action in subsequent years. Needless to say, the material power of the sultan and of his own mamluks was much increased at the expense of the other elements.

This may have been indicative of the lessening of the threat of Mongol invasion. For fifty years the Mamluks had been preoccupied by the serious proposition of a war of conquest once the Ilkhan's army crossed the Euphrates. This reduction in troops, together with the relaxing in discipline in the tibaq, hint at a retreat from the position of constant defence, presumably reducing the strength of the Mamluk sultanate in the long term.

The Ilkhan Ghazan had died in 1304, soon after the defeat in Syria, and his brother Oljaitu had succeeded. At first Oljaitu professed peace but soon, after converting to Shi'ism, declared his intention to spread this persuasion westwards. The conquest of Syria was again planned and new embassies were sent to Europe, but there was no serious action beyond this. Oljaitu later returned to the fold of Sunni Islam, and his vacillating lost him the confidence of his allies. Oljaitu did encourage raids by Armenians into Syria, and there was one by Mongols in 1312, but these accomplished nothing more than renewed Mamluk reprisals against Cilicia.

In 1316 his son Abu Said succeeded as Ilkhan. At eleven Abu Said had already been a provincial governor, able to assert his authority against all opposition. But he was a man of peace and a devotee to music. He sincerely made peace with an-Nasir as two Muslims together, and both made the Hajj together one year. An-Nasir married into the Ilkhanate's ruling family. The Mongols of Persia from Arghun's time were now becoming a more settled people, not so quick to make war, and as Muslims many were unwilling to fight the Mamluks. A few years after Abu Said's death in 1334 the Ilkhanate fell apart and in its place several petty states warred against each other. An-Nasir rejected an offer from the sultan of India of a joint attack on the region, but he sent some military aid to support Hasan the Great, who had seized Baghdad, against his rival Hasan the Less. Mongol Persia was never reunified.

The Seljuk sultanate of Anatolia had itself collapsed in 1300, and Anatolia was now dominated by a number of small principalities, the Ottoman and Qaraman amirates the most significant. An-Nasir accepted homage from some Turcoman chiefs of both Anatolia and Iraq but sent no more soldiers. Such precarious ventures were not worth the lives of his mamluks, he said, and thought it better that the Mamluk sultanate remained untouched by this fragmentation. An-Nasir did send out some expeditions: apart from those against Cilicia he ordered a force into Nubia to install another Muslim puppet ruler. He also sent troops to the aid of the King of Yemen in suppressing a revolt. There were also a number of diplomatic exchanges with Muslim and European princes. The missions between the sultan and King Jaime of Aragon were particularly successful, although an-Nasir thought little of Jaime's suggestion that he should give the Levantine coast to the Christians.

The third reign of an-Nasir Muhammad saw more political stability and prosperity than at any time since that of Saladin. It was an atmosphere that encouraged investment and more constructive pursuits. The traveller Ibn Battuta, who visited Egypt twice in this reign, said much in praise of Cairo and the prosperous and well-ordered society he found there. In his long reign, an-Nasir managed to reduce the hold of the Mamluk amirs on government. He had never been a mamluk and had only been installed twice as a stop-gap device, yet he survived three usurpers and many plots to remove him, and successfully controlled many powerful and restless amirs. The decline of serious enemies on his borders was very fortunate for his regime, and while he was not renowned as a military commander he had less need to be than previous sultans. Throughout the reign of an-Nasir, political stability and prosperity had never been so much in evidence – nor would they be again. It was a stable atmosphere which encouraged more constructive pursuits, and is considered the zenith of the Mamluk sultanate.

Although the practice of succession by usurpation was halted, when the son of a sultan did not last long on his father's throne it only fell into abeyance. It is true that for forty years after his death no amir attempted to usurp any of his descendants, even though many sought control over them. An-Nasir had certainly established the Qalawunid dynasty as legitimate rulers, consolidating the successes of Baibars and Qalawun and creating a well-run state, to the prestige of his own house. When an-Nasir died in 1341, there was no suitable successor.

6

THE RIVER AND THE CITADEL

'Prestige lasts at best four generations in one lineage,' wrote Ibn Khaldun, the fourteenth-century historian and sociologist. The vigour with which a ruling dynasty was founded did not usually extend to later generations. There were already many examples of this in Islamic history, but even as he was writing the descendants of Qalawun were providing yet another.

An-Nasir Muhammad left fourteen sons and eleven daughters, out of whom eight sons would succeed. He probably gave little time to his family, being preoccupied with state affairs, and made no attempt to train any of his sons for government. In fact he did not even name his successor until just before his death. At one time he proclaimed that his favourite son, Anuk, would succeed him, but he withdrew this soon afterwards and Anuk died a year before his father.

An-Nasir's sons were mostly either underage or inexperienced. They showed little ability as rulers and for most of the time it was one or other of the senior amirs who controlled the government, often one of the dead sultan's sons-in-law. Other factions of amirs intrigued against the regent, and at different times groupings such as an-Nasir's concubines and other harem elements dominated. The sultans themselves might try asserting their own authority but they were for the most part arrogant and impulsive youths, often given to alcohol and sexual excesses, and no match for the intriguing of their amirs. They could be deposed if the amirs considered them too much trouble.

A few days before an-Nasir died he named his second surviving son, Abu Bakr, as heir and the amir Qusun as regent. When the sultan died Qusun immediately arrested his rival, the amir Beshtek. Abu Bakr was soon committing acts of unwarranted cruelty, and because he was difficult to control Qusun had the young sultan arrested, deposed and exiled to Qus along with some of his brothers. Later he would have Abu Bakr strangled.

Qusun then placed on the throne an-Nasir's seven-year-old son Kujuk, having gained the Caliph's assent. Kujuk 'reigned' for just five months, his only action to simply hold the pen while Qusun guided his hand to sign state papers. Qusun went on eliminating his many rivals, until the amirs Tushtimur and Qutlubugha realised that they were on his list and revolted. They drove out Qusun, dethroned Kujuk, and wrought terrible reprisals on Qusun's supporters.

The two amirs conducted their coup in the name of Ahmad, an-Nasir's eldest son. Aged thirty and reputedly deranged, Ahmad had been exiled to Kerak by an-Nasir after a homosexual scandal and warned his amirs against ever elevating him. But the victorious amirs now thought him the best choice as figurehead. Ahmad was difficult to understand. He arrived in Cairo dressed as a Bedouin, having acquired the lifestyle of the desert Arab from them, and would only consult with the retinue he had brought from Kerak. His behaviour was abrupt and inconsistent. Almost immediately after promoting both Tushtimur and Qutlubugha, who had put him on the throne, to the highest offices Ahmad had them arrested and beheaded. Ahmad only lasted ten weeks as sultan. He grew fearful of the amirs and ran off to Kerak. The amirs used his flight as a pretext to depose him in his absence and proclaim his brother Ismail in his place. Ahmad refused to hand over the sultan's regalia and Ismail was forced to send armies to Kerak against him. After two years and seven campaigns Ahmad, who defended Kerak against the amirs, was finally captured and executed.

The reign of Ismail was quieter and more benign than most at this time. He had made a number of agreements with the amirs, but soon the influence of his stepfather Arghun al-Alai was increasing over the royal offices. The harem also established itself as a rival political focus in this time and the eunuch Anbar as-Saharti, the sultan's tutor, enjoyed considerable influence too. Ismail eliminated his two brothers and former sultans: Kujuk was strangled, and Ahmad beheaded on secret orders when Kerak was taken. Soon afterwards, in 1345, Ismail fell ill and died, reputedly on seeing Ahmad's severed head brought to him. Sorcery was also rumoured.

Two more brothers, Shaban and Hajji, followed in their turn, both arrogant, reckless and cruel. Shaban was elevated through the influence of Arghun, and made his own agreements with the amirs. Harem politics soon encroached, when a faction of slave girls headed by the Bedouin songstress Ittifaq gained influence. When the covenant with the amirs broke down after two years the amirs rebelled, deposed and executed Shaban and exiled Arghun. Hajji acceded in September 1347 under a similar arrangement with the amirs. He was also under the influence of the concubines and eunuchs, and secretly married Ittifaq. The amirs eventually decided to remove the women from the Citadel and Hajji was left alone to spend his time on the roof talking to the pigeons. When some Circassians revolted in December 1347, Hajji was killed in the fighting as they stormed the Citadel.

Twelve-year-old Hasan, whose mother was the daughter of Tankiz al-Husami, now followed. He would reign twice, the first time as no more than a puppet in the hands of intriguing amirs. The period of harem politics having come to an end, the

Mamluk amirs now fought it out again. Until 1350 two brothers, the amirs Beybogha and Manjak, were the most powerful, until Hasan had the latter arrested in the former's absence. In 1351, as Hasan was obviously showing signs of taking control of his own government, the amir Taz al-Mansuri, now leading the amirs, had Hasan deposed and imprisoned in the empty harem, along with two other brothers. Taz then had a younger brother, Salih, created sultan.

Salih, said to have been a pleasant and reasonable youth, was also sultan in name only. For three years Taz retained control in his name, but in 1354 the amir Shaikhu seized control in Taz's absence. He gave Taz a provincial governorate, had the Caliph depose Salih and then reinstated Hasan, having made agreements with him. Shaikhu ruled in Hasan's name for three years, and then was assassinated in unexplained circumstances. The amir Sarghatmish took his place, but was soon arrested and executed on the sultan's orders.

Sultan Hasan was as vindictive and self-willed as most of his brothers, although he is said not to have indulged in alcohol and womanising as they had done, and was in fact noted for his devotion to his wives. Al-Maqrizi considered him one of the best of the Mamluk sultans. The mosque he built in Cairo at the foot of the Citadel is considered one of the most beautiful buildings in the world. On his command the governor of Aleppo launched a new offensive on Cilicia, which came close to destroying the little kingdom altogether.

Had he ruled longer, Hasan might have been listed as one of the more successful Mamluk sultans. But he aroused the suspicion of the Mamluk amirs by raising civilians to the same rank. He first made ten of the awlad-an-nas amirs of One Hundred and gave them Syrian governorates. He also gave certain powers to some of his eunuchs and some assignments to women. It is possible that he was planning to reduce the influence of the Mamluk amirs and build a power-base with those born in Egypt, but his actions created dissent among the amirs. A sultan who showed too much independence from the standing clique of senior amirs – and, much worse, sought to limit their powers – was asking for trouble, as had long been established. Surprisingly, until the end of his reign there were no revolts against him.

Hasan's impetuous nature proved his undoing. In March 1361 it was whispered to him that the amir Yalbugha al-Umari al-Khassiki, once a mamluk of his own household, was trying to kill him. Hasan publicly humiliated Yalbugha before establishing that there was no truth in the rumour. Yalbugha rose in revolt soon afterwards and, seizing the Citadel, eventually captured the sultan. No more was heard of Sultan Hasan, the only one of an-Nasir's sons who had shown any promise as a ruler. It is likely that Yalbugha had him murdered in prison.

Yalbugha, now in power, appointed himself Grand Amir. As a child sultan would be easiest to control, he passed over Hasan's remaining brothers and chose one of an-Nasir's grandsons, Muhammad, son of the slain sultan Hajji. Two years later he removed this one, declaring him insane. Next the Grand Amir picked Shaban, son of Husain ibn an-Nasir who had recently died. Sultan at the age of ten, Shaban the Second would reign for fourteen years and eventually succeeded in maintaining some order, despite many mishaps and his own shortcomings.

For the first three years Yalbugha governed in Shaban's name, committing acts of noted cruelty which alienated even his own mamluks, the Yalbughawis, who then became increasingly unruly and mutinous. But in 1366 a crisis developed when some Yalbughawis revolted and to escape their patron's wrath appealed for the protection of Shaban. The sultan, desirous of a more active part in government, agreed. Yalbugha, already uneasy about Shaban's assertiveness, tried to have the boy sultan deposed. The Caliph stalled on giving assent to this action and the Grand Amir was soon confronted by a popular revolt on Shaban's behalf. The Yalbughawis, their position vindicated, killed Yalbugha soon afterwards.

While the act of mamluks turning on their patrons was viewed with horror at the time, and is often taken as a sign of the erosion of the mamluk system, this in fact expects more of the institution than was possible. Throughout its existence the mamluk system was not as sacrosanct as may be believed. The reliance of mamluks on their patrons was a vital component of the relationship and was not by any means unconditional. There are instances of mamluks being uncooperative and even close to revolt long before this time, and serious mismanagement of one's mamluks could easily produce the effects as seen. The Yalbughawis continued rioting and talked about killing the sultan too, but Shaban's supporters put down the rebellion. They killed many of the rebels and others were either imprisoned or driven into exile.

Shaban carried on from that point as well as he could. The following years were less unstable and fewer unpleasant incidents took place. His first mistake was to pardon the remaining Yalbughawis and to find them positions in his government. In 1377 Shaban made another mistake by going on pilgrimage, only to hear on reaching Aqaba that the Yalbughawis had again revolted. He returned to Cairo but had to go into hiding. The rebels found and killed him soon after, once he had hidden in the city and was exposed. There followed a civil war where several amirs rose and fell.

Poor leadership, with the sultans either puppets or failing to assert themselves while amirs jockeyed for political power, did not allow for stable government. The mamluk system was no longer as simple and the amirs' loyalty to their patron's sons as sultans had a wide interpretation. Countless rebellions and conspiracies flared and were suppressed with ferocity. Husain, an-Nasir's youngest son, led such a revolt in 1347. There was often fighting in the streets of Cairo between the mamluks of opposing factions.

Coinage became debased in that time also. Shortages in precious metals brought about the mixing of copper with silver in minting dirhams. The standard ratio of twenty silver dirhams to the dinar changed to thirty, and rose further still, never to stabilise again despite the efforts of later rulers. The economy suffered further.

Two major catastrophes also came about in this period, both from outside. The first of these was the arrival in Egypt and Syria in 1347 of bubonic plague, or the Black Death as it was known in Europe. There had been plague several times before in Egypt, but now the toll was far greater than ever. Although al-Maqrizi's estimate of 900,000 dead in Egypt is considered an exaggeration, numbers were very high. In some regions there were not enough left alive to gather the harvest, irrigation schemes fell into disuse and for two years plague killed so many that the entire Near Eastern region suffered from depopulation for centuries afterwards. The pestilence returned several times in the following century and beyond, each outbreak a serious disaster. At the same time came fruit disease and cattle murrain and many animals died of the plague too. In some of these years the Nile failed to rise, and food shortages became the norm.

Crusading from the Christian lands still went on in a muted form. The early Mamluk sultans had destroyed the Frankish states, but the Franks of Europe refused to accept what was to them a terrible affront to Christian belief. Much of this was good intention and came to nothing when the practicalities were discussed, but the Europeans seriously believed they would regain the Holy Land and this desire only declined on the discovery of the New World.

The Mamluks' scorched-earth policy of destroying the Levantine coastal towns and settling warlike tribes in the region had frustrated Frankish plans of a new landing. The Mamluk army would have been a match for the Europeans, unlike the petty, fragmented resistance the First Crusade had encountered, and if the Franks had landed in Palestine again they might not have remained there for long.

Nevertheless, Christian campaigns against the Muslims continued in a different form. The Armenian Kingdom of Cilicia was still a military and commercial threat. Deprived of its Mongol allies, the little kingdom had been received into the Roman Catholic fold in its search for protection, and its king was now linked by marriage to the Cypriot royal house. But these measures proved ineffective, and successive Mamluk expeditions had whittled down the state. When Sis finally fell to the Mamluks in 1375 Cilicia ceased to exist altogether, its last king, Leo VI, a prisoner in Cairo, and Mamluk governors were appointed to its towns as in Syria.

In the eastern Mediterranean two insular powers carried on the fight. The Kingdom of Cyprus, ruled by the Lusignan family since its capture by Richard the Lionheart during the Third Crusade, became the Mamluks' most active enemy. There were also the Knights Hospitallers who had set up their base on Rhodes, their rivals the Templars having been suppressed by the Inquisition in 1314. As naval powers both harassed Muslim merchant shipping, and occasionally raided the mainland, knowing that the Mamluks were such poor sailors that they would not counterattack.

When Peter I of Lusignan came to the throne in 1359, seaborne crusading from Cyprus intensified. As heir Peter had already made forays on the Anatolian coastline and as king he mounted expeditions to the Syrian shore, doing damage and leaving with captives and plunder. In October 1365 Peter set out on his most ambitious campaign. He had toured Europe to recruit for a large crusade and found a limited response, but with the support of the Hospitallers and a fair-sized force Peter landed and captured Alexandria. He chose his moment well. The flooding of the Nile had cut the city off from Cairo, the city's governor was on pilgrimage, and Yalbugha's quarrel with his mamluks was intensifying political uncertainty. Peter's motives are not clear. He either wanted to regain Jerusalem by negotiation, seizing the Nile Delta by the traditional strategy, or was simply attracted by the wealth of Alexandria. It is believed that he was interested in damaging Western trade with Egypt to the economic advantage of Cyprus.

But after taking the city he was clearly prepared to march inland, scenting a spectacular victory over Islam. There was an outside chance that he might have taken Cairo, but the other leading crusaders presented him with a dose of reality. He needed far more troops to accomplish this venture. By taking Alexandria he could secure a landing for a larger army from Europe, but no such army was due to appear, and the existing crusading force was all Peter could rely on. Even then many crusaders were leaving for home, having decided that the crusade had been accomplished. Peter reluctantly decided to withdraw from Alexandria. He put the city to the torch, slaughtered 20,000 people and sailed away with 5,000 prisoners and most of the city's wealth. Peter continued to ravage the Muslim coasts until his assassination in 1369.

The Mamluks vented their fury on their Christian subjects, seizing their property as reparations. Yalbugha had a fleet built to counterattack Cyprus, but the Yalbughawis' revolt overtook his plans and the expedition never sailed. The Mamluks spoke of revenge for this outrage; their own prestige as protectors of Islam had been damaged. But it was a long time before this vengeance would be enacted.

Such an insecure and disappointing period finally ended in 1382 when the former Yalbughawi amir Barquq finally persuaded his fellows that a strong, mature leader was needed as sultan. By this time it was obvious that to defer to the line of Qalawun was to admit irresponsible youths, incompetents and puppets to the throne, who could be used and disposed of by dominant factions of the Mamluk military. Barquq had been involved in both the Yalbughawis' rebellions, but after Shaban's murder he participated in the subsequent power struggles between the amirs Ainabak and Qaratai. Despite not having been a sultan's mamluk, Barquq had risen in the period between the two revolts by skilful intriguing from the rank of common faris in 1365 to that of Amir of One Hundred by 1379. Once he removed the other contenders, having them drugged at a feast and imprisoned, Barquq took command in the name of Shaban's son Ali, another child sultan.

For three years Barquq sought to establish his position in the usual manner. His most serious opponent was his brother (or possibly his blood brother) Baraka, who had risen with him from the ranks, but when Baraka revolted in 1380 Barquq had him imprisoned and executed. The sultan Ali died in the Citadel the following year under suspicious circumstances and Barquq replaced him with his eleven-year-old brother Hajji. In 1382, Barquq felt secure enough to call for his own accession and Hajji was deposed, Sultan al-Malik-al-Mansur Barquq al-Yalbughawi al-Uthmani taking his place.

Barquq was a Circassian, the first of his race to become a Mamluk sultan, with the possible exception of Baibars al-Jashnakir. He began what is known as the Burji, or Citadel, line of Mamluk sultans, who ruled until the conquest of 1517. Now that the Mamluk succession is usually divided into the Bahri and Burji periods, the first hereditary and the second elective, this division is somewhat simplistic. The River and the Citadel regiments were distinct entities in Qalawun's time, but even then the original Bahri regiment was ageing. The Roda barracks no longer played any part in politics after the thirteenth century and the sultan's mamluks were quartered at the Citadel.

Perhaps a more accurate division would be that of the Bahri regime from 1250 that produced Baibars and Qalawun, Aibak being something of an exception, followed by the hereditary sultanate of the Qalawunids. From 1382 the pattern of succession was that of usurpation, when the son of each sultan would first follow his father while the amirs would struggle among themselves for supremacy and the winner would usurp the hereditary sultan. Strangely enough the principle of hereditary succession was never formally abandoned but no hereditary sultan after this point was followed by a third generation, and only Barquq's heir reigned more than a few years.

From Barquq's time the Mamluks were Circassians rather than Turks by majority. There is no clear explanation for this.

It has been suggested that the supply of Turks diminished in the fourteenth century as a result of so many Turkish boys taken as slaves, disrupting the male-female ratio in their homelands. The Mongol devastation of the Steppes in that time has also been cited. The Circassian preference for their own race certainly aided this process. The Turks themselves could countenance other races, as the presence of Mongols, Anatolians and Circassians among their retinues testifies. There is no basis in Muslim thought for racial discrimination. The Circassians in contrast preferred their own race when raising mamluks and advanced them as their own positions improved, often taking advantage of the other races' lack of partiality.

According to tradition the Circassians were descendants of the Ghassanids, an Arab tribe who entered the Caucasus Mountains during the time of the early Arab conquests and settled there when they lost their way home. This is however the result of a practice of creating fake ancestries in Islamic culture and the Circassians were in reality a mountain people, pastoral in their lifestyle, and with different traditions than the Turkish herdsmen of the Steppes. Their loyalties were determined by a framework of sworn brotherhood, which was at times broken.

In contrast to the Turks the Circassians were hardly renowned as a race for their martial skills. Some Circassian mamluks had been purchased for their civilian trades, such as bakers or sailors. They still served as mounted soldiers in the mould of the original Turkish mamluks, but may not have been as successful. Many Circassians found political intriguing and treachery to have been their element. Nepotism, or indeed any close family association among the Mamluks, was rare in the Bahri period. Younger brothers of sultans and amirs, brought to Egypt and purchased in the slave markets, would be sent to the tibaq with the other boys, and could not count on any preferential treatment. Circassian Mamluks who rose in status might have their relatives brought to Egypt and given positions of authority, some even made senior amirs with the minimum of military training.

There had been Circassians among the original Salihi Mamluks, long before Qalawun bought large numbers in order to counterbalance the Turkish Bahris, and both Khalil and an-Nasir Muhammad continued this policy. Hasan sold many of his Circassian mamluks to reduce expenditure, as he considered them of inferior quality. His successors reversed this policy and many Circassians became amirs in the time of the later Qalawunids. There were still Turkish mamluks after 1382, but few appear associated with important events. Barquq still bought Kipchaks, and had inherited many unfreed Turks from his predecessors, but he himself gave preference to Circassians, despite his wife's exhortation to strike a better racial balance among his following. Yet his most favoured amir, his brother-in-law and Grand Amir, was Taghri Birdi, a Turcoman from Anatolia and the father of the historian of the same name. As the Mamluk military class was confined to the first generation, the Turks were supplanted fairly quickly and by 1412 few remained, mostly the older ones, survivors from previous times. Ibn Taghri Birdi, writing in the fifteenth century, suspected that his contemporary sultans Tatar and Barsbai gave advancement to Circassians simply because they were Circassians, and certainly not for their merits.

When Barquq first became sultan he brought a period of comparative stability and the Mamluk sultanate was again respected in the region. He received homage and tribute from the rulers of Baghdad, Tabriz, Mosul and several other petty amirates of Iraq and Anatolia; since the Ilkhanate had ended there were few enemies of the Mamluks in either Iraq or Anatolia. He conducted many public works, including the aqueduct at Arrub in Palestine and a large madrasa on the main street of Cairo near to that of Qalawun. Barquq's drinking of alcohol in public with his retinue offended Muslim piety, but he was otherwise respected as a bringer of order.

After a long apprenticeship in intrigue and rebellion Barquq proved adept in intercepting conspiracies. Before he had been long on the throne he discovered a plot in which some amirs planned to replace him with the Caliph. Barquq had the conspirators executed but could only content himself with imprisoning the Caliph himself, given the need for his support. Throughout his reign there were many arrests, imprisonments, tortures, assassinations and exiles, often without due cause but simply in order to assert his supremacy. Barquq had only to suspect a conspiracy in order to turn on anyone. He once had his chamberlain nailed to a plank and paraded around Cairo on a camel, purely on suspicion.

He still had his own khushdashin to deal with, some jealous of his elevation, and at best hard to manage. Some in fact were plotting against him, although his problem was knowing which ones. Barquq's behaviour, which bordered at times on paranoia, brought down his government in 1389. Yalbugha an-Nasiri, Barquq's khushdashin, then governor of Aleppo, learned that the sultan had suspected him of conspiring against him and was planning his murder. Yalbugha contacted his counterpart in Malatia, the amir Timurbugha al-Afdali, known as Mintash, who definitely was considering rebellion. The two amirs raised the revolt together and many discontented elements joined them. It is likely that dispossessed Kipchaks supported this rebellion. Barquq, unable to resist such opposition, accepted Yalbugha's terms of surrender, which guaranteed his life against Mintash's wishes. Barquq was deposed and imprisoned at Kerak. Yalbugha refused the sultanate when offered, and the two victors finally agreed to restore the previous sultan, Hajji ibn Shaban.

Hajji was now an adult and expected to rule by his own will, but soon showed himself unable to control his two kingmakers. Within a year Mintash rebelled again and fought a civil war with Yalbugha. When Mintash sent his men to Kerak to have Barquq put to death the people of the town heard of it and liberated the prisoner before they arrived, Barquq had become a popular hero during those troubled months and he rallied those discontented with the new regime, including Bedouins and Druzes. He quickly defeated his two enemies, first supporting one against the other and then having both captured and executed. After nine months Barquq was sultan again.

Hajji, deposed a second time, was held under house arrest in the Citadel and left to carry on as he wished, his main interests being alcohol and sadistic practices towards his slave girls, and Barquq only intervened to curb his worst excesses; Hajji often had his personal band play loudly to drown out the cries of his slaves. The last of the Qalawunids commanded no personal credibility whatsoever, and usually presented himself as a drunken exhibitionist at Barquq's feasts. There was no further attempt to reinstate him.

Barquq's second reign differed little from the first, although no more serious rebellions appeared. The comparative stability he restored was much appreciated. But late in this time there came a new and unexpected threat from the Mongols. Long after the Persian Mongol state had disintegrated the armies of Timur the Lame, known to the west as Tamerlane the Conqueror, came out of the lands further east. A descendant of one of Genghis Khan's retinue, Tamerlane sought to emulate the Great Khan and having begun likewise as a teenage outlaw, he died ruler over a vast Asian empire. In 1388 Tamerlane was ravaging Iran and Iraq and took Baghdad, forcing the Jalayrid sultan Ahmad ibn al-Uwais to take refuge at Barquq's court.

When Tabriz was added to the Timurid empire in 1394, with the ruling Black Sheep Turcomans defeated, Tamerlane sent to Barquq the customary demand for his submission, written in rhymed verse. Barquq, in the spirit with which Qutuz had answered Hulagu, imprisoned Atilmish, Tamerlane's ambassador, had his four companions executed, and sent a similarly boastful reply, also in rhymed verse. Tamerlane prepared to invade the Mamluk sultanate. His army was not ready to meet the Mamluks, and he became involved in an attack on Mardin in eastern Anatolia, whose ruler showed signs of insubordination. This gave Barquq time to gather his resources. He looked for allies, accepting an offer from Tokhtamish, Khan of the Golden Horde.

The Ottoman sultan Bayazid in western Anatolia sent money, which was much needed.

But when Tamerlane was ready he marched north instead. He all but destroyed the Kingdom of Georgia, and then campaigned against the Golden Horde after Tokhtamish marched on him, afterwards returning in 1396 to his capital of Samarkand. For the next few years he was preoccupied with plans for conquering India, but he would return to meet the Mamluks later. When Barquq reached Aleppo with his army in September 1394, he heard that Tamerlane had left. It looked as if Barquq had driven off the Mongols, and this bolstered the sultan's prestige. The Jalayrid ruler had retaken Baghdad a few months before with Mamluk aid. The role of the Mamluk sultan as defender of Islam had re-emerged, and Barquq had thus restored credibility to the Mamluk sultanate, even without fighting.

When Barquq died in 1399 he had achieved a degree of political stability and restored confidence in the Mamluk sultanate. Hereditary monarchy has always had one flaw: rulers may not inherit the qualities that saw their parentage fit to rule. An able and conscientious chief minister to act on their behalf is the best arrangement in such circumstances, but this was hardly possible when amirs were continually plotting to unseat them, as with the later Qalawunids. Barquq restored the basic definition of the sultan as the chief executive in Islam whose word was the ultimate command. But sultans do not live forever, and more instability would follow.

7

CIRCASSIAN RULE AND MISRULE

Barquq's usurpation of the sultanate may have ended the effete and inept ruling dynasty the Qalawunids had become, but his accession did not repudiate the principle of hereditary succession, even though in practice every hereditary sultan after him was usurped by the most senior amir. Despite all else, the Mamluks never abandoned the principle of primogeniture. Surprisingly, Barquq's son Faraj did reign longer than most hereditary sultans and by his own will most of the time.

The day before he died Barquq convened a meeting of the senior amirs, the Caliph and the chief qadis where he gained the assent that the nine-year-old Faraj would succeed him, naming his amir Aitamish as regent. Barquq was more attached to his family than previous Mamluk sultans; he brought his aged father Anas from his homeland to live in Egypt, along with some of his other relatives whom he created amirs. In the event six of Barquq's own mamluks would succeed him in turn as sultan, even though he planned for his own dynasty. As soon as Faraj was installed a conflict developed between the regent Aitamish and the

amir Taghri Birdi on one side, and the amir Sudun, a relative of
Barquq, on the other. Many of Barquq's other amirs, the Zahiris,
expecting another usurpation, declared their loyalty to the family
of Barquq. This saved Faraj from being immediately deposed, but
his subsequent thirteen-year reign did not state the best case for
any return to hereditary succession.

An-Nasir Faraj was no docile boy sultan. He lived in constant
fear that his father's amirs were plotting to remove him, often
with some justification, and such insecurity caused him to
grow up suspicious, treacherous, cruel, alcoholic and probably
deranged. His own mamluks were Anatolians, as his mother had
been, and were resented by the Circassian majority. As impetuous
young men they played on their patron's insecurities. In 1400,
when Faraj reached ten, he declared himself of adequate age
to rule and dismissed Aitamish from the regency. He quickly
set about arresting several amirs, some of whom he had
just promoted to senior positions, and as a result other amirs
boycotted the sultan's court, fearing arrest in turn. Although
the Zahiris and the sultan later made peace with assurances of
mutual loyalty, Faraj still listened far more to his own mamluks
and looked warily at the amirs. Soon afterwards the amir Tanam
az-Zahiri, governor of Damascus, rebelled on the pretext of the
behaviour of the sultan's companions, and many other Zahiris
joined him. The revolt collapsed when some governors went back
over to Faraj, and Tanam, Aitamish and several other Zahiris
were captured and executed. Taghri Birdi as Faraj's maternal
uncle was spared but forced to live in retirement in Jerusalem.

Before Syria had recovered from this insurrection, Tamerlane
returned with his army. Having heard of Barquq's death the
Mongol leader, now advanced in years but still very active, set
out again from Samarkand, confident that he could win Syria
this time. The rulers of the western Islamic lands prepared their
defence. The Ottoman sultan Bayazid I proposed an alliance
to Faraj, which may have been the best course of action, but
Faraj's mamluks reminded him that the Ottomans had seized

the Mamluk-held town of Malatia shortly after Barquq's death and persuaded him to reject Bayazid's offer. When Tamerlane devastated the town of Sivas in eastern Anatolia, burying the entire Ottoman garrison alive, the Mamluks did nothing. When the Mongols crossed the Euphrates in September 1400, destroying the Syrian frontier town of Ain Tab, the amirs in Cairo were still behaving as if nothing was happening, quarrelling over fiefs and commands, plotting against Faraj and similar activities.

Lack of responsible leadership was disastrous when faced by the likes of the Mongols, and the Mamluks should have kept their eyes open to this new Mongol threat. On 30 October Tamerlane took Aleppo, destroying the Mamluk garrison after a short siege and allowing his men the customary orgy of looting, rape and carnage. On hearing of it the Mamluks quickly prepared for action; Faraj mustered all his resources, even calling Taghri Birdi out of exile and making him governor of Damascus. As Hama suffered the same fate as Aleppo, the Mamluk army hurried to defend Damascus.

In the closing days of 1400 the armies met near Damascus himself. The Zahiris, who had cut their lances short so that they could stab one enemy after another more quickly, scattered the Timurid force, killing many before they regrouped. A few days later the Mongols tried again and succeeded in driving away the Mamluk left flank, but the rest stood firm and beat the invaders back to their camp, after which Tamerlane was forced to call a truce. The Mongols were far from defeated, but the battle was running in the Mamluks' favour. Some of Tamerlane's soldiers were changing sides while some Mamluk amirs had retaken Aleppo, massacring the Timurids in occupation. The troops Tamerlane had sent against Tarabulus were killed by villagers showering rocks on them. There was even a rumour that half the Timurid army was ready to desert to Faraj, but this last was a ruse engineered by Tamerlane.

In any event the Mamluks were holding their ground, and might have at least caused the Mongols to withdraw had they continued in this manner. But the amirs were still quarrelling and plotting as usual. When Faraj noticed that certain amirs had disappeared, and heard a new rumour of a plot to overthrow him, he panicked. With his retinue he immediately took off for Cairo, where he believed a coup was under way. The Mamluk host soon fell into a state of confusion, especially when several amirs and qadis who went after the sultan to bring him back were killed on the way by rebellious Druzes. Deprived of its leadership, the army disintegrated and the troops drifted back to their homes. Abandoned with the Mongol army at their gates, the Damascenes prepared to defend themselves. Taghri Birdi, whose suggestions had been consistently ignored throughout the campaign, urged a concerted resistance which proved effective.

But Tamerlane resorted to treachery. Adopting the pose of a pious Muslim ruler, he negotiated with the men of religion in the city including Ibn Khaldun. He offered the people of Damascus their lives in return for their submission and tribute, at which point the Damascenes opened the gates. The Mamluk garrison in the citadel refused to surrender, and Tamerlane spent nearly a month overcoming them. But once he had the city completely under his control, Tamerlane quickly forgot his promises, releasing his troops to do as they pleased. Following an outburst of atrocities – mass murder, torture, rape, looting and senseless destruction – large areas in Damascus were put to the torch and many famous buildings destroyed, including the mosque of the Umayyads.

Against expectations, Tamerlane seems to have decided against conquering the Mamluk empire at that time. It was, after all, a long way from Damascus to Cairo and such a campaign would involve some planning and resources. Perhaps he thought the Ottomans the more serious enemy and felt his left flank was secure after the victory in Syria. Having devastated northern Syria, he marched away. In September 1401 he vented his wrath on Baghdad for having thrown off its submission; the city was again reduced to charred ruins, with the customary pyramids of human skulls erected among them. By the following year, in July 1402, he reached central Anatolia. At Ankara he defeated the Ottomans – so heavily, in fact, that it took them some time to recover their military strength – and took Bayazid prisoner.

Tamerlane never returned to fight the Mamluks, dying in 1405 on the way to conquer China. He had made his mark on Syria, however: a trail of death and destruction and a breakdown in the Mamluk administration. Although Taghri Birdi soon returned to Damascus, as did his counterparts to the other governorates, there was much damage done and he returned to a ruin. Damascus never rose again to its former splendour.

Tamerlane's invasion was only one of the catastrophes that characterized Faraj's reign. As soon as the invaders had gone, the Mamluk amirs were fighting each other for control of the government. To be in a position to gain influence over Faraj, the amirs Yashbak ash-Shabani, Nauruz and Inal Bey each in turn rose and fell, perhaps to return to prominence later. Civil war became the norm, and the lives of the civilian population were often disrupted. The Circassian Mamluks in the government campaigned to have the other races excluded; Taghri Birdi as an Anatolian was unpopular at court and was dismissed and reinstated from his office several times. There was famine, plague, brigandage and general instability. The warring amirs continually aggravated all this with their fighting and extortion. Businesses were disrupted and everywhere peasants feared to work on the land. The Franks raided the coasts, a force of Cypriots and French under Charles d'Albret, Marshal of France, ravaging Alexandria in 1403 and then Tarabulus, Beirut and Sidon.

Sultan Faraj, now in his mid-teens, was hardly developing the qualities of an able ruler and his earlier experiences had made him alcoholic, paranoid and easily enraged. He would have many people arrested and executed purely on suspicion. Once he personally beheaded a wife he had recently divorced and her new husband, apparently out of pure spite. He also offended Muslim orthodoxy by having his likeness struck on coins. Worse still, he promoted his tutor, the young scholar Ibrahim ibn Ghurab, not only into the military class, which was unusual for a civilian official, but to the grade of Amir of One Hundred, and made him president of the council of amirs. Predictably, this offended the established order.

In 1405, during some horseplay at a drunken party in his bath, some of the sultan's Circassian mamluks held Faraj underwater too long, and only an Anatolian mamluk's intervention saved him from drowning. Convinced this was part of a plot to kill him, Faraj disappeared. Not knowing his whereabouts, the amirs replaced him in his absence with his younger brother Abdul Aziz. But Faraj reappeared from hiding two months later, and no one complained when he retook the throne. Faraj later had Abdul Aziz and his other brother Ibrahim poisoned, preventing their use in any further usurpations.

In 1407 a new revolt began when the amir Jakam had himself proclaimed sultan in Damascus and nearly all the governors of Syria recognised him. The only governor to remain loyal to Faraj was Shaikh al-Mahmudi, who governed in Safad. Shaikh defeated the rebel army at Gaza and killed Jakam battle. Having restored Faraj's authority in Syria, Shaikh soon welcomed his sultan in Damascus. Far from expressing gratitude, however, Faraj tended to treat his best supporters as enemies. He promptly had Shaikh arrested and thrown into the prison at the Zuwaila Gate in Cairo, which often held those sentenced to death. He also ordered the arrest of seventeen other amirs, including Yashbak and Taghri Birdi, some of whom were also loyal to him. Shaikh escaped from prison soon after; Yashbak did too, but he was recaptured and killed. Shaikh seized Damascus and reaffirmed his loyalty to Faraj, although this the sultan rejected. After the mediation of Taghri Birdi, since restored to favour, Shaikh was eventually pardoned and created governor of Tarabulus.

Over the next few years Faraj continued his purges and unwarranted executions. In his last year he had a hundred Zahiris halved at the waist for no apparent reason. In 1411 his policy of turning on his most faithful supporters brought about his downfall. Shaikh, on hearing that Faraj was again preparing to arrest him, declared himself in revolt, joining with Nauruz and other discontented elements, including a large part of Faraj's army. In April 1412, after a campaign in Syria, the rebels besieged Faraj in Damascus. The young sultan had lost nearly all his willing support, Taghri Birdi having recently died, and he surrendered after a fiasco of a battle, following which he was deposed and imprisoned. The victorious amirs, on a decision opposed by Shaikh alone, had Faraj murdered in captivity.

Although Shaikh led the winning faction he was far from ready to claim the sultanate himself. There were too many potential opponents, in particular Nauruz, his equal in rank. With the sons of Barquq now all dead, there was no designated successor nor any hereditary claimant. There was again a need for a nominal sultan, at least until a candidate could establish himself with enough support. During the fighting, a successor had already been chosen: the Caliph al-Musta'in Billah. As the rebels besieged Faraj in Damascus they announced at a crucial time that the Caliph had deposed him. Al-Musta'in, who was their prisoner at the time, protested, and the amirs offered to make him sultan in return for his compliance. After the defeat of Faraj, al-Musta'in agreed to remain titular sultan for a time although not even he expected to control the Mamluk amirs. The Abbasid Caliphate was a thing of the distant past, this line of shadow-caliphs in Cairo only existing for the purposes of Baibars I and his successors. There had once been a plot in Barquq's time to replace him with the Caliph, but that plan itself was ill-conceived. Al-Musta'in simply provided the gravitas that made the situation look more stable than it was while Shaikh consolidated his position.

As atabak, Shaikh ruled over Egypt for five months in the Sultan-Caliph's name while he prepared his own succession. At the same time, however, Nauruz was the virtually independent ruler of Syria. Not even Al-Musta'in expected to keep the position, instead requesting that he remain Caliph after Shaikh became sultan. This was agreed, but when Shaikh did take his place he later deprived al-Musta'in of the Caliphate and had him imprisoned.

On becoming sultan, Shaikh laboured to restore order in his realm and to eliminate the many abuses that had grown in Faraj's time. Famine, plague and high food prices were common, and lawlessness had become normal in many areas. Shaikh had wheat prices fixed and gave aid to the poor and needy. He also gave support to religious foundations, and promoted music and poetry. But first he had to deal with Nauruz, who had mobilized on hearing of his former ally's usurpation. From March 1414 Shaikh campaigned to regain control of Syria. By June he had Nauruz under siege in Damascus. He succeeded in having his rival come out to negotiate after swearing an oath guaranteeing safe conduct; this oath was delivered in such faulty Arabic that the qadis could easily declare it invalid. As a result, when his rival emerged Shaikh had him arrested and put to death. Shaikh had Syria again.

Shaikh's rule as sultan was considered more benign than most, and government went on in a more reasonable manner. Ibn Taghri Birdi considered him one of the better sultans; as an orphaned child he knew Shaikh's generosity. Shaikh was nonetheless dishonest at times, and often seized the property of important officials, as did many Mamluk sultans. He was also a noted drunkard from his youth.

Shaikh's reign saw a renewed expansion of Mamluk territory in eastern Anatolia. A number of campaigns against the Turcoman amirate of Qaraman had by 1419 regained former Cilician territory around Tarsus and near Caesarea. In the first half of the fifteenth century the Circassian sultans sent several expeditions into that region in a new drive for the expansion of territory, which may have been a continuation of the Mamluk conquest of Cilicia and the need to maintain the new borders. The Mamluk sultanate became increasingly drawn into the mountainous lands to the north of Syria, somewhat out of its comfort zone, and into campaigns against a host of new enemies.

For most of Shaikh's reign there were still some Zahiri amirs and some of Faraj's former mamluks, the Nasiris, who supported the claims of Barquq's family to the sultanate. But on the death in 1417 of Faraj's son, also called Faraj, this movement lost its impetus. On the whole there were comparatively fewer internal uprisings while Shaikh was sultan. Typical of the Burji sultans, the amirs were khushdashin of the ruler and were at once supporters and potential rivals.

When Shaikh died in 1422 he was succeeded by his son Ahmad. He had at first wanted to be succeeded by his older son Ibrahim, who was of an age to take responsibility, but Ibrahim had died in 1419. Consequently the Zahiris, Barquq's mamluks, reasserted themselves and the five sultans who followed came from their ranks. For eight months after Shaikh's death the Zahiri amir Tatar worked to establish himself as virtual ruler, with his khushdashiyya's tacit support. Tatar won popularity by distributing treasure to the army and removing Shaikh's mamluks, the Mu'iyadis, from their positions. There were many arrests and executions as he dealt with other opponents. When he had eliminated Grand Amir Altunbugha, Tatar married Shaikh's widow and declared himself sultan. With an extensive education in Islamic law, Tatar might have made a successful sultan, as many believed he would, but this promising reign was cut short with his death from illness three months later. The amirs replaced him with his young son Muhammad.

Less than four months on, another Zahiri amir repeated the pattern. Janibek as-Sufi, the Grand Amir, was speedily unseated by the Zahiri amirs Barsbai al-Duqmaqi and Tarantai. Having imprisoned Janibek, Barsbai was obliged to defeat Tarantai before assuming the sultanate while Muhammad ibn Tatar was allowed to revert to private citizenship. Barsbai reigned longer and more successfully than most of the Burji sultans. Although the customary payment to the troops was not made on his accession to the sultanate in April 1422, he kept their allegiance. Barsbai abolished the custom of his subjects kissing the ground before the sultan, although he soon re-introduced obeisance in a less-undignified form. Some of his successors insisted on the original practice.

The most prestigious event of Barsbai's sixteen-year reign was the Mamluk conquest of Cyprus. Ever since Peter of Lusignan's attack in 1365 the Mamluks had vowed revenge on this outpost of seaborne crusading from the West, and even in the time of Baibars I the Mamluks understood that the island was a base for attack by the Franks. But no expedition had ever set sail since the early period, despite renewed raids on the mainland in Faraj's reign. Cyprus had been secure for so long because the Mamluks had little maritime sense, the sea not being their element. The Franks, either Cypriots or Catalan corsairs using the island as a base, had become very bold in their piracy; they even stole merchant ships from the harbour at Alexandria, and there were rumours of a new invasion. In 1422, when the Franks seized a ship carrying the new sultan's ambassador and gifts for the Ottoman ruler, Barsbai ordered a counterattack that was long overdue.

Three expeditions sailed for Cyprus. In July 1424 a Mamluk raiding party landed at Limassol, sacked the town and departed with loot and prisoners, and a similar foray took place the following summer. Finally in 1426 a large fleet transported a Mamluk army and their horses to Limassol. They ravaged the island, burned Nicosia and plundered wherever they went. They defeated the Cypriot forces at Choirokoitia with very little fighting.

King Janus of Cyprus, taken prisoner, was brought to Cairo to be publicly humiliated, and his banners dragged in the dust. Barsbai only released him when he had agreed to pay a large ransom and an annual tribute, and after he had sworn that he was the sultan's mamluk. For some time a Mamluk garrison remained on the island. Of the Mamluks' Christian enemies in the eastern Mediterranean only the Hospitallers on Rhodes remained, but the shock of the Mamluks seizing Cyprus was enough for their Grand

Master to make a peace treaty with Barsbai. The Knights gave the Mamluks no trouble for some time afterwards.

At the same time, the eastern Anatolian region was again cause for concern. Emerging from the dispute between members of Tamerlane's family after the conqueror's death, Shah Rukh, one of his sons, succeeded after a coup in ruling his father's empire from Herat. But his authority over the western region – western Iran, Iraq and Anatolia – proved at best nominal, and two rival confederations of Turcoman tribes disputed supremacy in these regions. The Qara-Koyunlu and the Aq-Koyunlu, or the Black Sheep and the White Sheep Turcomans, were distinguished by the fact that the Black Sheep had never accepted vassalage to the Timurids whereas the White Sheep did, and that they were respectively Shi'ite and Sunni Muslim. To the west of Mamluk Anatolia lay the decaying amirate of Qaraman, which at least insulated the Mamluks from border tensions with the emergent Ottoman sultanate that now stretched through western Anatolia and into the Balkans. The Dulqadir (or Zu-l-Qadr) amirate also bordered on Mamluk territory. In Shaikh's time the Black Sheep Turcomans were the most aggressive. From their centre near Lake Van they spread, seizing Baghdad in 1410. Eventually their khan, Qara Yusuf, claimed supremacy over all Iraq, Azerbaijan and western Iran, and menaced Mamluk Syria. But by the reign of Barsbai the Black Sheep's aggression had faded, and the White Sheep rose from eastern Anatolia, gaining ground at the expense of their rivals.

From 1429 Qara Yelek, Khan of the White Sheep, raided the frontier region of Mamluk Syria and temporarily occupied Ruha. In 1433 Barsbai was obliged to lead an army against Amid, the Turcoman capital. According to Ibn Taghri Birdi's eyewitness account as a junior halaqa officer on the campaign, Barsbai and his amirs conducted the campaign with marked incompetence and a pathetic lack of military sense. Uninspired, the troops showed little enthusiasm. Despite such a poor show of Mamluk strength, Qara Yelek eventually agreed to a nominal submission to the sultan and to keep the peace. A temporary revival of the Black Sheep kept Qara Yelek busy for a while afterwards. Until the last year of the Mamluk sultanate, none of its sultans would lead an army into battle again.

Shah Rukh occasionally attempted to assert his hegemony over the Mamluks. He demanded that his name be inserted in the khutba after that of the Caliph, and insisted on draping the Kaaba as the Mamluk sultans famously did. He was too far away to be a serious threat, despite inciting the Turcomans to raid Syria. Barsbai answered his arrogant demands with equally contemptuous responses. He had one of Shah Rukh's envoys flogged, and when another came from Herat in 1436 with a robe of investment for Barsbai as Timurid governor of Egypt the sultan had him ducked in the Citadel horse pond.

In addition to these enemies, the ousted regent Janibek as-Sufi gave Barsbai considerable trouble. Amir Janibek had escaped from prison in Alexandria the year after his overthrow and went to eastern Anatolia where he united the many elements opposed to the sultan. For several years this renegade Mamluk waged his private war against Barsbai, often fighting together with White Sheep and Dulqadir forces. He was finally captured and died in prison at Aleppo in 1437, less than a year before Barsbai's own death.

In Barsbai's reign there appeared obvious signs of deterioration in discipline among the Mamluk troops. Their effectiveness in warfare was already in question, and slovenly and unruly behaviour was now much in evidence. Even the sultan often appeared in public in casual clothes. The lesser mamluks of the sultan's army showed this indiscipline by abusing their officers, rioting in the streets, robbing the Egyptians, looting, and raping women and young boys. Unable to control them, Barsbai offered concessions but this only encouraged them. When the Mamluks retook Ruha from the Turcomans in 1429 the amirs promised its citizens no reprisals, but as soon as the troops re-entered the city they pillaged, looted and raped as if it were an enemy conquest, turning this Mamluk border city into a ruin. The amirs had shown no control over their soldiers. Many such instances of poor discipline were witnessed in Barsbai's reign and afterwards.

When Barsbai died in June 1438 the usual usurpation process followed. Grand Amir Jaqmaq al-Alai, another of Barquq's mamluks, soon replaced Yusuf ibn Barsbai, who had succeeded his father. But Jaqmaq had moved too quickly, and the Ashrafis, Barsbai's mamluks, rose against him. There was a brief civil war, but with the support of the remaining Zahiris, together with the Mui'yadis (Shaikh's ousted mamluks), Jaqmaq suppressed the resistance of the Ashrafis. This accomplished, az-Zahir Jaqmaq ruled peacefully, seeking the most conciliatory course of action in every dispute. He often allowed abuses to go unpunished. Once he even agreed to Shah Rukh's demand to drape the Kaaba, much to his amirs' annoyance.

Between 1440 and 1444 Jaqmaq sent three expeditions against the Hospitallers on Rhodes, aiming to repeat the success of Barsbai in conquering Cyprus, but no decisive victory came from these seaborne campaigns. Once the Mamluk forces ravaged the island but could not take the Knights' fortress. The Hospitallers continued to harass Muslim shipping until the Ottomans finally took Rhodes in 1523.

By the 1450s the Zahiris, in the ascendancy from Barquq's day, were either dead or old men. Jaqmaq himself was eighty when he died in 1453. Over several reigns newer groupings of amirs had been created from the mamluks of one sultan or another and most had lost influence when their patron died. Such groupings still hoped to return to power, and might make alliances or support one or another to this purpose. The Mui'yadis of Shaikh had returned to the limelight in Jaqmaq's reign, and served in government alongside his Zahiris. But like the Nasiris of Faraj, the Mui'yadis were now ageing and few in number. There were still many Ashrafis, loyal to Barsbai. As the Zahiris tied to Barquq gradually disappeared, alliances between dispossessed groups of amirs increasingly dominated politics, as each sought to regain lost wealth and position. When Jaqmaq's son Uthman succeeded him at the age of eighteen, he began his short reign by dismissing the Mui'yadis and paid large amounts to Jaqmaq's Zahiris. The Mui'yadis joined with the more numerous Ashrafis and other malcontents and revolted against Uthman. For a week Cairo was a battleground, until the Caliph was finally persuaded to depose the young sultan.

In March 1453 the victors agreed to elevate the atabak Inal al-Alai. Inal was the last of Barquq's mamluks to become sultan. He was in fact inherited by Faraj before his release, and was therefore identified as a Nasiri. He was not a very successful sultan, preferring to placate opposition; whenever the mamluk troopers revolted, Inal always gave way to their demands. He looked for new ways to meet the higher financial toll that resulted, and it was soon difficult to find someone to take on the thankless task of managing the treasury. Inal once had an official flogged until he accepted the post of wazir.

In 1458 King John II of Cyprus died, and his heiress Carlotta's claim was disputed by her illegitimate half-brother James. Inal, as overlord, decided to support Carlotta but the common mamluks rioted in protest and Inal agreed to endorse James. Carlotta resigned her claim to a relative, and in turn the island passed by a complicated inheritance to the Venetians, who annexed Cyprus in 1473. Inal's action was the last deliberation the Mamluks made over Cyprus. The Cypriots still paid tribute to Inal's successors, but the island consequently passed out of the sphere of Mamluk control.

As the junior mamluks continued to riot, the senior amirs continued in their intriguing. When Inal's son Ahmad succeeded in 1461 he was unseated and imprisoned after a month by a coalition of four factions of amirs. At thirty, with several years' administrative experience, Ahmad was no helpless child sultan, but he lacked in political strategy and a power-base among the amirs.

To avoid a confrontation, Jaqmaq's Zahiris and Barsbai's Ashrafis, who formed the most powerful factions, agreed on Khushqadam, who had served as Ahmad's Grand Amir.

Khushqadam was an Anatolian Turcoman and a Mui'yadi, few of whom still lived. As with Inal this made him easier than most to replace if desired, for he had few supporters. But Khushqadam lasted for six years, presiding over an undistinguished reign in which corruption was commonplace and the sultan would have people tortured on request if the price was right. On his death in October 1467 the Ashrafis, still in the ascendancy, replaced him with Yalbai, another Mui'yadi.

But Yalbai, known as *al-Majnun* ('The Lunatic'), proved incompetent and did not establish any power-base. Before the year ended the Zahiris revolted, exploiting this poor choice to gain advantage over the Ashrafis. Deposing Yalbai in December 1467, they installed their own khushdashin. the Albanian amir Timurbugha, thus regaining power themselves. Timurbugha might have made a successful ruler. He began his short reign by releasing from prison the deposed boy sultans of previous reigns, but he had inherited serious financial problems and as the treasury was empty he could not make the usual donation to the troops. This the sultan's mamluks resented. As there were now too many factions to please, Timurbugha could barely give a payment to the Zahiris and complete the payment ordered by Yalbai.

In January 1468 the sultan's mamluks revolted. They proclaimed the Mui'yadi amir Khairbak sultan, but the revolt collapsed when crushed by Timurbugha's commander Qait Bey az-Zahiri. The Zahiris then hailed Qait Bey as sultan, and Timurbugha, misunderstanding this, announced his own abdication, requesting only that he be allowed to live in Alexandria. Whether this is true, and Timurbugha's staunchest supporter unwittingly supplanted him, or whether either Qait Bey or the Zahiris seized an opportunity is not clear.

The most significant achievement of al-Ashraf Qait Bey was to remain sultan for twenty-eight years, the longest since an-Nasir Muhammad. This was good for the Mamluk regime, allowing the various factions to fade away as prominent amirs died or retired. Qait Bey's own mamluks eventually held the senior positions, as if by default. He was much loved by the people, particularly for his charitable acts and public works including many mosques, schools, roads, irrigation schemes and similar projects in both Egypt and Syria, and generosity towards religious foundations. The fort he built at Alexandria is still in use by the Egyptian army. Yet Qait Bey would rob orphanages and monasteries of their funds as often as he donated to them. Taxes on dhimmis were raised severely. The sultan might extract money by flogging court officials until they paid large amounts, on one occasion personally beating the wazir. He once had the eyes of an alchemist put out when he failed in his assignment of turning lead into gold. There were serious economic problems, and raising revenues required harsh measures. In reality the decline of the Mamluk sultanate was proceeding, and Qait Bey did little to prevent it.

The northern frontier was still far from secure. Uzun Hasan, Khan of the White Sheep, had finally crushed the Black Sheep in 1466 and had gained ground from the Timurids in Iran. But it was Shah Suwar, ruler of the Dulqadir amirate of Albistan, who posed the most active threat to Mamluk Syria. From 1467 Shah Suwar repeatedly struck at Aleppo, Damascus and other towns, and continued until 1473 when he was captured and executed in Cairo. For a petty Turcoman prince to have given the Mamluks such trouble for so long was one more slur to their prestige.

The White Sheep now threatened Syria. In 1482, Ruha was again occupied. Qait Bey found an ally in this conflict in the Ottoman Sultan Bayazid II, while the Venetians gave the White Sheep their support. The Mamluks were humiliated by defeat several times, but lost little to the Turcomans in the long term, and peace was finally made in 1485. The White Sheep were then split by civil war and undermined by the Safavids, a Shi'ite movement rising within their territory. The Mamluks meanwhile fought a war with the Ottomans following a suzerainty dispute over eastern Anatolia. This conflict had no decisive outcome, and ended six years later with a truce and both sides staying where they had been at the beginning.

Qait Bey was the last Mamluk sultan to be widely revered and respected. He may not have been outstanding as a ruler, but he achieved almost three decades of political stability. When he died in 1496 his fifteen-year-old son, another an-Nasir Muhammad, succeeded him. Strangely enough, just as Barquq had been succeeded first by a son and then in turn by five of his mamluks, Qait Bey was followed by his own son and then five mamluks, albeit on a very different timescale. It seemed at first that the usual pattern of stop-gap heir followed by usurpation would take place as the amir Akbrindi prepared his coup, but a revolt by rival amirs blocked him.

Muhammad was an arrogant degenerate, and his retinue riotous and uncontrollable, but his father's amirs, the Ashrafis, soon broke into rival factions and their infighting enabled him to remain sultan over two years. But when he attempted to raise a bodyguard of African slaves armed with muskets, the amirs were finally moved to action, fearing for their hegemony. In November 1498 the amir Tuman Bey headed a conspiracy that had Muhammad murdered while riding; he was offered a drink when dismounting from his horse and stabbed as he drank.

The amir Tuman Bey may have been ringleader but he did not have enough support for his own accession. His fellow amirs chose Qansuh ibn Qansuh, Qait Bey's brother-in-law, probably because he was the most senior amir. A year later a new rebellion which included Tuman Bey's faction unseated him. Still lacking enough of a personal following, Tuman Bey nominated his khushdashin Janbulat al-Ashrafi as sultan.

Early in 1501, Tuman Bey had overthrown Janbulat and finally named himself sultan. He then set about liquidating any amirs that looked like possible rivals by murder or imprisonment and accordingly he was soon offending his own barrack comrades. As Tuman had committed the fatal error of being too obvious about breaking the power of the established amirs, the Ashrafis rebelled within three months of his accession. With no real support,

Tuman Bey escaped into hiding. He was discovered a few days later and killed trying to escape.

But the Ashrafis had by then kissed the ground before their comrade, the amir Qansuh al-Ghuri. Qansuh was already sixty, though remarkably active for his age. He had to be browbeaten into accepting the sultanate. Perhaps his lack of involvement in the politics of recent years had influenced that choice, or else he was probably installed as yet another stop-gap sultan. Qansuh reigned for fifteen years. He inherited a decaying empire, fraught with serious economic reverses and threatened by new enemies. He did all he could but had no new ideas or notable talents, and his most significant achievement was to avert every attempt to unseat him. Qansuh al-Ghuri was the penultimate Mamluk sultan. He met his end defending his empire against its conquerors. He was much commended for all his efforts, even if they produced no significant results.

Succession by usurpation naturally produces strong leadership, but at the same time it encourages others to revolt. Every time a usurper gained the sultanate he not only had to beware of plotters and intriguers but had to placate or marginalize those advanced by previous sultans. Such internal strife did not lead to good government, and it was only in Qait Bey's time that the factionalism finally came to an end. However, by now the Mamluk sultanate had larger problems concerning economic decline and emerging enemies. Given its diminishing military strength, these issues would throw the entire empire into peril.

8

THE MAMLUK STATE

Although this book has mostly concerned the activities of the Mamluk ruling class, the government of the Mamluk sultanate was far more sophisticated than a simple matter of sultans, amirs and wazirs. Rather than a mere self-perpetuating body of military adventurers, government was complicated, often paradoxical and more subtle than it looks at first glance.

Many government institutions were inherited from the Fatimid and Ayyubid periods, and some may have dated from Byzantine times. Their principles were theoretically dictated by the law of Islam, but the formal show and the reality of the Mamluk regime were very different, and produced many contradictions. It was customary in this time to divide those involved in government into three groupings: the Men of the Sword, the Men of the Pen and the Men of Religion (otherwise called the Men of the Turban).

The mamluks were first soldiers, having risen as Islam's defenders against the Mongols, but to run an empire involved more than brawn. It was the sultan whose word decided all, but technically speaking he was not the sovereign ruler. The Caliph was the designated head of state; the Commander of the Faithful, who always preceded the sultan in state ceremony. In the Friday prayers, the khutba was always recited first in the name of the Caliph, and then that of the sultan, his executive officer. The Caliphate dated from the earliest times in Islam, when on the death of the Prophet in AD 632 his friend Abu Bakr became his *khalifa* or 'successor'. Medieval Islam made no distinction between temporal and spiritual leadership, and the Caliph was simply leader of the Muslim community. The Abbasid clan gained the Caliphate in 749, by which time it had become hereditary. The Shi'ites, who had disputed the succession the previous century, recognized rival Caliphs descended from the fourth Caliph Ali.

From the ninth century the Caliphs had theoretically delegated their authority to the Seljuks and later to the Ayyubids. The sultan, the executive authority in Islam, would provide good government over the lands of Islam so that the religion may flourish, would defend Islam from its enemies, and would lead the jihad, where new lands would be 'opened' or conquered so that Islam may spread. The Caliph in Baghdad would invest a sultan by a written patent and by the black robe of honour, the Abbasid livery. The caliphs were mostly obliging in this, without many real powers over Muslim princes beyond Iraq, but their endorsement gave rulers the status of legitimacy. When the Mongols took Baghdad in 1258 they murdered the Caliph and his family, and although there were rival caliphates by that time the Mamluks saw this as a potential destabilizing of their authority. Four years after the destruction of Baghdad, Baibars al-Bunduqdari had a surviving Abbasid enthroned as Caliph in Cairo. Dependent on the Mamluk rulers, these caliphs conferred the title of sultan on each in turn so that no challenge to their legitimacy could be made by Muslims. This not only made Baibars and his successors more secure but increased their prestige. They became protectors and overlords of the region of the Holy Cities, and as far west as

Tripoli and Tunis the name of the Mamluk sultan was recited in the khutba.

The Caliphs of Cairo had no choice in the investiture. They acted as instructed by the amirs in power, and would at times be called on to depose a sultan under similar circumstances. Qalawun never even bothered to have the Caliph endorse his own accession. The Caliphs could do little more than delay action on the changeover, as al-Mutawakkil I did in 1366 when Yalbugha demanded that he depose Shaban. They knew that the sultans could imprison them or make life very difficult, or even replace them with another Abbasid. Although he theoretically headed the religious hierarchy, the Caliph was not admitted to court except for a monthly state visit. The sultans kept them out of sight except for public festivals, sometimes under house arrest or in exile in Upper Egypt as in the Qalawunid period.

The sultan was at least in theory bound by the tenets of Islam, but the qadis could do little to bring any effective censure against him. The sultans might pillage orphanages and dervish monasteries to raise money; they could treacherously break promises and ignore Muslim virtues of clemency and compassion. The chief qadis may protest, but as they themselves depended on the sultan's goodwill they had to agree to what they could not prevent. The sultan's personal conscience dictated his own observance of the Shari'a.

The real check on the sultan's authority could only come from his amirs. The narrative has shown the importance of relations between the sultan and the small group of senior amirs who served as his immediate advisors and lieutenants. They were often his former barrack comrades who supported his government. In return they expected the highest positions, the privileges and revenues that went with them, and consultation on major decisions. Having such resources at their disposal they could take to rebellion should this relationship break down, and even remove a sultan should they so desire. Some sultans, such as Kitbugha, lost the support of their fellows when they made too many decisions without referring to them. The real government of the Mamluk sultanate was therefore the *atabakiya*, or council of senior amirs, a junta of senior officers. The amirs might appoint one of their number as sultan, perhaps the oldest or most respected, or else someone who was either personally or politically weak and could be more easily manipulated. Alternately the sultan might only govern by playing the various factions of amirs against each other, as the former mamluks of Barquq often did.

The atabakiya would resist the sultan raising his own mamluks to positions of power. By the nature of the mamluk system sultans trusted those they had personally raised from slavery above all, and while a sultan's khushdashiya were essentially his comrades-in arms, experience shows they may have their own agendas and were more likely to betray that trust on issues of personal ambition. The Mamluk sultanate began when the Salihis' master died and his heir was set on replacing them with his own mamluks. Qalawun placated the Bahris by reversing Baibars' policy of advancing his own Zahiris, but still succeeded in making his own mamluks amirs, although he kept them in secondary roles for a time. On his accession a new sultan would usually begin by promoting some of his own to the grade of Amir of Ten. It may take time to augment them further, as any attempt to change the existing order would be resented; the Mansuris had the sultan Lajin promise not to elevate his own mamluks and eventually revolted when he broke this agreement. Baibars had to win the assent of his fellow Bahris to become sultan in the first place. The Bahris continued as a powerful entity in the times of Baibars and Qalawun until the amirs eventually died. It would take time for a sultan to build a reliable support base, and in the later period few ruled long enough.

A new sultan would build his army by purchasing new slaves and buying up his predecessor's un-freed mamluks, as he could trust those he had freed above his former comrades. But even these were not blind followers; they expected rewards and possibly consultation too. On their patron's death their positions became insecure. At a pace dictated by opportunity a new sultan would advance his own mamluks and other supporters and would set about removing the last sultan's protegees. In the Circassian period one set of sultan's mamluks after another would be speedily evicted from the Citadel barracks as soon as a new sultan appeared.

There was constant tension between the mamluks of the reigning sultan, known as the *mushtawarat*, and those of the dead sultans, the *qaranis*. For the latter, finding their power and material wealth seriously curtailed, would often intrigue to recover it. In the fifteenth century there were often several groupings of qaranis, often creating temporary alliances, or joining rebellions against the ruling group. The sultans were obliged either to play the qaranis against each other or send them on campaigns, keeping the mushtawarat at home. Shaik's Mui'yadis returned to participate in Jaqmaq's government by supporting his accession.

There was never established any formal procedure for choosing a Mamluk sultan. There was at least a nominal adherence to the principle of hereditary succession, and many sultans took pains to have their sons recognised as heirs, often creating them joint rulers with themselves. Hereditary monarchy was an accepted principle in Islamic society, as much as it was in Europe, and the dynasty of Qalawun did last four generations, but only after an-Nasir Muhammad capitalised on the shortcomings of his usurpers. Each time the amirs would be divided between those who supported the claim of his dead patron's family to the sultanate and those who claimed that strong, capable leadership was needed. The sons of sultans were seldom sufficiently mature or politically astute to control a band of ruthless and powerful amirs, and they usually lost the throne once an amir emerged in undoubted command.

It did not really aid the prestige of the Mamluk dynasty to be a line of upstarts. When the Ilkhan Ghazan occupied Damascus in 1299 he presented his claim as legitimate Muslim ruler by demonstrating to the city's ulema that they could all recite his own genealogy from Genghis Khan, whereas none of them could even name an-Nasir Muhammad's grandfather.

Court ritual and protocol were highly stylised. There were several pieces of regalia, probably from Fatimid tradition, among them a gilded saddlecloth borne before the sultan in processions and a parasol topped with a silver-gilt bird held over him by the wazir. There were also definite rules concerning the dress of amirs and court officials, according to the occasion. In processions the sultan would usually ride on horseback while all others walked. Robes of honour were used very often, especially when conferring promotions and appointments. The newly invested would afterwards ride in triumph from the Citadel wearing the robe. There were many ceremonies, in public and at court. On the first day of each lunar month the sultan received the four chief qadis at his court, and at another point in that period the Caliph was admitted. There were ceremonies at the several Muslim festivals. At the time of the inundation of the Nile each year the sultan and his court visited the Nilometer on Roda, where the rise of the river was observed. Other scheduled events, each with elaborate customs, took place throughout the year.

It was the *atabakiya*, that group of Amirs of One Hundred, that effectively ruled the Mamluk empire, often above even the sultan. Between them they held the largest number of mamluks and the most senior positions. In the beginning there were twenty-four of them but their number declined as resources diminished, leaving eleven in Barsbai's time. By 1516 the number had risen again to twenty-four.

There was usually one amir who was senior in rank to all but the sultan. In the early period he held the position of Viceroy of Egypt, or of atabak, and had many important duties, including hearing petitions, giving judgment and leading processions, especially in the sultan's absence from Cairo. He would sign documents jointly with the sultan. The viceroy could later be known as the Grand Amir (*al-amir-al-kabir*, or *al-amir-al-umar'u*), and would be the most favoured and powerful of the amirs. He was often a possible successor as sultan, and would at times control the government in the name of a weak ruler.

The atabak, or Commander of the Army, had similar importance. Officially the atabak commanded the army on campaign and gave advice in council but had no further duties. The office was usually filled by a senior amir, on some occasions by whoever effectively controlled the government, such as Qalawun in Salamish's short reign. The title later became an honorific for the most senior amirs. A regent may have been appointed during a sultan's minority, with jurisdiction over all except the treasury. He would usually hold another office at the same time, usually as atabak or Grand Amir. An-Nasir Muhammad ruled without appointing a viceroy and also dispensed with the offices of wazir and atabak; his experiences with Salar and Baibars, and his style of personal government, dictated this choice. After his death the viceregal post reappeared, but it gradually diminished in importance and when it fell vacant in 1408 the office was never filled again.

There were several other offices which the senior amirs held. The encyclopaedist al-Qalqashandi lists twenty-two in the early fifteenth century. There were an acting atabak and Viceroy of Egypt, both with limited powers. There was a head of the advisory council, an amir of the council chamber, governors of Cairo, of Fustat, of the Citadel, viceroys of Upper Egypt and Alexandria, the Amir of Weapons, the Major-Domo of the palace, the Guard Officer who supervised the Citadel prisons and executions, and several others. The Chamberlain, a militarized office, performed important judicial and administrative duties. Amirs of One Hundred would also serve as provincial governors.

Second-grade amirs, those of Drums, occupied lesser offices. Some acted as deputies for their seniors, others were Amirs of the Hunt, of Banners, and other military and royal functions. As economic decline reduced the numbers of higher-grade amirs, the more important posts were filled by those of lower classes, and offices might be doubled.

The sultan's household, the *khassikiya*, undertook governmental duties besides their domestic functions. The High Steward had major responsibilities in the treasury, and the major-domo of the royal apartments commanded the royal mamluks. The khassikiya had served from the early days as a kind of officer training school, and in the Circassian period its role increased, and became the principal route to a senior position in government.

Besides the Mamluks other elements may at times have influenced the sultan's government. Eunuchs were included in the military class and could be Africans, Abyssinians, Indians or from the Mamluks' own homelands. They were also freed slaves who had proved themselves useful, as eunuchs were even more dependent on their patrons than other slaves. Some attained the ranks of lesser amirs. Many served in the sultan's household and occasionally held such important posts as Grand Treasurer, or tutor to the sultans' children. The sultan's wives, or other members of his family, may also influence affairs of state at times. In an-Nasir Muhammad's reign, and in the time of some of his sons, both eunuchs and the mixed-race slave girls of whom he was fond became influential. Anyone who wanted an *iqta* (fief) granted, or a petition heard, would be advised to go to the harem, where a eunuch or concubine could advance his suit for him.

The Mamluks were essentially a class of warriors whose material needs were supported by a largely agrarian population. This in fact parallels the ruling classes of Europe at the same time, where like knights and nobles the Mamluk faris and amirs were granted estates from which they could live on the labours of peasants. The sultan had the largest holding of all, which supplemented other revenues. It was fundamentally a feudal society inherited in part from the Ayyubids where holdings were calculated according to income and rank. From the proceeds of half a village, as was typically granted to the common faris, to a larger area comprising multiple villages that increased with an amir's seniority, the iqtas were standardized and circumscribed and included up to ten villages. The iqta's holder would usually expect a third of the income of ordinary land, and half of that of irrigated land. The halaqa also held iqtas, a single village supporting roughly a dozen.

The Mamluk feudal system had two major differences from the European model: an iqta holder did not normally live on his estate, and might never visit it except possibly to collect revenues. In practice the Mamluk lived in Cairo and either appointed or inherited a *mu'tazim* or tax farmer, who collected revenues from the peasants and rendered the expected amount at intervals. The mu'tazim kept all he collected above that amount and would often use his office to extort large amounts from the *fellahin* (peasants) to his own profit.

Nor were the iqtas allowed to become hereditary possessions, as happened at an early stage in Europe. They usually passed from father to son in Ayyubid times and under Aibak, but Baibars halted this practice, knowing that it would dilute the first-generation Mamluk corps. On the holder's death, an iqta automatically returned to the army office for reissue, and it remained the practice from that time. If a holder was transferred to another region he was granted a new iqta there, and the original was relinquished. On gaining a promotion a Mamluk would also have his holdings exchanged for estates of the appropriate size. Hereditary lordships were prevented by the nature of the mamluk system.

The sultans had the right to call a *rawk*, where all iqtas were recalled, reassessed and redistributed, although this only happened a few times. After the celebrated *rawk-an-Nasiri* of 1315 the sultan held nearly half the iqtas personally. It was possible through this policy to prevent large feudal groupings which could challenge the sultan's military strength, and made it easier to unseat opponents. But such policies also gave the holders little incentive to improve the condition of their possessions.

The Mamluk sultanate was founded with the intention of defending Islam from Mongol conquest, but once the Ilkhanate collapsed and before the Timurid invasions there was a great stretch of time where there was no such danger. The Mamluks simply grew rich on the peasants' labour. They must have seen that there was more to running an empire, however. It was thus the Men of the Sword who ruled over the empire and reaped the benefits, but the Men of the Pen attended to its actual administration. The civil service, long established and noted for its efficiency, maintained the empire's administration, even while the Mamluks were fighting their civil wars. Most civil servants were native Egyptians and Syrians. Some, such as the Jian family of Cairo, provided clerks in each generation. Many – the Jians included – were Christians, and others were Jews. They were at times ejected from their offices during periodic religious persecutions, often to be reinstated afterwards.

There were many senior officials from other lands. Those who had built a reputation in their homelands, or had come to Cairo as scholars, could enter the Mamluks' service in either an administrative or religious capacity. Ibn Khaldun is a noted example. Sometimes qadis functioned as civil servants. Many Egyptians made their fortunes in the civilian elite, often dishonestly, with the official an-Nashu in the reign of an-Nasir often cited. If a rich official died his wealth was often seized, as it was assumed that he had embezzled most of it.

The civil administration could be broadly divided into three departments: the chancery, the army office and the treasury. The wazir, or vizier, controlled all three. At times he may be an amir, at others a qadi. Al-Maqrizi outlined different protocols in the ceremonials if the wazir was a Mamluk. In the later period the wazirate remained a civilian office, which a scholar would fulfil. The wazir attended the sultan, reading dispatches and petitions, and acting as advisor. He had several deputies and there was a multitude of officials and clerks with areas of responsibilities.

The chancery enacted all the Mamluks' deliberations. There were strict rules concerning the dating and minuting of state papers. The army office supervised the allotting of fiefs, where authorized patents were issued. There were two separate treasuries, one for the state and the other supervising the sultan's privy purse, raised from the revenues of the royal estates. After the land redistribution of 1315, the second office became the more important, especially as money became scarce.

There were no statutory taxes, the government simply levied whatever tax they thought would draw the most at any one time. Taxes were nearly always high, and new levies often came when others already burdened the native population. There were taxes on livestock, on the cultivation of apples, lentils and other crops, on oil and sugar presses, on wheels and so on. Whereas some sultans forbade the selling of alcohol, others permitted it for a high tax. Taxes on dhimmis were harsh, and often raised as an act of persecution. There were many taxes levied for specific purposes, such as military campaigns, or to satisfy insubordinate Mamluk troopers' demands for pay increases. There were import and export duties. Goods crossing Mamluk territory brought a duty as high at times as a fifth of their value and the spice trade became the greatest source of royal revenue. From Barsbai's time state monopolies were imposed, the spice monopoly the first of these. There were also monopolies on emeralds, alum and other commodities, and such franchises were granted as gifts to amirs, whose desire to eke out as much profit as possible often destroyed them as commercial concerns.

Besides the qadis and other religious scholars who served in the civil administration, there were those designated Men of Religion. They represented the ulema, the community of religious scholars, and many held the positions of qadis, or of imams and preachers in the mosques. The chief qadis and their retinues headed this hierarchy. Although the four were theoretically equal in status, the Shafiite chief qadi was the primate and could appoint qadis in Egypt without consulting the other three. Although the Shari'a applied to all matters civil and religious, the qadis' jurisdiction was in practice limited and other courts, under the sultan and his representatives, increasingly absorbed the responsibility for criminal law and some civil actions, and the qadis were restricted to matters of religious affairs and family law. They could advise the sultan at his court, but he might not heed their counsel. There was a separate legal code for the Mongols who lived in Mamluk lands. The Christian and Jewish communities had their own courts too, and some autonomy. The Chief Rabbi and the two Coptic Patriarchs attended the court, but their presence as representatives of the dhimmis had far greater ceremonial importance than administrative.

The administration of Egypt itself rested on members of the three groups in conjunction. The country was divided into eleven administrative districts; seven in Lower Egypt, and four in Upper Egypt. Each district had a *khashif*, or inspector, usually a first- or second-class Mamluk amir, whose many responsibilities included irrigation, roads, fortifications, postal services and agricultural productivity. There were other khashifs who supervised labour on the maintenance of dykes, canals and irrigation schemes. There was a senior amir who served as governor of Alexandria, and others who governed in Cyrenaica and Qus, on the edge of Mamluk territory to the western and southern desert regions.

In each district was also a *wali*, or chief of police, who maintained law and order. He was usually an Amir of Drums with up to seventy horsemen at his command. Their duties included fighting rebellion and banditry, guarding city gates and protecting the trade and pilgrim routes, as well as watching against criminal activities such as theft and prostitution in the towns. The amir Khuja az-Zahir, appointed wali of Cairo by Barsbai in 1432, was particularly known for his meticulous discharge of his duties. He ordered the streets be swept and washed clean, and that all shopkeepers keep lamps in their shops. He promised that all wrongdoers that fell into his clutches would be halved at the waist if he caught them a second time, and he always kept his word. He restricted the mobility of women on the streets. Khuja was despised for his thoroughness, but Cairo was a cleaner and safer place while he was wali.

The *muhtasib*, or market inspector, managed the civil and commercial affairs of the town, jointly with the wali. They were native Egyptians and Syrians, and often educated; al-Maqrizi the historian held this position at one time in Cairo. Those of Lower Egypt were appointed by the market inspector of Cairo, or his counterpart in Fustat for Upper Egypt. Each town also had its qadi, with deputies. These were often Shafite, although qadis of other schools could be found in some places. For a long time the chief qadi of Alexandria was a Malikite. The parity of the four schools did not apply everywhere.

There were no concessions to the will of the people, not even the commercial classes. In the Ayyubid period the towns had mayors, but when the Mamluks came to power all references to these in the sources abruptly cease. There were guilds in each town for every trade but these were not autonomous; the wali appointed the guild masters and they functioned as organisations for mutual benefit rather than for protection of their trade. The sultan himself would appoint the heads of such select guilds as those of physicians and engineers.

Syria was an important gain for the Mamluks in 1260 when they defeated a Mongol advance force, but there were serious problems governing the region, especially when the Mongols were still on the far side of the Euphrates. Syria was difficult to govern from Cairo, as long distances and the Sinai Desert hampered communications and meant government was semi-autonomous, with military resources delegated, and this carried risks. Qutuz split the territory into several smaller units rather than create a large governorate that could rebel against Cairo. The 1260 campaign had also gained possession of Aleppo and Damascus, which an-Nasir Yusuf had held, and Qutuz gained the submission of the Ayyubid amirs of Homs and Hama, two petty principalities also in northern Syria. Baibars added Kerak and Safad to the provinces, and Qalawun Tarabulus (or Tripoli) when he took it from the Franks in 1289. Gaza was created a province much later.

In the larger provinces, from the time of Qalawun, there was a separate governor of the citadel who commanded the garrison. Qalawun gave the viceregal posts to the Bahris amirs and the military command to his own Mansuris. Many sultans followed this example, and like Qalawun changed both governors often. Few amirs held the same posting for more than three years. This limited the likelihood of rebellion, but certainly did not prevent it; indeed, many revolts against the Mamluk sultans began in Syria.

Each province was virtually autonomous. The viceroys held their own courts, miniature versions of the sultan's, with amirs, qadis and dhimmi representatives. Lesser-grade amirs, often the governor's mamluks, governed the smaller towns. As in Egypt the iqta system operated, as did the walis and market inspectors. The viceroys collected the taxes and revenues of the province. Part of this amount they forwarded to Cairo, but some used at least part of the remainder for the benefit of the region. They might build or repair fortifications, bridges and aqueducts, mosques, madrasas and irrigation schemes, or endow charitable foundations. Some of the viceroys of Damascus endeavoured to promote Jerusalem, the third Holy City of Islam, as a centre for religious learning. Several of them renovated the al-Aqsa Mosque and built or endowed madrasas. But such improvements were unusual. The brevity of tenure in these offices encouraged amirs to use them to amass personal wealth. A diligent reforming governor was often followed by one who did not share his interest in such schemes, and the efforts of one may easily come to naught through his successors' negligence.

The Viceroy of Damascus was the highest office in Syria, and ranked equal in precedence with the Viceroy of Egypt. The historical capital of the Umayyad Caliphate and the richest city in the region, Damascus had a distinctive character and the

Mamluks sought to maintain its loyalty. They encouraged the city to become the capital of learning and the arts. There were twelve Amirs of One Hundred in Damascus (this number later fell to eight), twenty Amirs of Drums and sixty of lower grades. There were also about 12,000 halaqa. The viceroy appointed the sub-governors of Baalbek, Jerusalem and Ramleh, although the sultans later took control over this.

An-Nasir Muhammad had the amir Tankiz al-Husami serve him as Viceroy of Damascus for twenty-eight years and gave him authority over all the other governors of Syria. Tankiz was of the same mind as the sultan in many things, and a close friend. An-Nasir could trust him to manage Syria on his behalf, but after the disagreement of 1340 and Tankiz's fall the sultans gave no other amir the same authority over Syria and appointed the governor with great care. The Damascenes fiercely stated their independent spirit through it all.

Aleppo ranked second in importance. The chief city in the border region and at the crossing of trade routes, Aleppo was later more successful than Damascus in commercial terms. Tarabulus, formerly Tripoli, capital of the central Levantine coastal region and its hinterland, came next. The other provinces were much smaller in size and resources. Hama began as a vassal amirate once its Ayyubid amir submitted to Qutuz and was confirmed as his governor. Hama remained an Ayyubid possession, until replaced by a Mamluk around 1300, although an-Nasir Muhammad reinstated the Ayyubid in 1310. The last Ayyubid prince of Hama died the same year as an-Nasir, and the sultans appointed Mamluk governors thereafter. Homs also had an Ayyubid prince under Mamluk suzerainty at first in 1260, but two years after that amir died Baibars had the province absorbed into the Damascus governorate. Kerak was a poor province, as was Safad; both had few resources. Gaza was created a separate province in 1333, having been part of Egypt before, and was then created a dependency of Damascus, with few officials and amirs, under Tankiz's control.

The Bedouins held the desert to the east of Damascus, as they did the Libyan Desert, with independence under the sultan's suzerainty, and a powerful tribe such as the al-Fadl would hold primacy and maintain order. Such suzerainty was often nominal, as Bedouins frequently rebelled, took up banditry or sided with the sultan's enemies, and this would happen more in times of weakness of the sultanate. Turcoman tribes defended fortresses in the border regions of the Euphrates, also under a similar suzerainty. In Aleppo there was always one senior amir, and some lesser, who were Turcomans. The region near Beirut was held in vassalage by the Buhturi tribe, who defended the coast from possible landings by the Franks. The Buhturi amirs were also hard to control.

As the Mamluks fought their way into the Taurus Mountains, they created a number of governorates in the conquered Cilician lands where towns such as Adana, Tarsus and Sis were governed by lower-grade amirs. In the fifteenth century the Mamluks expanded into eastern Anatolia, to include Malatia, Caesarea and at one time Albistan. These cities also became governing centres, but served mainly as frontier posts, for this was a region hostile to the Mamluks.

The Hijaz, the Red Sea coastal region that included Mecca and Medina, was ruled by the sharif. The Mamluks mostly left this vassal state to its own devices, glad to be styled protectors of the Holy Cities and the Pilgrimage. The kings of the Yemen had designs on this region, and a garrison of mostly veteran troopers was stationed at Mecca to provide a deterrent. The king of the Yemen himself was also the sultan's vassal. He paid tribute, although not always regularly, and occasional phases of insubordination gave the sultans concern. The Sudan was also a tributary state, and the Mamluks, mindful of security in Upper Egypt, often took an interest in its internal stability. After the conquest of Cyprus in 1426 its king came regularly to Cairo to pay obeisance to the sultan and to deliver tribute.

During the lifetime of the Mamluk sultanate, several other states came under its suzerainty, at least for some of the time, including the Qaraman and Dulqadir amirates, the Knights Hospitallers on Rhodes, the Jalairid and Ottoman sultans and several other principalities in the border regions of Iran and Iraq. It is not clear whether all paid tribute, but Mamluk suzerainty was a condition which many princes accepted voluntarily. It was more worthwhile to acknowledge the sultan as overlord, and possibly to render tribute, than to risk his enmity. At the very least a vassal ruler would find sanctuary in Cairo if ever deprived of his domain. The Mamluks occasionally intervened on behalf of one ruler or another, but their concern was mainly their own security and stability in the states on their periphery.

The Mamluks were by their nature predatory; they were, after all, foreign soldiers concerned largely with their own material gain and political power. This was not ideal when governing a large region, but the Mamluk sultanate somehow survived. The civilian elite were mostly very professional and their efforts did much to hold it all together through two centuries of rebellion, intrigue and invasion. But the attitude of the Mamluk rulers would gradually erode the stability of the state, and this eventually left them without adequate defence against the conquerors to come.

9

COMMERCE, SOCIETY AND RELIGION

For the native populations of the Mamluk lands, life was not much different from the centuries before or after. Much of it was harsh, but their masters did bring them some respite, at least in the early period. The native population conducted agriculture, trade and industry, from which the Mamluks benefited, and the Mamluk sultanate was the richest state in the Islamic world in its time. It was usually when the Mamluks interfered unduly with economic affairs that problems began.

The economy of Egypt and Syria was primarily agrarian. The land and the peasants who farmed it produced food, and also the incomes of the Mamluks themselves. For this reason the rulers devoted so much attention to irrigation schemes, dykes, canals and composite constructions of these, while agricultural productivity dictated their own financial prosperity. The flooding of the Nile each year was of paramount importance, and the water level shown on the Nilometer in the spring was used to determine food prices.

Besides its agrarian produce, Egypt was already a rich country long before the Mamluks. Its gold mines were exhausted by this time, but there were still other natural resources. Alum was an important commodity for its use as a dye fixative, in paint and in some chemicals. Among other commodities Egypt also produced and exported grain, leather, paper, sugar, cotton and other textiles, salt, copper, quicksilver, rosewater, carpets and oil. They even exported pigs, the consumption of which was forbidden by their religion, and the similarly proscribed wine made by the Christian inmates of a prison in Cairo for a substantial profit.

Syria produced many of the same commodities, and also such items as silk, glass and perfumes. There were saltworks all down the coast while the Beirut region produced olive oil and the mountains of Lebanon had cedar trees. Most towns had craftsmen of many kinds. Damascus has always been famous for its workers in wood and metal. Some of the larger towns had primitive factories, or at least enlarged workshops. In the early period an increase in population provided a rise in both manpower and consumers. Refugees from the lands the Mongols conquered, and later Mongol immigrants, gave impetus to economic growth. Craftsmen and merchants who came from Iraq provided significant benefits and often brought trade and their own expertise.

Almost every settlement had a market of some size. All along the Nile there were market villages not more than a day's journey apart and all over the empire there were similar markets. There was some variation in their frequency, depending on the value of the goods sold and the distance the traders travelled to them. Mecca was the main commercial clearing house of the entire Near East.

The Mamluk sultanate was well placed for trade with both East and West, benefiting frm the convergence of several important trade routes. The sultanate imported from Europe such much-needed commodities as timber, iron and weapons, and the Black Sea route was very important to both the Mamluks and the Europeans. From this region the Muslims imported amber (popular in female fashion), furs (important to masculine fashion) and slaves after Baibars made agreements with Michael Palaeologus. The Genoese merchants also travelled this route, bringing shiploads of Turks and Circassians to the slave markets of Cairo. The Italian mercantile city-states such as Venice, Pisa and Genoa had always been more interested in trading with the Muslims than in fighting them, and while commercial relations between the Italians and the Ayyubids had been long established, the early Mamluk sultans continued to encourage this trade. At times the popes forbade trading with the infidel, as did some European princes such as Philip the Fair of France, but such commerce still went on; in such times it could be conducted indirectly through either Cilicia or Crete. Peter of Cyprus' raid on Alexandria caused the Mamluks to cease trading with the Franks, especially as the Venetians aided Peter's expedition, but in 1370 some Franks, almost certainly Italians, negotiated with Cairo and succeeded in resuming commercial relations. The Italians otherwise traded regularly with the Mamluk sultanate, particularly the Venetians who were the rising commercial power in Italy. Others such as the Aragonese, Catalans and Provençals also came. Each mercantile power had a *funduq*, a guesthouse that doubled as a trading warehouse in Alexandria and some had consular missions in Damascus also. The Franks had some trade with the ports on the Syrian coast, although Alexandria was the main centre for trade with Europe.

At first the Europeans came once a year with the trade winds, but when the compass came into widespread use around 1300 the rhythm of commerce changed, and the Franks usually came twice a year. Since the period of the Crusades the Franks had become interested in many eastern goods: silks and other fabrics, sugar, glass, spices and many others. The Muslims were glad to sell them all.

The Mamluk lands also traded with the East; galleys from India, Zanzibar, Ceylon, Malaysia and even China sailed into the Red Sea, bearing gold, silver, precious stones, ivory, silks, drugs, porcelain, rare woods and, most significant of all, spices. The old Spice Route, which ran through the Persian Gulf, had suffered from the ravages of the Mongols; Baghdad and Basra, once important routing points, were destroyed. Only the Red Sea route remained for Eastern traders to move in safety, and although the Yemen was a trade rival Cairo got most of the benefit. Merchants travelling the Great Silk Road, overland from China via Samarkand and Nishapur, reached the Mediterranean through Aleppo or Damascus. The caravans might continue to Alexandria, and it was not safe to transport goods through Anatolia, an unstable region in this time, and again this was to the advantage of the Mamluks. In the Bahri period the Frankish states and Armenian Cilicia were both serious trade rivals, providing another reason for the Mamluks to destroy them. The Mamluks wrecked the Cilician port of Ayas several times, partially for commercial reasons.

Another important route passed through Nubia into Mamluk lands. Traders came from western and central Africa bringing gold from Mali and Ghana, the mines at Jenne having just become productive at this time, along with African and Abyssinian slaves. In addition nearly all the Western pilgrim routes, bringing Muslims each year to Mecca and Medina, passed through the Mamluks' territory. Besides the prestige of protectors of the Hajj, the Mamluks profited indirectly from the trade.

The most significant commercial focus in the Mamluk sultanate was in reality the transit trade where the convergence of trade routes made the region so successful as an entrepôt between Europe, Africa and Asia. To buy goods from the East, the Europeans had little choice but to trade in Alexandria or Damascus; their only alternative was a less reliable route via the Black Sea. At this time, of course, no one in Europe knew of a sea route to India. The Frankish merchants would usually buy goods in Alexandria as they were not allowed to deal directly with merchants in Cairo, the centre for trade from the East. The

Egyptian middlemen made enormous profits, as did the sultans; a twenty per cent tax on goods in transit was not unusual.

The spice trade was the most important single concern. Demand was high in Europe: food would otherwise be monotonous. Most spices came either from the central Muslim lands or from India and the Moluccas, and many a ship offloaded them to the Red Sea ports for transporting first to Cairo and eventually to Alexandria. Each year over a million pounds of pepper passed through the funduqs of Alexandria alone, as with cloves and other popular spices, and this brought great revenues. For most of the time the Mamluks and the Venetians held the virtual monopoly on spices between them, much to the resentment of the other mercantile peoples of Europe. Spices were sold in bulk in Venice and transported across the Alps. In Cairo the *karimis*, or spice merchants, became the richest and most influential of the native Egyptians.

The Mamluk sultans saw the need to promote trade. From Qalawun's reign they encouraged commercial operations in both East and West, and negotiated trade treaties with Christian princes. They issued licenses for foreign merchants and set up commercial houses in other lands. They built *khans*, or fortified travellers' inns, along the trade routes and did all they could to prevent caravan raids. They also taxed merchants heavily, although in the lucrative early period this was no great hardship. The Circassians, however, did serious damage to commerce. They embarked on trade themselves, the sultan and the amirs building their own factories and business houses and imposing higher taxes on private competitors. Following this the practice of monopolies began; in 1423 Barsbai established the sultans' own monopoly on the entire Egyptian sugar industry. The spice trade was similarly 'nationalised' soon afterwards, and many other concerns were eventually placed under government monopolies. Needless to say, the greed of the Mamluks damaged the industries they appropriated with their constant demands for money. By the end of the fifteenth century both trade and industry suffered from their actions.

Although the Mamluk sultanate was generally wealthy, there was a wide divergence in wealth and living conditions. There were many different races, religions and lifestyles, and great contrasts in wealth and social status. The Mamluks themselves were usually rich. A common faris came into fairly comfortable means once released, and senior amirs were known for their riches; when an amir's property was seized on their death or disgrace, the inventories often showed monies and possessions worth several million dinars.

Some of the native population prospered under the Mamluks – mostly the commercial classes, the Karimis in particular. Manufacturers and craftsmen made their fortunes too, as did some government officials. For most of the tradesmen, artisans and labourers of the towns and cities, incomes varied considerably and fluctuated according to the economy. In the rural communities of the fellahin, life was harsh and often unrewarding. For a fellah, little had changed from the time of the Pharaohs and nor would it for a long time. As tillers of the soil and herdsmen they struggled to survive and meet the demands of their Mamluk masters. They paid high taxes alongside dues to their feudal lords, and often supplied forced labour for the many ambitious building schemes. There was little they could do to improve their lot, although some might rise to become tradesmen. Many tried to escape to the towns, in such numbers that in the early period the Mamluks designated officers to pursue runaways. For the peasants of Syria there was little difference. Only in the region of the Lebanon was it any better. Here the peasants were free and held their smallholdings as tenants, giving a fixed proportion of their produce as rent to their landowners.

The Bedouins mostly stayed on the margins of this economic structure, although there was some overlapping. As they had always done, most of them roamed the less hospitable areas of the empire, herding their sheep and goats from one grazing ground to another, their allegiance to the sultan little more than nominal. They often fought amongst each other and periodically revolted against the Mamluks. Many Bedouins lived in the villages, working alongside the fellahin, but would also rise in revolt when their chiefs called them to arms. There were also numerous Turcoman tribes, similarly nomadic and living mostly in northern Syria. They also lived under Mamluk suzerainty, guarding the border regions. A few Turcomans became successful scholars, some even qadis, but they were usually considered second-class citizens, referred to as 'the Turcoman' whatever their achievements.

Many other peoples lived in the sultanate. There were Kurds, both remnants from the Ayyubid period and more recent refugees, also living usually as herdsmen. There were many Mongols, usually nomads or else members of the Mamluk corps. There were also Iranians, Anatolians and several other minorities both in the towns and on the land. Other immigrants came from all over the Muslim world, either to study Islam in the best schools or to seek opportunity for advancement.

The people held in the least regard were the African slaves, who were treated with contempt by everyone. They performed the most menial of duties and usually had mildly derogatory names such as Kafur ('Camphor'), Gawhar ('Jewel') or Miska ('Musk'). Abyssinian and Indian slaves seem to have done little better. It was mostly eunuchs who had opportunities for advancement. Sitt-al-Miska, the wetnurse, and the Sudani eunuch Gawhar al-Julbani, tutor to Barsbai's children, both rose enough in wealth and position to build mosques in their names. Otherwise, in contrast to a white-skinned Turkish or Circassian slave who could aspire to no less than the throne, most other slaves had little to look forward to; even the minority who were released had few possibilities.

In the early period, prosperity offset high taxes. There may have been thousands sleeping on the streets of Cairo at any given time but charitable works were a common preoccupation among Mamluks. Qalawun's Maristan was a prime example and Barquq built a similar complex. Many amirs would at least build a *sabil*, or public drinking fountain. Some would build a *sabil-khuttab*, where a large, walled fountain was surmounted by an upper storey holding a religious elementary school. The aged, the infirm, widows and orphans were often under the care of a religious foundation or dervish order which Mamluks might endow. Their charitable works contrasted with their violent, greedy and treacherous dispositions. It is said that many Mamluks sought to atone for their crimes in gaining high position by so many good works, hoping for a place in Paradise.

The more brutal aspects of Mamluk rule were almost daily occurrences. Public executions, with offenders beheaded or halved at the waist, and torture were common public spectacles. A favourite method in the later period was to have offenders nailed to planks and paraded on the backs of mules or camels. Despite their frequency, the public was often disturbed at such atrocities. There was little difference between these and public punishments commonly seen in Europe at the same time.

The status and condition of women in the Mamluk sultanate has only been the subject of research in recent years. In medieval Islamic society women were far from equal with men and had few rights of redress, but they did have certain personal rights as enshrined in Islamic law. They may have fared little better in Christian lands at the same time. The Turkish Mamluks, nomadic by origin, would consider their women to be their equals, but it was usual in this time in the lands of Islam to restrict women in all spheres, and both attitudes are in evidence in the Mamluk empire.

The Mamluks, if at all, usually married freed slave girls, often of Turkish or Circassian origin. Some sultans married daughters of qadis, or foreign princesses. If one of his slaves bore him a son, she may be freed and made his principal wife. In Islamic law a man could have up to four wives at one time, divorcing any at will. The consorts of Mamluk sultans held the title of princess. Some had influence in government, although usually indirectly. Some, such as Princess Toghai, an-Nasir's principal wife, were

1. The Citadel at Cairo. Built in the time of Saladin (1137–1193), the Ottoman-style mosque (centre, top) was added by Muhammad Ali. (Courtesy of Ahmed Al Badawy under Creative Commons 2.0)

2. The madrasa and mausoleum of as-Salih Najm-ad-Din Ayyub, constructed in the 1240s. (Courtesy of Ahmed Al Badawy under Creative Commons 2.0)

المُقابَلَةُ الرَّابِعَةُ فى دَوَرانِ الفَرَسِ ٥

This spread, next spread: 3–6. Pages from *Kitāb al-makhzūn jāmiʿ al-funūn* (*The Treasure That Combines All Arts*). This treatise on martial arts has been claimed as being written by figures including Miqdad ibn Aswad, a companion of the Prophet Muhammad celebrated for his feats during the Battle of Badr in 624, but is likely a Mamluk work of the 1300s. Depicted are flags, formations and practice drills, with lines of poetry at the top and bottom of the pages. (Courtesy of the Library of Congress)

وَكَيْفَ يَفْعَلُ مَعَ الغَرِيمِ إِذَا اكَبَسُوا

باب الرمي بالقبق وتبيينه والدخول فيه

وصفة اعلم انه يتخذ رمحا في قزبوص السرج البراني وتخط

في راسه علامة ويسوق ويلتفت ويرمي الى العلامة وذلك الادمان

ينبغي ان يحرس نفسه وركبته الا يتحى في القبق

ثم يرتب حلقة مثلثة باشاتها فيها إلى ما مشبّنة

في فعلها ودورها صنعوا وهذه مرسومة مكتوبة

صفة الرامي في الطوق من بين الخسارة

وتبطيله أن يضرب العنا يكس الفرس

Left: 7. A bust of the legendary sultan Baibars (d. 1277), scourge of the Crusaders. (Courtesy of Ahmed Yousri Elmamlouk under Creative Commons 4.0)

Above: 8. Baibars' badge of the lion *passant*. (Courtesy of LadyofHats)

9. The tomb of Shajar ad-Durr (d. 1257), wife of Sultan as-Salih Ayyub and the closest thing to a female Mamluk. (Courtesy of R. Prazeres under Creative Commons 2.0)

10. The Maristan on Bayn al-Qasrayn in Cairo, better known as the Qalawun complex. Built by Qalawun in 1285, it contained a mosque, an orphanage, a nursery, a public library, a children's madrasa, a lecture hall, a free public hospital and well-equipped laboratories. (Courtesy of Saliko under Creative Commons 2.0)

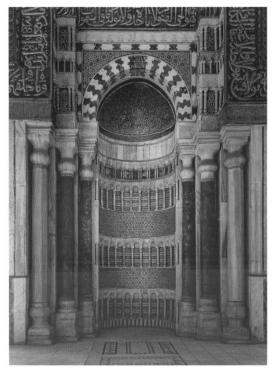

11. Also within the Qalawun complex is the mausoleum that holds the remains of Qalawun and his son, an-Nasir Muhammad. (Courtesy of Keladawy under Creative Commons 2.0)

12. A manuscript depiction of the siege and capture of Tripoli by the Mamluks under Qalawun in 1289. Lucia, Countess of Tripoli and Bartholomew, Bishop of Tortosa can be seen sitting at the centre of the fortified city. (Courtesy of the British Library under Creative Commons 2.0)

13. The enormous Mosque-Madrasa of Sultan Hassan, completed in 1363 during the Bahri period. (Courtesy of Mohammed Moussa under Creative Commons 2.0)

14. The Fort of Qait Bey, Alexandria. This citadel was built in 1477. (Courtesy of kmf164 under Creative Commons 2.0)

15. The Sabil-Khuttab of Qait Bey, built 1479, on Saliba Street in Cairo. Where some amirs installed sabils – kiosks where water was distributed free of charge through a grille – others added a khuttab above, where Quranic learning was offered. (Courtesy of R. Prazeres under Creative Commons 2.0)

16 The entrance portal of the *wikala* of Qait Bey, a caravanserai built alongside the Sabil-Khuttab. (Courtesy of R. Prazeres under Creative Commons 2.0)

Above: 17. The Kaaba, the stone building at the heart of Islam's most important mosque, the Masjid al-Haram in Mecca, Saudi Arabia. For a time the Mamluk sultans were honoured with the task of draping the *kiswa*, the cloth that covers the Kaaba. (Courtesy of Richard Mortel under Creative Commons 2.0)

Right: 18. An inscription in the Kaaba dated 1423 made by the Sultan Barsbai. It reads, 'In the name of God, the Most Compassionate, the Most Merciful. Our Lord, accept from us that you are the All-Hearing, the All-Knowing. Draw nearer to God Almighty by renewing the marble of this noble and honorable house. The poor servant of God Almighty, the honorable Sultan King Abu al-Nasr Barsbay, Custodian of the Two Holy Mosques. May God reach his hopes and adorn his deeds with good deeds. The year eight hundred and twenty-six AH.' (Courtesy of Adnan al-Sharif under Crative Commons 2.0)

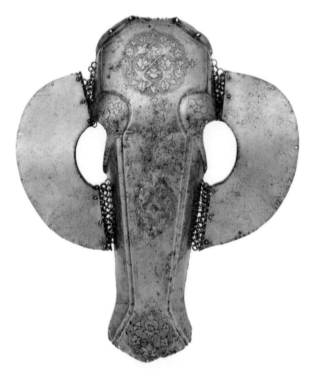

19. Mamluk horse armour, fifteenth or sixteenth century. (Courtesy of the Metropolitan Museum of Art)

20. Mamluk chain mail, fifteenth century. (Courtesy of the Metropolitan Museum of Art)

21. Mamluk shield, fifteenth century. (Courtesy of the Metropolitan Museum of Art)

22. Mamluk sword, pre-1419. (Courtesy of the Metropolitan Museum of Art)

23. The Mamluks had a system of blazons or emblems representing the roles of courtiers. This example dates from the rule of Qait Bey in the late fifteenth century. (Courtesy of the Metropolitan Museum of Art)

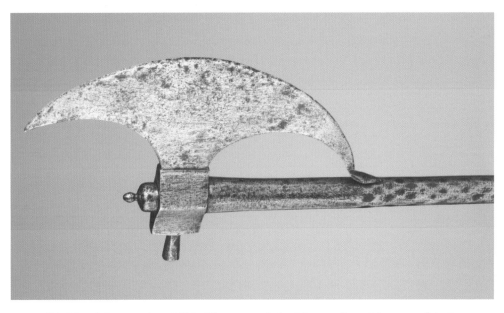

24. Mamluk axe, *circa* 1500. (Courtesy of the Metropolitan Museum of Art)

25. 'Mamluk on Horseback' by the French painter Carle Vernet and dating to the French invasion of Egypt, where they faced the Mamluk war machine. (Courtesy of the Metropolitan Museum of Art)

26. Dirk Langendijk's painting of the Battle of the Pyramids in 1798, when Napoleon's army defeated a Mamluk force three times its size. (Courtesy of the Rijksmuseum)

much loved by the people for their charitable works. Otherwise some could exact influence upon the sultans, such as the Bedouin songstress Ittifaq and an-Nasir's other slave girls.

Shajar-ad-Durr is a striking example of a woman who ruled effectively when she was allowed. The Bahri amirs were glad to support her, but given the circumstances of their coming to power the endorsement of the Caliph was essential; when this was refused she could not remain sovereign ruler, although she continued to quietly manage the civil government. This is typical of the status of women according to the constraints of Islamic culture and what occurred in practice. Ibn Battuta was outraged when he saw Egyptian ladies, wives of merchants as well as amirs, appearing in public without their veils, and their husbands' deferential manner causing them to be taken for their servants. The same traveller also recalls sitting at the feet of two respected female religious teachers in Damascus.

In contrast, another fourteenth-century traveller, the Florentine Leonardo Frescobaldi, describes seeing Egyptian women so heavily veiled that only their eyes could be seen, and some even covering these with transparent cloth. There were decrees issued periodically which ordered that women veil themselves in public, imposing many restrictions on their activities outside the home. Women were sometimes forbidden to attend social gatherings on the Nile or to visit cemeteries. It is likely, however, that the frequent repetition of such decrees indicates that they were often ignored. In fact, throughout the fourteenth century there was much commentary on the revealing nature of women's fashion, at least by the standards of the day. One curious incident took place in 1389 during the Qalawunid sultan Hajji's brief restoration. Kumushbugha, the new governor of Cairo, not only issued the usual restrictions on women's activities but ordered that their dresses, the present fashion being voluminous, be made from a very limited amount of cloth. Barquq countermanded the order when he returned, but the 'Kumushbugha dress', known for its shortness, continued to be seen for some time afterwards.

It is in fact yet to be established how the status of women under the Mamluks compared to life in other Islamic societies in this time, and whether that of the Mamluks' own ladies differed from that of the wives and daughters of the middle classes. There is at least some evidence that their lot was a little better in some ways and that they faced fewer restrictions. When the Ottomans later conquered Egypt, they secluded and repressed women to an extreme.

Recreations and pastimes for all people varied considerably, from picnics (particularly in the orchards of Damascus) to illegal gambling and drinking sessions in secluded places. Activities included hunting, falconry and archery. It was always a popular spectator sport to watch the Mamluks themselves showing their martial skills at the hippodrome. Apart from jugglers, acrobats and other popular entertainers, the fine art of storytelling was popular, tales of the hero Baibars al-Bunduqdari being among the most acclaimed. By the end of the thirteenth century a sophisticated form of shadow-play had become well established. Puppetry was also popular at the time, with the famous character Karagöz ('Black Eye') first seen.

It was also a common though macabre entertainment to visit cemeteries and tombs. Pilgrimages to the graves of the Companions and Muslim saints had long been common practice, but in this period people often came to pay homage to the sepulchres of dead Mamluk amirs and sultans, princesses and other highly regarded individuals. There was a fascination with the dead and their final resting places, which may have contributed to many Mamluks building elaborate tombs and mausolea for themselves, often as part of their mosques. There was frequently a partisan sentiment involved; when Baibars heard that the tomb of Qutuz attracted a large following, he had it destroyed.

The entire issue of religion was complex, and paramount for the Mamluk rulers. They were all avid supporters of orthodox Islam, sometimes to the point of fanaticism. They were nearly

all converts, having received their first religious instruction in
the tibaq – of the sultans only Barquq claimed to have had a
Muslim father. Many sultans and amirs performed the requisite
good works. Every sultan, and many amirs, gave money to
have a mosque built, and several from this period still stand in
Cairo. Most of these were *madrasas*, or college-mosques suitable
for learning. Only az-Zahir Mosque, which Baibars built, was
designed as a congregational mosque for Friday prayers.

The Mosque of al-Azhar was founded in Fatimid times,
until Saladin's day a Shi'ite establishment, and fell into disuse
under the later Ayyubids. In the early Mamluk period it was
re-established as a Sunni school of learning when Baibars had
it renovated and raised its status. Under the Mamluks al-Azhar
flourished as a school for religious teaching, and it is still one
of the most respected institutions in the Muslim world today.
From the Mamluk period students came from all over to study
at al-Azhar, both young men seeking higher education, and older
'postgraduates' involved in particular courses of enquiry. Eminent
scholars, such as the Moroccan savant Ibn Khaldun, also came to
teach there.

In al-Azhar, and in many madrasas of Cairo and Damascus, the
Arabic language maintained its primacy. While the language of
the rulers was Turkish, Arabic would otherwise have lost ground.
A finer understanding of Islam was also maintained, as fanaticism
and superstition became widespread in this time. The shaikhs (the
heads of dervish houses) often protested against the excesses of
the Mamluks, for while the Muslim values of compassion and
forgiveness were ignored and the Mamluks seized the property of
the deceased – disregarding the needs of widows and orphans, to
say nothing of their heirs – the ulema would always reaffirm the
Muslim standpoint. There may be little they could do about the
Mamluks' behaviour, but they at least kept these principles alive.

At the same time there was some interdependence between
the Mamluks and the scholars. While a scholar relied on the
patronage of an amir or sultan to gain the office of qadi or a

teaching post, the Mamluks would need the moral support of the qadis. The sultans and amirs might need to buy this with generous gifts, or by a bout of persecuting dhimmis or Shi'ites.

As protectors of the Hajj, which assembled annually at Damascus, a powerful Mamluk amir with an armed guard always escorted the pilgrims. One distinctive feature of the Hajj in this time was the *Mahmal*. When Shajar-ad-Durr was queen she was too busy to lead the Pilgrimage, so she sent an empty litter to represent herself. Baibars repeated this practice, and it became established thereafter, few Mamluk sultans daring to leave Cairo for too long given that a rebellion could easily depose them in their absence. Every year a camel bore a tent-like structure at the head of the procession. Worked with gold embroidery, it contained two copies of the Quran enclosed in silver-gilt cases. The Mahmal continued into recent times, travelling alongside the black-and-gold cloth from Cairo which draped the Kaaba.

There were four separate schools of Islamic law, theoretically equal in status, although the Shafite chief qadi took precedence. Each of the four, Shafite, Hanafite, Malikite and Hanbalite, were based on the teachings of Islamic jurists of previous centuries on the practical application of the Shari'a. The qadis of the different schools usually worked well together, although the Hanbalites' continual insistence that theirs was the only true interpretation caused friction. A qadi who made an important pronouncement in Islamic law was awarded the title of Shaikh of Islam, and took precedence over even the Shafite chief qadi, and when no longer in office.

The Hanbalite teacher Ibn Taimiya, who died in Damascus in 1329, clashed repeatedly with the Shafites on points of law and theology, causing him to be removed from his position several times, despite the patronage of an-Nasir Muhammad. Ibn Taimiya's teachings had a major influence on the fundamentalist Wahhabi religious movement of recent times.

Mysticism grew in popularity in this period, and became more closely linked with established religion. There were many Sufi orders, with as many as seventy-eight dervish monasteries in Damascus at once time. Sultans and amirs often consulted the shaikhs.

For all the religious fanaticism of the time Cairo remained a city tolerant of heterodoxy and freethinking, and heresies were often heard. Yet the Mamluks periodically persecuted deviants from Sunni Islam, and this atmosphere of free expression was often deceptive. Many Shi'ite groups flourished in Syria. In the Lebanon there were still Nusairis, now known as Alawites, in modern times prominent in the government of Syria. The Assassins, once conquered by Baibars, had lost their capacity for terrorism but continued for a time as an Ismailian sect. There were other Shi'ite groups, mostly survivals from Fatimid times. The Mamluks may have intermittently persecuted Shi'ites, but never succeeded in forcing them all to adopt Sunnism. Also in the Lebanon were the Druzes, a post-Islamic religion whose adherents rebelled at times. In 1305 Ibn Taimiya issued a fatwa against all non-Sunni Muslims and an-Nasir Muhammad's troops defeated the Druzes at Keserwan, after which they were forced to comply with the outward observance of orthodox Islam. The Druzes survive into the present day, but chafed under the yoke during Mamluk and later Ottoman rule.

The treatment of non-Muslims in the Mamluk sultanate proved a sad affair, contrasting with previous times when a degree of tolerance was the norm. In the seventh century, when the early Arab conquests were under way, Caliph Umar issued a decree ruling that Christians, Jews and Zoroastrians could continue to worship under Muslim rule. As an alternative to the choice of conversion or death those of other monotheistic religions could become *dhimmis*, or 'protected peoples'. This involved a tax, restrictions on building churches and synagogues taller than mosques, on carrying weapons, and distinctive dress. The Pact of Umar was really designed to keep the two communities apart, and was less harshly enforced in practice. In places the *jizya* or tax on non-Muslims was lower than those they had paid before the conquests.

The extent of religious tolerance varied in the early centuries in Islamic civilisation, but on the whole there were few problems. During the period of the Crusades and the Mongol invasions, relations between Muslims and dhimmis tended to cool and the non-Muslims were accused with some justification of aiding the enemies of Islam. In the early years of the Mamluk sultanate treatment of the dhimmis was still mild, and few restrictions were in evidence. Many Christians and Jews served in the civil administration. But there were instances of severe unprovoked persecution. Qalawun purged the civil service of non-Muslims, and Khalil once ordered universal conversion to Islam on pain of death. Nevertheless, for most of the early period the dhimmis had little interference from the Mamluks.

In 1301, however, according to al-Maqrizi, 'a misfortune befell the people of the protected religions', the first of many such. A Moroccan wazir on a state visit to Cairo complained to the regents Salar and Baibars al-Jashnakir that he had seen Muslims paying deference to a Christian riding horseback in the street. 'How can you hope for victory,' he put it to them, 'when the Christians ride among you on horseback, wear white turbans, humiliate the Muslims, and have them run in their service?'

Such an indictment, disproportionate as it was, caused Salar and Baibars to summon the senior qadis, and to listen in particular to the most narrowminded. They subsequently confronted the heads of the dhimmi communities with the Pact of Umar, which could not be questioned. The regents then proclaimed that a strict version of the Pact be enforced throughout Egypt and Syria, threatening bloodshed if the dhimmis did not comply.

Thereafter Christians were enjoined to wear blue turbans, and Jews yellow, and their women to wear veils of the same colours. Samaritans wore red turbans. Dhimmis were forbidden to ride horses, only donkeys, and to leave the centre of the road to Muslims. Nor could they carry weapons. They would wear bells around their necks when they visited public baths. They were not allowed to raise their voices in worship, and many churches and synagogues taller than mosques were pulled down. Except in Kerak, where the governor ignored these new regulations, dhimmis all over the empire suffered these privations and worse. In Cairo mobs attacked the houses and shops of dhimmis, pulling down the tall houses, and even demanding that their shop counters be lowered.

When an-Nasir came to full power in 1309 the dhimmis petitioned him to revoke the decree. He would have done so, but his chief qadis persuaded him against it and persecution of Christians and Jews continued. During an-Nasir's reign and afterwards Christian monks were on several occasions accused of starting fires. Terrible reprisals were taken, many monks being burned alive and sometimes Jews with them. Mobs, believing that the sultan willed it, pulled down churches and synagogues and mobbed dhimmis. Some European princes called for the better treatment of Christians. An-Nasir did make some concessions to the dhimmis, but these were minimal in the context of the times.

Throughout the life of the Mamluk sultanate there were phases of persecution, usually followed by long intervals of vague tolerance. After Peter of Cyprus' invasion of 1365 the government seized the property of dhimmis to pay for damage. At this time, as on several other occasions, Christians and Jews were expelled from their posts in government service. As there were so many, and with such expertise, they could not be replaced so easily and were usually reinstated soon afterwards. After such pogroms died down the dhimmis would pick up the pieces and live without too much hardship, until the next wave of persecution.

In 1354, Amir Taz issued a new decree in Sultan Salih's name which not only reaffirmed the Pact of Umar but introduced new restrictions. A dhimmi riding in the street must, on seeing a Muslim, dismount and turn to face the wall until he passed. Two years later Jews were forbidden to practise as bankers. For a time dhimmis were not allowed to meet for worship, as this was considered an opportunity to conspire against the Muslims. They were continually accused of plotting, and their sullenness was often construed as a rebellious disposition. Similar decrees were issued, and new restrictions, new taxes and occasional enforced conversions were ordered. In Jerusalem, Jews were only allowed to renovate their own home on payment to the authority of a fee several times the value of the house itself. By 1500, large areas of the city had become crumbling ruins. In 1389, shortly after a mass conversion under duress, several thousand Copts reaffirmed their Christianity, and the Mamluks ordered the death penalty for apostasy.

By the fifteenth century it had become an accepted act of piety to persecute Jews and Christians. Shaikh once won popular acclaim by summoning the Coptic Patriarch and lecturing him soundly over the alleged persecution of Muslims by Christians in Abyssinia, even though there was no link between the Egyptian and Abyssinian churches. During an outbreak of plague shortly afterwards a mob destroyed a Christian monastery in the Sinai Desert as an act of atonement.

There were two Coptic churches, observing the Melkite and Jacobite rites, and with separate patriarchs. The Chief Rabbi led the Jewish community and appointed the head of the Samaritans. In the fifteenth century two Coptic patriarchs attempted to reform their churches. Gabriel V, who became Patriarch in 1409, reformed the liturgy and produced an effective explanation of the rite. He was succeeded in 1427 by John XI, who proclaimed the union of the two churches, although this did not come about in practice. John also sent a delegate to the Council of Florence in 1439, where the union of Eastern and Western churches was discussed.

During the last generation of the Mamluk sultanate the Jewish community received an influx of European Jews. In 1492 King Ferdinand and Queen Isabella expelled all non-Christians, as did the king of Portugal four years later. Many went to Jerusalem where the Jewish population increased many times over. The European and Jewish communities tried to live together, but differing backgrounds and outlooks caused tension.

There were other, smaller Christian churches. The Maronites in the Lebanon region do not appear to have been recognised by the Mamluks. The status of the Catholics of Frankish descent in Palestine is not clear either. Nor did the Armenian Gregorians of Cilicia have autonomous status, and the Ottoman sultan Selim I later promised them this in return for their aid against the Mamluks.

There were monasteries of all Christian denominations across the Mamluk lands, and they kept Christianity alive in this dark period. But both the Christian and Jewish communities sank into decline, both in numbers and creative vitality. Continual persecution gradually had its effect, and the pressure to convert was high. The dhimmi communities continually lost their young people to Islam, and eventually shrunk to the minorities they have since become.

10

LETTERS, ART AND ARCHITECTURE

The achievements of medieval Islam in the sphere of discovery and learning are manifold and impressive, and the world is indebted to Muslim civilisation for its achievements in mathematics, science, medicine and many other subjects. Although medieval Islamic civilisation is often believed to have passed its peak with the destruction of Baghdad in 1258, the Mamluk sultanate still allowed learning and the arts to flourish for a time. They may not have shone as brightly and by the time of the Mamluks the creative impetus in Islamic learning was almost exhausted, but there were still some new achievements and perhaps the Mamluks can be credited with the preservation of what had been achieved.

Under the Mamluks education was always a major concern. They themselves would at least receive an elementary education while in the tibaq, although comparatively few became very literate. Some of the Burjis attained a high standard in further learning, such as the Sultan Tatar who became adept in Islamic law. The awlad-an-nas were often educated privately on their fathers' wishes. Senior Mamluk amirs gave financial support to public education, from the elementary schools to the madrasas, and some gave scholars their patronage.

There was much writing throughout the period in all arts and sciences, and on more 'practical' subjects such as equitation, archery and navigation. There were many encyclopaedists, such as the civil servant al-Qalqashandi (d. 1418), whose book for government officials is an important source for the period. The scholar Jalal-ad-Din as-Suyuti (1445–1502) produced 561 works on almost every subject, including theology, sciences, history and rhetoric. Many other scholars distinguished themselves as historians, geographers, cosmographers or scientific writers. Abu'l Fida, the last Ayyubid prince of Hama (1273–1332), wrote books in history and geography. Ibn Khallikan (1211–1282), produced among others what was reputedly the best general biography ever written. But most other writings were of little real value; almost entirely repetition of works already produced. Some books tended towards the realms of fantasy, or at least departed from the principle of responsible enquiry.

But it must be said that the Mamluk sultanate was one of the few places in the Muslim world where learning stayed alive. When Ibn Battuta visited Basra in 1327, in the region the Mongols had devastated, he could find none who could recite the Friday prayers or even speak Arabic with proper grammar. The Mamluk lands remained a stronghold for the preservation of learning, while even there it mostly stagnated.

In the field of medicine and the associated sciences there was still plenty of activity, and medical knowledge still overshadowed that in Europe. The hospital in Qalawun's Maristan, together with its older counterpart in Damascus, led the way in medical research. Its dean Ibn an-Nafis (d. 1289) discovered the pulmonary circulation of blood three centuries before its credited discovery in Europe by William Harvey. The concept of psychology first appeared at this time as well. Early in the Bahri period, al-Attar produced a major work of pharmacy.

Ophthalmology attained at this time a higher standard than ever before, and expertise in the Mamluks' region was renowned. The Aleppine oculist al-Khalifa displayed such confidence in his own skill that he once showed no hesitation in removing a cataract for a one-eyed man. Many of the eminent physicians, including al-Khalifa, al-Attar and an-Naqid, were Jewish, and accordingly suffered during the periodic persecutions of dhimmis. In 1448 there was a law proclaimed under Jaqmaq forbidding Muslim and dhimmi doctors to treat those of the other religions, and as Jews were prominent in this field this was a disaster to medicine. Despite this medical practice was also, by the fifteenth century, suffering a tendency towards charlatanry and superstition. *Zar'iraja*, a debased form of 'occult science', was on the increase, and witchdoctor methods tainted medical practice.

Amid the intellectual stagnation of the period, there was one original thinker whose work is still of value: the historian and sociologist Ibn Khaldun (1332–1406). This Moroccan scholar, whose full name was Abd-ar-Rahman Abu Zayd ibn Muhammad ibn Muhammad ibn Khaldun, had already become an accomplished savant and politician long before he came to Cairo. He first taught at al-Azhar before Barquq made him the Malikites' chief qadi. Faraj would dismiss and reinstate him several times, and he eventually died in the role. When Tamerlane was besieging Damascus in 1401, Ibn Khaldun was lowered down the city walls in a basket to call on the ruler at his camp. The Mongol leader was much impressed with the Moroccan, even though he did not assent to the scholar's request to take him back to Samarkand. It was a momentous meeting. Ibn Khaldun later took part in negotiations with Tamerlane over the surrender of Damascus but astutely fled to Cairo before the expected massacre.

Ibn Khaldun had written his most important work before he came to Egypt. This, completed in five months, was entitled *The Book of Example and the Commenced Diwan and History of the Days of the Arabs, Persians, Berbers and their Contemporaries Who Possessed Sovereign Power*. Apart from the volumes on the Berbers, it is only the introductory volume, known as *al-Muqaddima*, which is of any real value. This was the most original and significant work of the entire period. The Muqaddima embodies the first attempt by a historian to show a pattern in the changes occurring in society and government. Breaking from traditional methods and with a new terminology of his own devising, Ibn Khaldun wrote of the effects of the environment on the character of peoples and set out to explain the rise and collapse of ruling dynasties. Concerning the latter he showed the importance of what he called 'group solidarity' (*asabiyya*), by which a dynasty gains power, though it is dispensed with once established, after which supremacy cannot last. The text is a study of social and political groupings rather than of an individual.

Although Ibn Khaldun advocated a rational approach his was not a secular view, showing instead the presence of God in all things, but any degree of freethinking was suspect at this time; a friend of the scholar who expressed similar ideas was lynched as a heretic. Until comparatively recently Ibn Khaldun remained unknown to the West. His analytical methods were only approached in nineteenth-century Europe, but he merits the title of the true founder of the science of historical enquiry. Aside from an autobiography and a number of school exercises, Ibn Khaldun wrote little else. Otherwise he meddled in the politics of both Egypt and North Africa, practised as qadi and taught a number of students.

Ibn Khaldun's methods notably influenced Taqi-ad-Din Ahmad, known as al-Maqrizi, whose writings are important sources for the Mamluk period. Al-Maqrizi (1364–1442), a Syrian scholar who served in Barquq's reign as market inspector for Cairo, wrote several books. Most were historical, but there were also works on archaeology and topography. His most significant work, *The Book of Entries into the Knowledge of the Dynasties of the Kings*, became a celebrated history, dealing mainly with the Ayyubids, the Bahri Mamluks and the early Burjis. Al-Maqrizi also planned an eighty-volume history of Egypt but ended up writing only sixteen. Reflecting his former master's influence, this scholar's 'sociological' approach contributes to his work's value as an important historical source. He also wrote several histories, a book on the famines of Egypt, and other works on a wide range of subjects, particularly one on the lives and habits of bees.

Al-Maqrizi was in turn tutor to another important historian, Yusuf Abu-al-Mahasin, known as Ibn Taghri Birdi (*c.* 1410–1470). As the patronymic suggests, his father was the Anatolian Amir Tahgri Birdi, sometime army commander and brother-in-law to Barquq. On his father's death in 1412, Ibn Taghri Birdi was taken under the protection of his sister, Faraj's Grand Princess, and later grew up as protege of the Shafite chief qadi. Ibn Taghri Birdi was celebrated as 'Holder of the Two Merits', being a Man of the Sword and a Man of the Pen. He was created an Amir of Five and served as a junior officer with the halaqa on Barsbai's eastern Anatolia campaign in 1433. As a scholar he produced many books on literature, music and philosophy, and a number of historical and biographical writings. His most advanced work was *The Stars that Glow: On the Kings of Misr and Cairo*, written soon after a seven-volume biographical dictionary on the sultans and important amirs. In this chronicle Ibn Taghri Birdi continued al-Maqrizi's narrative up to the accession of Qait Bey in 1468, two years before his own death.

The works of al-Maqrizi and Ibn Taghri Birdi are the principal narratives through which the Mamluk period is researched, although historians also make use of as-Suyuti or al-Qalaqashandi along with other writings. After Ibn Taghri Birdi had concluded his chronicle the most coherent narrative can be found in the journal of Ibn Iyas. Also of the awlad-an-nas, Muhammad ibn Muhammad ibn Iyas wrote an account of the closing years of the Mamluk sultanate, ending on his death in 1522 after the Ottoman conquest.

One more writer deserves mention, although he only lived in the Mamluk lands for short periods. Muhammad ibn Abdullah ibn Battuta (1304–1377), a scholar from Tangier, became a renowned traveller of the medieval world. When on pilgrimage to Mecca in 1325, the young man stayed in Cairo and a conversation with a qadi aroused a desire in him to travel more widely. After completing his pilgrimage he continued travelling for the next twenty-five years, to India, Persia, Anatolia, central Asia, Spain, West Africa – in effect all over the Muslim world. His accounts of China and Constantinople are questionable and some untruth is no doubt present in his work. Ibn Battuta first visited Egypt at the high point of an-Nasir Muhammad's reign, and again shortly after that sultan's death. He gave impressive accounts of Cairo ('the mother of cities') and Damascus ('surpasses all other cities in beauty'). He also describes the ruined condition of the coastal towns of Syria, so long after the destruction of Outremer.

Even the Arabian Nights stories reached us through transcriptions during the Mamluk period. Originating in an oral storytelling tradition, they were first written down at this time, the flavours of fourteenth-century Cairo transposed to the Baghdad of Harun-ar-Raschid. There were many poets, as poetry had enjoyed a strong tradition among the Arabs since pre-Islamic times. Of these only al-Busiri (1212–c. 1296) proved to be of any distinction. The writer Ibn Damiya developed the popular art of shadow-play towards the creation of an Arab theatre, but after his death in 1310 none continued his efforts.

As always in the lands of Islam there was no shortage of scholarly and literary activity in the Mamluk period: Cairo, Damascus and other cities teemed with scholars and students. Since the days of the Arab conquests when Caliph Umar declared that Muslims should seek knowledge from wherever it could be found, men of learning were much respected and rich Muslims might support and sponsor scholars. But little proved remarkable, and most was repetition from previous writings. Apart from Ibn Khaldun, there was little produced at the time that has been translated into European languages or contributed much to knowledge and understanding. However, learning continued in this era and the Mamluks at least protected an environment where it flourished, if in a prosaic and repetitive form, and much of it was not lost.

The Mamluk sultanate also had its artists and craftsmen, many of whom came as refugees from the Mongols in the early period. For this reason the style of painting identified with Samarra in Iraq became widespread in the Mamluk lands, although such a style was becoming popular in Syria beforehand. Miniatures, usually illustrating manuscripts, were the most significant examples of painting in this time. Many such illustrations still exist, such as the 'Fables' of Bidpai and a bestiary.

The most important illustrated text was that of the *Maqamat*, or 'Assemblies' of Hariri. The Assemblies, painted around 1300 by an unknown Syrian artist, is a reproduction of a twelfth-century collection of fifty anecdotal stories and is now in the British Library. It has eighty-four illustrations, which show many 'human interest' scenes, such as hunting, theft, banquets and others. Its style is typical of the period, a transplanted and highly idiosyncratic 'Samarra style'. Colours were painted in rich, deep shades. Drawn on geometric patterns, the figures appear in a much-ornamented fashion. Out of scale, houses and camels are painted in smaller proportions to the human characters. The sky is usually shown as a segment, often with moons and stars on it, or the sun with a face. Birds often appear, flying over the characters' heads, and other animals are shown, including fish, which is unusual in Islamic art. Cups and other Mamluk heraldic symbols are often also seen in the pictures. Many of the human figures have a distinctly Mongol appearance; there was already a growing tendency for artists to look eastwards for inspiration, but it was accelerated after the Mongol invasion. Detailed scroll-folds in the figures' clothing, depicting such delicate materials as watered silk, are a distinctive feature of Mamluk painting.

In contrast with the bright and lively painting of earlier times, artists of the Bahri period produced a wooden, expressionless artform where the formal, elaborate style detracted from the creative vitality. The animals looked far more lifelike than the humans. This style may have been in keeping with the formality of the Mamluk sultanate, where everyone's place was clearly circumscribed in elaborate ceremonial and protocol.

Chiefly due to the settlement of Eastern craftsmen, some of the best glassware and pottery of the time was produced in Egypt and Syria. The city of Raqqa on the Euphrates, known for its distinctive style of pottery, was destroyed by the Mongols in 1260. Wares of what was later known as the Raqqa style, either unglazed or decorated with a design of green and blue glaze, appeared all over Syria and Egypt once the Mamluks rose to power. Enamelled glass was a popular technique and highly fired glazes in dark brown were characteristic of the Mamluk period also. Many Mamluk mosque lamps in this style have survived. Decoration with arabesques and geometrical patterns, and also birds, animals and Mamluk heraldic devices such as cups and tables, appear everywhere in craftwork, as they do in painting. Copies of such lamps are on sale as souvenirs in modern Egypt. Arabic script was also much in use and calligraphy, always a prestigious art in Islam, also flourished in this time. At first the angular Kufic script was much used, but the Nakshi design eventually superseded this as the most popular form of ornamental writing.

Metalwork and woodcarving, always common in Syria, is also much in evidence. Silver and gold inlaying of brass and other metals in their finer decoration became an intricate art around this time. A copper basin now in the Louvre, incorrectly known as the 'Baptistry of Saint Louis', is in fact the best-known example of Mamluk inlaid metalwork, created between 1320 and 1340. It is inlaid with gold and silver, partially in Arabic characters where its maker Muhammad ibn al Zayn signed it. It bears human figures, including what is believed a portrait of Salar, an-Nasir's Mongol regent, on its side. The basin came into the possession of the French kings by the eighteenth century and was used as a font to baptize royal children.

Both Egypt and Syria produced fine textiles. Carpets with geometrical and garden designs were produced in Cairo, often wrongfully called Damascene carpets. When the Mongols brought silk working in the Chinese style, this encouraged the development of the Egyptian gold brocade technique. Decorations of animals, Arabic script and heraldic symbols, usually in relief, were again often produced. Silks and damasks were exported to Europe, where their style of embroidery was carried over to Renaissance tapestry, and the gold brocade method into the making of church vestments.

If the Mamluks contributed anything of worth to posterity it was the many architectural triumphs they financed. They may not have in fact designed the buildings, but they used their wealth to make them possible. Almost every sultan and many senior amirs built at least one mosque, and often also dervish monasteries, alms houses, religious schools, sabils and other constructions. An-Nasir Muhammad and Qait Bey were the most prolific builders. It was considered the act of a pious Muslim who had gained material wealth to promote religious and charitable work, and the senior Mamluks often had at least one project that they funded and promoted. Some of their works are counted among the most beautiful buildings in the world, and many still stand.

Many of the Mamluk mosques were madrasas, or college-mosques. Every town needed a single mosque where the entire community could gather for Friday prayer, and most were already built by this time. The madrasa, usually a smaller construction that included facilities for teaching, was first brought from Syria by Saladin as part of his campaign to suppress Shi'ism, and such a foundation often lent itself to promoting learning and charity. Many such madrasas would have the founders' tombs built into them. This practice was not in accordance with Muslim tradition. It may have originated from Turkestan, where some Ayyubids followed it, or else it could have been a survival from Pharaonic times – the native Egyptians still buried their dead in elaborate tombs.

There were many dedicated mausoleum mosques in Cairo, rather than madrasas that included the founders' tombs. Some stand outside the city in two groups, one of which is erroneously called 'the Tombs of the Caliphs'. Some of these were occupied by orders of dervishes, who prayed for the dead Mamluk's soul in gratitude for his patronage, and some sultans built even larger complexes with multiple purposes. The Maristan, at once a mosque, library, school, hospital and mausoleum of Qalawun, is a noted example. Apart from a similar building commissioned by Baibars al-Jashnakir, few others of this kind survive.

The Mamluks' buildings, both religious and secular, still dominate the urban landscape of the old city of Cairo and together with the Fatimid and some Ayyubid edifices, many of the buildings of the *medina* (city centre) date from the Mamluk period. The Cairo skyline shows the elaborate minarets and stylized cupolas that characterise Mamluk building. Such a style of architecture had many inspiring influences: the Syrian Nurid type which Saladin brought to Egypt, through Persian, North African, Byzantine, Anatolian and even Frankish styles. Perhaps the style of Turkestan was the prime influence, and the Mamluks attracted Eastern builders and architects to Cairo. In the later days, Ottoman influences appear.

The ubiquitous cupolas traditionally associated with Islamic building first came from Turkestan in this era. They were usually onion- or helmet-shaped, as on the mosques of Barquq, Barsbai and Qait Bey, or, as on the mosque of Princess Toghai, a barred dome. A few had twin domes, notably the mosque-mausoleum built by the regent Salar and his friend Sanjar al-Gawli, where both finally came to rest. In the fourteenth century builders discovered the method of building domes with stone. Minarets were usually cylindrical, or polygonal, and often built in three distinctive sections, often higher than previously, perhaps topped with an onion-shaped piece. Stalactites (*muqarnas*) and projections also characterised Mamluk architecture, as did stylized battlements. A few of the later minarets have double-pronged points at the top of the minaret.

At first mosque ground plans followed a traditional model: a rectangular open court with shaded porticoes on each side, as was the pattern of the mosques of Baibars, an-Nasir Muhammad and Shaikh. But the madrasa-style mosques initiated a new form, where the central court or *iwan* was built on a smaller scale, with four square courts radiating from it in a cruciform design. These smaller courts were used as classrooms, sometimes allotted to each of the four religious schools or else used at different times of the day according to the sun's position. In some madrasas of the Burji sultans the iwan disappears altogether, as the school aspect of the madrasa was paramount. The iwan might have a fountain as its centrepiece.

Porphyry and chalk from the Muqattam Hills provided the main building materials. Building in different hues of brickwork in alternate courses produced a ribbed effect. Façades were often elaborate, that of az-Zahir a particular example. Polygonal geometric shapes, arabesques and animal motifs decorate the interiors. Heraldic devices also appear. The Lion, or Panther, of Baibars al-Bunduqdari is shown, usually in relief, on everything he commissioned. Wooden carvings, such as latticework, and elaborate carvings of minbars, or pulpits, adorn the insides of the mosques.

There are so many examples of the Mamluk style of religious building that it is difficult to choose the best. The two three-storey minarets that top the Zuwaila Gate are part of the al-Mu'ayyad Mosque. When Shaikh was arrested under Faraj's orders he was placed in the Zuwaila prison, and after escaping and becoming sultan he built this mosque in place of the prison as thanksgiving for his deliverance. The 'Blue Mosque' of Aqsunqur is another important example. There are simply too many buildings, all showing distinctive Mamluk styles, to enumerate and evaluate here.

Almost certainly the most impressive is the mosque of Sultan Hasan. This cruciform madrasa-mausoleum was built on a scale with measurements twice the usual proportions. It has tall, smooth walls, with windows reaching as far as the root sill, and is closed off with a *muqarnas* vault. Battlement designs top the walls. The minarets, one of which rises above the main entrance, are as tall as 81 metres and divided into sections by polygonal platforms. The original dome was in wood, since replaced by a marble version. The entrance is a massive gate in a deep and richly ornamented niche, accessed by a free stairway. Shaikh appropriated the original grand doors for his own mosque. According to tradition, Hasan took the marble facing of the Great Pyramid to face his mosque. The central iwan is shaped almost as a perfect cube and is dominated by a fountain, since rebuilt in the Ottoman style. The rooms surrounding the cruciform plan were either dormitories or self-contained miniature madrasas for each of the four schools. Hasan's tomb is on the side of the building facing Mecca, although given his obscure end it is unlikely that Hasan was interred there; although two of his sons rest there. The entire interior is richly decorated, with both Kufic and Nakshi script and with wooden and gold-inlaid bronze ornamentation.

The Mamluks also commissioned military buildings. Although they added little to Saladin's defences of Cairo save for some refortification, they were responsible for several formidable fortresses in Syria, and the reinforcement of some earlier strongholds. Baibars rebuilt the Ayyubid fortress of Sheizar, which overlooked the Orontes, having taken it from the Assassins. The Citadel of Aleppo was again rebuilt under the Mamluks, with such impressive fortifications that it cost Tamerlane 10,000 men to overcome it. The Fort of Qait Bey, still in use in Alexandria, is another example. Mamluk military architecture is characterised by deep, thick, square outer walls, again with heraldic motifs much in appearance.

All but a few of the Mamluk palaces in Cairo have since disappeared. These were usually built around an inner courtyard, with one long great hall in the upper storey that often served as the harem. A perforated wooden cupola was usually erected in the centre of the roof. In the cities of Syria the upper storey would be T-shaped, with mosaic panelling. Cairene houses had projecting upper storeys, their windows with bow-shaped wooden lattices allowing women to look out onto the streets without being seen. This basic design is still the pattern for Cairo's townhouses.

To an extent through the Mamluks' efforts, medieval Cairo became the most impressive city in Islam in their time. Ibn Battuta spoke of it in the most laudatory tones. Ibn Khaldun wrote that 'he who has not beheld Cairo knows not the grandeur of Islamism. It is the metropolis of the universe, the garden of the world.' The Mamluks as a political grouping were hardly endearing, but they did leave such architectural wonders, which merits them some commendation.

In the mid-thirteenth century the Mongols had reduced Iraq and Iran to smoke-blackened wilderness. The Mamluks halted the Mongol advance at the Euphrates and held the frontier there, and in doing so not only protected society but enabled the scholastic and artistic achievements of Islamic civilisation to flourish for a little longer.

11

MATTERS MILITARY

Above all else Mamluks were soldiers, and rather than rulers of civil government their prime concern was fighting the potential enemies of their empire. Such a role was essential to the maintenance of stability in the entire region at that time, and the Mamluks in the main succeeded in this. In the Bahri period they saved Syria and Egypt from devastation at the hands of the Mongols and ended the presence of the Franks in the Levant, among other achievements. In truth their performance as a military force was patchy, and perhaps the standards set by the original Salihis were not maintained.

In many ways the Mamluks resembled the knights of Europe and the samurai of Japan. They were maintained materially by a feudal economic system and followed a code of behaviour, in their case a martial version of the principles of Islam where those who fell in valiant combat were assured of Paradise. They even had their distinctive system of heraldry. Most of all, they were an elite cavalry, well trained and well equipped, their tactics coordinated effectively. Such a force would be more effective than a much larger number of untrained fighters.

The first Mamluks were Turks, whom as-Salih Ayyub often chose for their reputed pugnacious nature. A Turk and his horse always made a formidable combination, according to writings from the early period of the Arab conquests. He could manoeuvre in the tightest situations, mount or dismount with a leap, call a horse to him and ride hard at the enemy. Both could survive a long campaign in the most inclement conditions, the horseman even subsisting on mare's milk and the horse on shoots and leaves. Turks were accordingly considered the best soldiers in Islam. As-Salih Ayyub also recruited slaves from other races, but they were trained according to the expectations of Turks.

The tibaq system made soldiers of slaves. Once they had completed the early process, designed to indoctrinate them in the values of Islam, they received the most rigorous military training from the age of about fourteen. Over five years or so, those who had attained proficiency both in equitation and using an array of weapons would be released from slavery. As a hybrid of the harsh nomadic tribesman and the well-trained knight, a Mamluk faris could certainly produce results.

Turkish cavalry warfare was a fast-moving affair. They could manoeuvre quickly and easily in battle, attacking from the rear and at the flanks, encircling the enemy, loosing their arrows and riding quickly out of range. At close quarters they used their swords and lances as well on horseback. The Franks discovered this to their cost in the early period. The Mamluks broadly followed the same light cavalry tactics, their extensive training in formation discipline being to their best advantage. Mamluk armies went into battle in a three-section formation. In the centre the best Mamluk troops and the command saw the most fighting. The two flanks were often populated by lower-quality troops who might flee the field when hard-pressed while the centre fought on, as at Homs in 1281.

Mamluk soldiers wore light armour, not wishing to slow down their horses; it was usually mail armour, or mail enforced with metal splints. Sometimes they wore lamellar armour, plates of iron, rawhide or horn laced into rows with thongs, often with mail sleeves attached. It appears that most Mamluks did not usually wear helmets but preferred either to wear a turban or a yellow brimmed hat in the early period, or else the triangular fur-trimmed hat that amirs often sported. Illustrations to the many equitation manuals of the time often show Mamluk horsemen wearing turbans. The helmets they did wear at first consisted of a simple covering for the crown of the head, usually of hammered iron and tapering to a point. This basic design might be extended to protect the ears and the nape, or have attached a leather covering to protect the neck and throat. This original design was gradually extended to cover the face too, as a nasal appeared, and mail covered the mouth. In Qalawun's time a characteristic tall, conical helmet appeared, sometimes plumed, and the face enveloped by a curtain of mail, leaving only two reinforced eye-openings. Helmets became more stylised as time went on, the ones worn at the end having a metal peak over the eyes. Examples of all these designs survive.

Shields were usually round and made either of metal or of wood reinforced by hide or metal. Kite-shaped shields in the Norman style were also used throughout the Islamic east, probably in imitation of the Byzantine model. Lances were short and light, either of steel or steel-tipped wood, and might have a pennant or streamer. Lances could also be thrown like spears. There are instances of troopers cutting their lances short so that they could stab more of their enemies more quickly. The bow was a Mamluk faris' effective weapon, about 3 feet long and made of wood and several layers of horn. A faris would be trained through a progression of five bows of different strengths before he could master the bow used in battle. He would carry, either on his back or hanging from his belt, a quiver of about thirty arrows, sometimes holding extra flights in his boots. He could loose arrows as far as 300 yards, or a little over half that distance with a fair margin of accuracy. A Mamluk's arrow could not pierce armour, other than possibly chainmail, but the bows they used were the most effective before the appearance of the English longbow. The crossbow was used at the time and there is some evidence of Mamluks using them in both war and hunting, but most sources appear to indicate that they preferred the conventional bow, and that the crossbow was a common infantryman's weapon.

The sword was most often used at close quarters. Rather than the inferior-quality swords produced in Egypt, the Mamluks might acquire those imported from India, China, Malaysia or even Scandinavia. Many of those imported first went to Damascus to be inlaid with gold and silver before resale by the process known as 'Damascening'. The Mamluks' swords usually had straight blades. The scimitar, the traditional Islamic curved sword, did not come into general use until the fifteenth century, although most swords had at least a slight curve before this. They were sheathed in a scabbard, either over the left shoulder or at the waist. A faris was given exacting and extensive training in the use of the sword. He would first be made to strike varying amounts of soft clay, up to 1,000 times a day from the same position. He would eventually be able to strike through a bar of lead with a single blow. He was further trained to cut through a prescribed number of sheets of paper, or of individual reeds, so that he could vary the extent of the blows he inflicted, either to disarm, wound, mutilate or kill. He also learned to fight with two swords at once. Battle-axes were mostly ceremonial weapons but sometimes used in combat. Troopers at times carried maces, either iron or steel, with spherical or polyhedral heads. They may also have carried daggers.

Like a modern standing army the Mamluks were required to undergo daily combat training, on training grounds around Cairo. They competed in complicated lance games, in archery and in feats of military skill. These training grounds fell into disuse in the fifteenth century, despite the efforts of Qait Bey and other later sultans to revive their activities.

The sultan's own mamluks, the *julban*, comprised the most important part of his army. There would be four kinds, and the ones utilised most would be those the sultan had raised and freed. If the sultan had previously been an amir, those original mamluks would be the nucleus of his command. Increasingly important in the Circassian period was the *khassikiya*, the corps of pages, selected from the julban for service in the sultan's household. They were regarded as the elite troops, usually by virtue of their close association with the sultan. They often gained promotion before they had proved any military skill and were senior amirs before their experience merited it. Whenever a new sultan came to the throne many of his predecessor's mamluks were still in the process of training; the new sultan would purchase these by a legalistic procedure, and eventually release them himself. These, and other mamluks of previous sultans entering the service of the successors, were known as the *saifiya*. The sultan may have performed the crucial act of releasing them, but he did not rely on them as much as those who began in his service. The other group, the *qaranis*, the mamluks released by a previous sultan, have already been discussed. They may have been a political threat to reigning sultans, but they could still serve as his soldiers. It is unlikely that he could reward them very well for their efforts, and many sultans kept the qaranis busy rather than risk their rebelling, and so they might be involved in thankless campaigns. It was difficult to remove these experienced soldiers without destabilising the army, although mass evictions from the Citadel barracks characterised the changing of Circassian sultans. During Barquq's brief deposition, Mintash and Yalbugha attempted to exterminate his mamluks.

The numbers of mamluk troops a sultan held in his service could vary considerably. Baibars expanded the royal mamluk corps during his reign, and in the early Bahri period there was said to be never less than 10,000. Qalawun was said to have commanded over 20,000, although this is probably exaggeration. Qalawun certainly did expand his army when he founded the Burji regiment and the second Bahri corps. In contrast, the rawk of an-Nasir in 1315 shows fiefs distributed for only 2,000 royal mamluks and forty amirs.

Whatever the true figures, there was certainly an increase under the Bahris. Under the Burjis, however, numbers fell as financial resources dwindled. In the later days the sultans found it difficult to raise a thousand troops for a campaign. To the mamluks the sultans commanded those of the amirs could be added for campaigns. It is unlikely that every Amir of One Hundred actually maintained a hundred mamluks; their incomes in the later period did not always allow them to do so. But taking this number as a standard it would mean a total of 2,400 mamluks in the Bahri period and 1,100 in the fifteenth century. In reality the amirs' mamluks would probably have totalled nearer half these figures. The mamluks of Amirs of Ten and of Drums also need to be counted and these also fluctuated but could have been as many as several thousand, altogether about as many as the sultan. It seems that an-Nasir had tried to counterbalance the numbers of the amirs' mamluks in his rawk with those in his service. The sultans' mamluks had no specific duties. There were Bahris stationed at various times at Kerak and Qus, and a Mamluk garrison on Cyprus after 1426, but this was not common practice. Veteran mamluks were often stationed at Mecca, as a deterrent to the king of Yemen challenging the sultan's suzerainty.

It was often difficult to make a campaign set out, while the troops would expect a donative before they moved. They would need to go periodically to their fiefs to collect revenues, and would object to being on campaign too long. Campaigning in winter was almost impossible, for the Mamluks suffered heavily from the cold. Troops on garrison duty during campaigns would often return early. From Barsbai's time discipline was generally poor.

The sultan had other military resources at his disposal. He could if he so desired call every able-bodied man to arms, as

Qutuz did in 1260. This was far from desirable except in extreme circumstances, and a smaller, more suitable military force was really needed to support the Mamluk troops on most campaigns.

There was the *halaqa*, or 'ring', a survival of Ayyubid times when they formed the elite troops, though they were now relegated to an auxiliary role. Most were horsemen and probably had some training in weapons, although not to the extent of a Mamluk faris. Like the Mamluks they received the income of a landed estate, although much smaller. The awlad-an-nas, the sons of Mamluks, formed the elite of the halaqa. It was a traditional occupation, and many served as a matter of course, such as Ibn Taghri Birdi. The main body of the halaqa were otherwise the sons of Egyptian and Syrian merchants and artisans, and some other relatives of Mamluks. There were also some *nouveau riche* elements who bought their way into the corps, for it was the only part of the feudal military class open to non-Mamluks. This group also included irregular troops, such as Bedouin Arabs. Some Bedouin shaikhs were allotted fiefs and made honorary amirs, and only commanded their own people. There were also Turcoman contingents, some Druzes and other subject peoples. Mercenaries from other lands also served.

On campaign a Mamluk Amir of One Hundred would notionally command 900 halaqa in addition to his own mamluks, each sub-unit of 100 halaqa led by their own commander, or *bash*, and each group of forty having their own lesser officer *(muqaddam)* and sergeant *(naqib)*. There were about 24,000 halaqa in the early Bahri period, and they were often called on, especially on Baibars' and Qalawun's campaigns. But they were considered less useful in the fourteenth century, especially as the threat from the Persian Mongols subsided, and they were downgraded and considered surplus to requirement. When the two land surveys ordered by Lajin and an-Nasir Muhammad reorganised provision for the army, the fiefs for the halaqa were much reduced, particularly in 1315, and they received less productive iqtas.

The halaqa continued afterwards in a much reduced form, chronically underpaid and holding less prestige. The institution did not disappear altogether, although it was mostly the awlad-an-nas who carried on with it, few able to find alternative professions; so much that the halaqa as a whole was usually referred to as the awlad-an-nas by the late Burji period. They were still called on some campaigns: Barsbai took them to Amid in 1433. Otherwise they were required by this time to pay for exemption from military service, which may be more desirable for both sides. In 1468, when Qait Bey was raising an army against Shah Suwar, he summoned all the awlad-an-nas to Cairo, and ordered each one to draw a bow. Those who could do so would either serve on the campaign or pay the exemption, but the ones who failed this test were deprived of their fiefs. There were attempts later in his reign to turn the awlad-an-nas into a corps of musketeers, but by then they were not very much taken into account.

Syria had no regular forces, apart from the Bahris at Kerak in the early period, and each province had a number of Mamluk amirs and halaqa. The figures varied: in Damascus one authority claimed there were twelve Amirs of One Hundred, eighty more junior amirs and 12,000 halaqa, while another claims there were eighteen Amirs of One Hundred and fifty-one junior amirs. In Aleppo there were six to nine senior amirs, while the other governorates had fewer fiefs and smaller forces. Gaza had only two Amirs of Drums and 1,000 halaqa. At different times economic factors may have meant periodic reductions, and this may explain the discrepancy of figures. The amirs were usually the governor's mamluks, and the halaqa was enlisted locally. A governor of a province such as Aleppo or Damascus had considerable military resources at his disposal, and too often used them for rebellion against the sultan.

It took over a month for an army to march from Cairo to Aleppo, although an army on the move was well organised with food depots, horses and camels prepared before the army set out.

There were two camels to every Mamluk and three to every two halaqa. The armies also had qadis, military police, surgeons and physicians. There was always a large baggage train, usually of camels. The armies moved on written orders.

As in Christendom, siege warfare was a major concern where it was difficult to dislodge an enemy securely entrenched in a fortified town or stronghold. The Mamluks used siege engines such as battering rams and siege towers. The arbalest, or giant crossbow, was probably a Muslim invention. In particular, the giant catapult was an important siege weapon. Four different types are mentioned, but nowhere in the sources is the difference between the four explained. When Shaikh was besieging Faraj in Damascus in 1412, the catapult he used reputedly needed 200 camels to bring it to the walls.

Again as in Europe, mining below the walls was often used, either to enter the city or to cause part of the walls to collapse. There was always a contingent of sappers from Aleppo, whose inhabitants had a reputation for such skills. Mining – and countermining – was often used, and subterranean combat was by no means unusual. Each side used noxious gasses from sulphur and ammonia to drive out their enemies.

The Ayyubids and their predecessors had fortified the cities and castles of Egypt and Syria, and the Mamluks usually either extended or maintained the fortifications, building little themselves. Such fortifications were usually of rubble faced with stone. Every large town had a citadel; a fortress either inside a city wall, or against the walls themselves. This was the final stronghold, the last possible refuge for the defenders, and the station for the Mamluk troops. The citadel of Aleppo is the most impressive example of Mamluk fortification. An Ayyubid building, it was destroyed by Hulagu and rebuilt in 1292. The citadel towers 165 feet above the city on a steep mount surrounded by a deep moat. It was almost impossible to scale the mound under siege conditions, which made the drawbridge and stairway the only route. It is believed that the Europeans learned a great deal of castle technology from the Muslims in the time of the Crusades.

From the early times Muslim armies made use of naphtha, or 'Greek Fire', a substance similar in effect to napalm, which clung to whatever it burned. Naphtha was held in earthenware pots, either to be pitched at a target or used as a primitive flamethrower. There were usually some halaqa who served as 'grenadiers' for this purpose.

It is in fact debatable how successful the Mamluks were as soldiers, and how much they owed their successes to factors outside of their control. Their victory over the crusaders in 1250 showed an astute sense of strategy on Baibars' part. As we have seen Ain Jalut, where the Mamluks won acclaim as the force that halted the advance of the Mongols in their path of destruction through the Islamic lands, was not the spectacular defeat of the vast Mongol hordes as believed; Hulagu had withdrawn the main body of his army beyond the Euphrates and it was a smaller screening force that Qutuz and Baibars engaged, and even then they were hard pressed.

The Mamluks however provided a competent defence of Syria while the Mongols threatened to assimilate the region into the Ilkhanate. When Hulagu's successors did invade, the Mamluks mostly defeated them save for Wadi-al-Khaznadar. The Franks of Europe did not invade in strength after 1250 and did not impede the final destruction of Outremer. How much of the military successes and failures could be attributed to the attitudes of their commanders? The Mamluks were noted for infighting; Faraj's abandonment of the 1402 campaign lost Damascus to the Timurids. There were similar failings on the Mongol side, when religious conflict kept the Ilkhans occupied, and the splintering of the Mongol empire reduced their resources. The Franks and Armenians were never numerous enough to mount any serious defence.

When the threat from the Ilkhanate was clearly coming to an end the Mamluks scaled down their military capacity. An-Nasir

Muhammad not only reduced the feudal provision for the halaqa but relaxed the harsh regime in the tibaq. Now that the need to keep an army at the ready was much reduced it stood to reason that resources could be better deployed. The tibaq system produced brutal, self-reliant and obedient soldiers and it is questionable whether a successful formula should be tampered with. The Mamluks expected no new enemies to appear, and never envisaged that Tamerlane would pose a new threat of the magnitude of Hulagu. The pressure to maintain an army of such hardiness and discipline was eased. It was to the Mamluks' good fortune that Tamerlane did not return to follow up his conquest of northern Syria after the 1402 campaign.

As time went on there were two areas in which the Mamluks showed serious inadequacies, both of which contributed to their undoing. These were naval warfare and the development of gunpowder. For some time Islamic peoples had little to do with the sea, apart from north African pirates and also traders and travellers, and it was some time before they turned their attention to building navies. Saladin raised a fleet from practically nothing and maintained it against the Franks, but after his death it fell into disuse. When Baibars identified Cyprus as a supply source for Frankish Syria and a base for seaborne marauders he did send a flotilla of ships full of soldiers, but this came to nothing. Baibars had built a large fleet, again practically from scratch, to attack Cyprus and cut the supply route to Outremer, but his expedition of 1270 failed, most of his ships wrecked. There were several other attempts by Mamluk sultans to build a navy, but always from nothing after long periods without naval activity. It was difficult to find craftsmen capable of building ships, and timber had to be imported. It was also difficult to find adequate sailors.

The Mamluks considered warfare as cavalry tactics with infantry support, and war at sea was almost alien to their thoughts. They even used the term *ustuli* ('seaman') as an insult. They were suspicious of any warfare that separated them from their horses, and disdained the idea of fighting in ships.

The Mamluks mostly unwilling to sail, crews had to be raised either from foreign volunteers (largely north Africans) or from pressgangs, the latter method bringing the most unsuitable elements. The Mamluks sought to defend the shores by fortifying the Delta and by a scorched-earth policy along the Syrian coast, but it was eventually obvious to them that they could not ignore Cyprus, nor the base the Hospitallers maintained on Rhodes. The Franks often attacked Muslim shipping and at times raided the sea coast. Crusading in the fourteenth and fifteenth century was chiefly a seaborne activity, and Peter of Lusignan's occupation of Alexandria was a particularly terrible disaster. Cyprus and Rhodes were centres from which the Franks menaced the Muslims for a long time.

While the Mamluks remained decidedly landlubbers, Cyprus lay tantalisingly out of their reach. Although they vowed revenge after 1365, it was not until 1424 that any Mamluk ships sailed for Cyprus and it took three annual expeditions before they succeeded. Barsbai's conquest of the island in 1426 was in reality the act of transporting a land army across the sea. The Mamluks never learned the arts of sea warfare. They never achieved naval supremacy in the eastern Mediterranean. Nor did they repeat their success against the Hospitallers on Rhodes. The Mamluks were the first to mount cannon on their ships, but this did not turn them into a major naval power. It came to the attention of Qansuh al-Ghuri while he was sultan that the Portuguese were harrying Muslim shipping in the Indian Ocean. Once again the Mamluks despatched a fleet to the defence of Muslims but failed to make any headway, leading to a severe loss of prestige for the Mamluk sultanate.

It has been debated, as suggested by the modern scholar David Ayalon, whether the slowness of the Mamluks to embrace the use of gunpowder and firearms laid them open to eventual defeat and destruction. This was later challenged; slow development of this technology meant that neither the Mamluks nor the Ottomans could become the gunpowder empires to be seen a little later.

Gunpowder was first used by European armies in the thirteenth century, but its first mention in Mamluk sources was in 1342, when the deposed sultan Ahmad used cannon to defend Kerak during a siege. There are scant references for some time afterwards, but it appears that both cannon and handguns came into more widespread use about the reign of Barquq. Experiments on creating musketeer corps in Qait Bey's time were probably encouraged by improving firearm technology and in the Mamluk period firearms were still in a primitive stage of their development. Cannon was at first more valuable as a psychological weapon, mostly making noise and smoke rather than actually doing damage. Technological improvements came slowly.

It was a major operation moving large, cumbersome cannon on campaign, and while they would be useful in sieges and possibly coastal defence and on ships, they could slow down a campaign considerably. The nature of Mamluk military strategy made such guns useless in the fast-moving campaigns characterising their warfare. Of course the big guns would be effective as siege weapons.

Shortly before the Ottoman invasion in 1516 Qansuh al-Ghuri had many more cannon made, even ordering the building of several foundries dedicated to this purpose. But he did not use any at Marj Dabiq, and seems to have wanted them for coastal defence against the expected attack by sea. Tuman Bey tried to use them at Raidaniyya in a static defence against the advancing Ottoman army, but this proved ineffective in the event given the poor strategy he employed.

Mamluk ambivalence towards the use of handguns cost them effective use of this weapon at the time, but there were practical considerations. It was true that the Mamluks scorned the gun as a common infantryman's weapon and took pride in their skills with sword, bow and lance; such traditional skills justified their supremacy. But at that stage firearms could not be so easily assimilated into the Mamluks' tactics. The handheld weapon of the time, the arquebus, was cumbersome, and very difficult for a faris to carry on his pony. To fire such a gun, and possibly to load it as well, the trooper would need to dismount, and as Mamluk military tactics were dependent on fluid, fast movements and skilful manoeuvring, there was no room for this.

To adapt to the use of firearms would therefore mean a complete revision of military methods, and might have even challenged the political status of the Mamluks. At the same time in Europe new infantry weapons were already affecting the indispensability of knights. Mamluk troopers would hardly consent to part with their horses and their bows, to be reduced to what they considered a common foot soldier. African slaves, generally considered the lowest of all, carried the arquebus and this shows the contempt the Mamluks had for handguns. The Africans were simply given the gun and told to fire it; no training was attempted.

In 1490 Qait Bey, considering the Ottoman threat and their better use of firearms, ordered that the awlad-an-nas learn to use the arquebus. Again there was no provision for training, and such a corps of arquebusiers never saw action. At the same time Qait Bey also tried to revive the long-abandoned training programme of the Mamluk faris, as an attempt to promote traditional equestrian warfare, which encouraged the Mamluks to look down on the arquebusiers still more. The amirs pressurised Qait Bey to disband the corps of musketeers, but he remained convinced that it was indispensable.

Muhammad ibn Qait Bey appeared to favour this new technology and the arquebus was eventually reallotted to the black slaves, possibly in an attempt to offset the strength of the Mamluk corps. The amirs eventually disposed of him, their anxieties over this business probably proving an important factor. Qansuh al-Ghuri gave the gun back to the awlad-an-nas in 1510, but the Africans gained it again after Marj Dabiq.

The Ottomans had acquired firearms much later than the Mamluks had done, and could see better their possibilities now that they were more advanced technologically. But even then firearm technology had not yet advanced enough for the gun to replace more conventional weapons. The Ottoman armies used both cannon and handguns on their campaigns but they also employed light cavalry tactics with mounted archers as often as the Mamluks did. Marj Dabiq was not so much a victory of firepower over outdated feudal cavalry methods as Professor Ayalon suggested, but a battle decided by conventional military strategies. It was a battle the Mamluks could still have won, as will be shown in the next chapter. Although Ottoman cannon and muskets did the Mamluks damage, they were not the decisive factor. After Marj Dabiq, when the Mamluks tried to defend Cairo, Tuman Bey II made a frantic effort to organise the defence around the use of cannon, but it was too late to learn this new warfare. There were not enough guns available and there was no time to train soldiers to the required standard. His plans to adapt cavalry strategies around the deployment of cannon proved disastrous. Perhaps if Tuman had used traditional Mamluk warfare methods he might have won this battle. Or else if he had had more time to train his armies in the use of guns. Raidaniyya was far more a failure in planning than a clash of technologies.

After the Ottoman conquest, and when advances in firearm technology made guns more portable and more easily used on horseback, the Mamluks used them. By the eighteenth century it was common to see a mounted Mamluk wearing a brace of flintlock pistols and with a carbine slung over his back. They still used their bows, lances and swords as much as before, however, even as late as the French invasion of 1798. It was really the threat to their equestrian military lifestyle that made the Mamluks wary of firearms in the time of the sultanate.

Psychological warfare as practised in that age was an effective weapon. The Mongols were masters of this, cultivating their reputation of invincibility and committing the most horrific atrocities on all who did not immediately submit to them. The

Mamluks acted in exactly the same way, discouraging resistance with displays of terrible carnage. Many potential enemies would submit to avoid their wrath. As instruments of this form of warfare the Mamluks also used drums and sometimes other musical instruments in battle. The effect of the drumming at the height of the battle was tremendous, often shattering the composure of the enemy and famously throwing the Bedouins' horses into confusion. A Mamluk army was truly formidable to behold, its mounted soldiers well equipped and well disciplined; such was the force that Baibars and Qalawun inherited from as-Salih, and which they perpetuated. However, standards fell and the Mamluk sultanate ended in military defeat. The Mamluks gained the credit for halting the Mongol conquest, which gave its sultan the highest prestige, but by 1517 the Mamluks' real prowess did not match it in the final analysis.

12

DECAY AND DEFEAT

The Mamluk sultanate ended in military defeat and conquest, but it was certainly in a state of severe decay long before it faced the Ottoman advance. It had gone the way of so many other dynasties, where a vigorous beginning and a peak in powers gave way to a long and slow decline, ended with the emergence of a new regime. In most other cases the descendants of the founder did not live up to his ability, and their shortcomings encouraged the process of deterioration. The Mamluks were in a way different: they were nearly all first-generation upstarts and accordingly maintained the vigour of the sultanate. When the Qalawunids failed in the third and fourth generations to produce decisive leadership, the *de facto* practice of usurpation by the most powerful amirs made a return.

But the Mamluks themselves, by their system of recruitment and their predatory manner, caused serious damage to their realm in the long term. Although Mamluk mismanagement was partially to blame, economic factors did the most damage. Many of these were outside the Mamluks' control, but they did not handle the changed conditions very well.

Depopulation was a common factor in the fourteenth-century Near East, and this had serious consequences. Plague caused much of this, and the slowness of the population to make up the losses created a long-term demographic decline. The first outbreak of the plague in 1347 took a phenomenal number of lives. The chroniclers tell of thousands of deaths both human and animal, ungathered harvests, frantic migrations towards Anatolia, and disruption to ordinary living. Plague returned to Egypt and Syria sixteen times before 1517, often striking again soon after a region had recovered from the last outbreak, and it was expected every seven years or so. Children, eunuchs and foreigners suffered the most. Mamluks, themselves northerners in an uncongenial climate, were often affected. In 1347 about a thousand mamluks died, as did nearly all of a corps of drummers, and the halaqa disappeared completely for a time. Such epidemics might happen when the sultan needed his army, and plague handicapped many campaigns in this way. Mamluks would refuse to leave Cairo during outbreaks while they feared a rival faction taking control in their absence and preferred to risk dying instead.

Other natural disasters also visited Egypt and Syria, often at the same time as plague or political instability. In 1301 an earthquake brought destruction. There was cattle murrain, fruit disease and other agrarian disasters. Many times the Nile failed to rise, bringing famine to the land. The native population, impoverished and undernourished, suffered accordingly.

There is much evidence of a dramatically shrinking population in the second half of the Mamluk period. Between the rawk-an-Nasiri of 1315 and a similar count taken late in Barsbai's reign, over 300 villages had ceased to exist. Whole quarters of Cairo and Alexandria were deserted ruins by 1500. In Syria the pattern is repeated: large areas near Hama and Antioch uninhabited and everywhere hundreds of villages either abandoned or scarcely populated. Aleppo seems to have been an exception, probably due to its flourishing trade.

Such depopulation was in part the cause of the decline of Egyptian and Syrian industries from the mid-fourteenth century. Not only were there fewer consumers in the region, but skilled craftsmen became more difficult to find and many had to be lured from other lands, and those remaining demanded higher wages, often for poorer standards of workmanship. All this contributed to inflationary trends. In the early fifteenth century traditional industries such as textiles, sugar and glassware all but collapsed. Europeans, whose technologies now surpassed those of the East, brought unequal competition. European textiles, paper and other goods flooded the Muslims' markets, leaving little opportunity for the struggling native industries.

Coinage was debased. As silver became scarcer in the late fourteenth century, the mints mixed it with copper, and the exchange rate between the silver dirham and the gold dinar fluctuated considerably. At times the copper coin replaced the silver one altogether, and further inflation ensued. New supplies of silver and Barsbai's reforms, which produced the *Ashrafi* as the new unit, alleviated this for a time, but there was never as much precious metal for the mints as in previous times. In 1440, dinars and most dirhams disappeared completely for a time and wheat was used as money.

Such economic problems had effects that plagued the Mamluk rulers in this later period. Revenues diminished as costs rose and iqtas declined in value. Commercial duties collected mirrored the decline in trade. Mamluk troopers felt the pinch, their pay usually either in arrears or advanced over a long period to meet increased costs. In the later days even the twice-weekly fodder ration was not always issued, as hay was expensive and difficult to obtain. A faris might sell his horse or his weapons in order to buy food.

It is easy to see why the junior Mamluks often rioted for higher pay, and why the amirs became involved in commerce and industry. Abuses of the mamluk system itself were many. Shaikh discovered during his reign that many of the sultan's mamluks had listed themselves as the mamluks of amirs at the same time, thereby drawing two incomes. Shaikh forbade this practice, but gave larger fiefs in compensation. It was also by no means unusual for a Mamluk to sell his fief, often to a civilian, thus leaving military service altogether. At first this sale of fiefs was forbidden, but by Barsbai's time the army office would demand a fee to sanction the transaction.

The Mamluks did not show much address to economics. They were no doubt conscious of the decline in incomes from certain sources, but they did little other than find ways of extracting more from the same. By Barsbai's time the granting of monopolies to amirs of lucrative goods was established, as was the compulsory purchase of the same commodities. The spice trade had long been an important means of raising revenue, but the sultans took control of it and amassed as much money as they could.

The sultans were always looking for new revenue streams, if only to keep their troops' loyalty. Besides these monopolies they created new taxes and raised the existing duties. They reduced the number of senior amirs, and gave more important positions to those of lower rank. Barsbai had only eleven Amirs of One Hundred, whereas the early Bahri sultans had twenty-four. Official posts and governorates were bought and sold at times, often to unsuitable incumbents. An amir could become Viceroy of Damascus by paying 45,000 dinars to Sultan Khushqadam; at the same time Safad could be bought for only 4,000. The office of wazir was for sale also, but economic conditions were so poor that few wanted it, and some nominees had to be flogged into accepting the position. Khushqadam even accepted bribes from amirs to allow them to torture and kill their personal enemies. It was normal throughout to seize the property of disgraced amirs and officials, and even those simply deceased on the vague assumption that they must have gained most of it by dishonest means. Many others were exhorted to part with their money on pain of death or torture. None of these dubious methods succeeded in solving the financial problems besetting the Mamluk regime from the mid-fourteenth century onwards, merely doing further damage to the general morale of the empire. While the Mamluks treated Egypt and Syria as their personal milch cow, those regions were being sucked dry by their demands. The Mamluks held back supplies of grain during famine in order to raise prices. The Egyptians and Syrians were continually suffering from such unreasonable demands.

The fellahin suffered some of the Mamluks' worst excesses. As the economic value of the iqtas depreciated, their owners still demanded more, and the peasants suffered further from the demands of the holder and his tax-farmer. The ambitious building works of the time, the mosques, canals and irrigation schemes, were nearly all conducted with unpaid forced labour, where thousands of peasants would be called from the fields for months at a time. And even then the Mamluks still expected the peasants to pay high taxes and duties without the opportunity to earn them and regardless of their own needs. Throughout the Mamluk period, especially in the fifteenth century, fugitive peasants came in thousands to the towns.

If the Mamluks had sought to improve their fiefs, they may have halted their decay. The irrigation schemes, the canals, dams and similar projects with which the early sultans concerned themselves were not continued in later times, and the existing ones were not always maintained. When a dam in the Fayyum collapsed in the early fifteenth century it was never repaired, even though this impoverished the entire region. The Mamluks were mostly concerned with how much money they could make from the iqta and had little desire to improve the lot of the fellahin. Unlike European fief holders they had little contact with their lands. Nor did they expect to hold the fief forever, as on their advancement it would be changed for a more profitable one and so they made little effort to improve it. Governorships were often treated in the same fashion, on a larger scale. There were some Mamluks who tried to repair the dilapidation. At a very late stage Qait Bey ordered that dams and canals be repaired and some governors and holders of iqtas put time and money into improvements. But changes in governorates and fiefs were often frequent, and their successors seldom continued such work. There was little incentive when they had no real stake for any length of time, and the Mamluk feudal system lacked continuity.

So many rebellions and civil wars also had a disturbing effect on economic and social conditions. Only the most significant revolts have been mentioned in this text, but many others took place together with Bedouin risings and raids into Syria by Mongols and Turcomans. The events of Faraj's reign caused much economic damage from which the Mamluk sultanate never recovered. After Tamerlane had turned northern Syria into a wasteland civil war repeated the process on the rest of the Mamluk territories. Rebels levied further sums of money to finance their revolts. Gangs of robbers and extortionists appeared, often allied with factions of amirs. Bedouins revolted several times. Law enforcement ceased to have any effect. Even though in the more stable reigns of Shaikh and Barsbai some attempt was made to undo the damage, a general state of deterioration was an obvious feature. The peasants often scattered into hiding, afraid to till the soil. The civil service, which had remained stable throughout previous disruptions, broke down in this period.

As a military institution, the decline of the Mamluk system itself was often attributed to the supplanting of Turks with Circassians, but this is simplistic. Ayalon pointed out that there is no reference in any of the contemporary sources to the military prowess of Circassians as a race, in stark contrast to all that was said of Turks. There may be comments on individual Circassians – Qait Bey was renowned in his younger days for his skill with the lance – but the Circassians were not as a whole known as a warlike race. However, the early writings praising the Turks' military prowess concern adult Turks enlisted into the service of Muslim rulers; the hardy, pugnacious boys discovered in the slave markets in the thirteenth century were likely candidates for as-Salih, Baibars and Qalawun but they or their buyers must have been selective even with the Turkish captives. Circassians, and for that matter Anatolians, Albanians and slaves of other races, were then trained in arms in the mould set by Kipchak Turks and only freed once they had attained the required standard. There is no race whose young men cannot, with the required training, be turned into effective soldiers. The Circassians may not have had the affinity with the horse, nor the long nomadic tradition of the Turks, but they could still be trained in the same way from an early age. Both as-Salih Ayyub and Qalawun thought enough of Circassians to recruit them, in the latter case in large numbers.

It must be acknowledged that the Circassian sultans and amirs tended to prefer their own race when selecting slaves. They did not lose sight entirely of the need for the best soldiers, but there is evidence that some were not chosen for their potential as troopers as the first criterion. The Mamluk corps was diluted when one slave or another was chosen for his skill as a baker, and when another was a younger brother of a Mamluk amir. The Circassians often brought their relatives from the Caucasus and raised them to senior roles, but this was not a prime cause. The real change took place when the threat of the Mongols subsided in the early fourteenth century. Rather than raise effective armies to defend the sultanate against the invaders, the pressure eased and the mamluk training system fell victim to the complacency of a long external peace.

It was an-Nasir Muhammad who began the dilution of this mamluk system when he 'improved' the tibaq regime. He thought that giving the trainees more affection and making their surroundings more comfortable would endear them to him more, but in the longer term these changes weakened discipline and reduced incentive for advancement. An-Nasir could keep firm control on his soldiers, but in his descendants' reigns the tendency towards laxity and poor discipline continued. He was far less concerned with raising warriors once he first made peace with the Ilkhan and then saw the Mongol state disintegrate in the 1330s. An-Nasir was even believed to have chosen slaves that resembled his friend the Ilkhan Abu Said. In the same spirit, the halaqa was seriously reduced in 1315; nobody expected a major invasion now.

The sultan's household became increasingly the main route towards promotion, whereas in earlier times amirs rose more often from the ranks by proving themselves on campaign. Timurbugha and Qait Bey both became senior amirs entirely through their service as secretaries to Jaqmaq, and many others similarly rose by gaining their sultan's favour as pages in his intimate household rather than showing merit as soldiers. The household proved far from adequate as an officer training school, where a sultan's mamluk would perform duties as a page or groom and be appointed a senior amir without any military training to speak of, with no experience of either warfare or command.

The period spent in the tibaq became shorter, and less rigorous; in Inal's time all restrictions were finally lifted. Many adults were admitted into the Mamluk corps with no training at all and relatives of Circassian sultans and amirs would be made amirs themselves with only a token stay in the tibaq, if not immediately. Military proficiency accordingly declined. Even the hippodromes where Mamluks once trained daily fell into disuse. The regime which had produced able and well-disciplined troopers was practically abandoned, and the Mamluks were mostly hiding their inadequacies behind tradition. Some of the campaigns of the Burji period showed noted military incompetence.

By 1375 the Mamluks had accomplished nearly all they could in the military sphere. They had defended Egypt and Syria from the Mongols, as they did against their Turcoman successors, and destroyed the Christian states on the edges. Tamerlane was an unexpected incursion and Cyprus a long-delayed security operation. Most campaigning after 1304 went on in eastern Anatolia, where the Mamluks found the mountains unsure territory and were unable to use their horses as effectively. Any attempt to expand across the Euphrates would have taken vast military resources, and the sultans mostly contented themselves with maintaining vassal buffer states against eastern enemies. Although a smaller force for campaigning would still be required in this later period, they had not paid the required attention to maintaining an effective army.

The falling standards that the Mamluks now observed came to the notice of their subjects. Barquq's drunkenness in public offended Muslim piety, and when Barsbai and others took to appearing in Cairo in ordinary dress the image of the Mamluks began to look increasingly seedy; even the mask of the illustrious Muslim ruler was slipping from the sultans. For the Mamluks' Egyptian and Syrian subjects, there was little reason to be loyal. Their masters were greedy, cruel and often dangerously violent, but there was little they could do about them. Once in Barsbai's time the citizens of Alexandria rose up and had the governor and his deputy publicly humiliated and afterwards executed, but this was unusual, and any popular revolt would bring harsh reprisals. Nevertheless, the natives gave the Mamluks little willing support when the Ottomans invaded.

The Mamluks came to power by insurrection and murder. This was not too unusual, but during the Burji period such a process repeated itself many times, and all attempts to found a ruling dynasty ended in usurpation. The Bahri sultans were accorded the reverence which the Ayyubids had enjoyed, but those following Barquq were very much first among equals, the support of their amirs essential to maintaining their position. It was too easy to advance a claim to the sultanate by force of arms; so many did it, and it encouraged many a senior amir to consider his own bid. The endorsement of the Caliph granted the essential legitimacy but was no barrier as he could be induced to change the sultan on instruction by the victorious faction. There were many groups of dispossessed Mamluks in the fifteenth century seeking to regain lost wealth and power, and intriguing with whoever might help them succeed. The atmosphere of intrigue, treachery and mutual suspicion, accompanied by bickering between amirs and shifting alliances among the dispossessed, was in no way conducive to healthy government and it contributed towards the Mamluks' cratering credibility.

When Qansuh al-Ghuri became sultan in 1501 he inherited an empire in an advanced state of decay. He may have been more responsible than some in the manner of Qait Bey, his former patron, but he was known for his extravagance. This was by no means unusual for Mamluk sultans, even in harsh economic times, but Qansuh in particular tried to maintain support by paying large sums of money to his troops, who always wanted more. He also financed several new schemes – canals, madrasas and pious endowments – without too much of a sense of the cost, and raised many new mamluks. His princess owned dresses costing over 30,000 dinars, and many other dependants benefited from his largesse.

In Qansuh's reign taxes were high and imposed on many commodities from waterwheels to dhimmis. There was robbery and brigandage, even in Cairo; there were the usual plots and revolts, and rioting by the lesser mamluks. There were scandals and many other unpleasant incidents. However, as Ibn Iyas' journal shows, business went on as usual, and there were even some pleasant interludes in these dark times. Qansuh might not have alleviated his empire's economic and political problems, but it was an achievement to have remained sultan for so long at that stage, while maintaining relative stability.

At the same time new threats made themselves known to the Mamluk lands. It would be simplistic to say that it was the compass and the gun that destroyed the Mamluk sultanate, but both are illustrative of the new forces at play. While life in the Muslim world remained very much the same, developments in Europe were advancing as new attitudes and technologies brought dramatic changes: Qansuh al-Ghuri never knew that he was a contemporary of both Christopher Columbus and Martin Luther.

In the new spirit of discovery, the Europeans were now looking away from the eastern Mediterranean and out into the Atlantic. New naval technology made longer sea journeys possible, and in this seafaring revolution Portugal led the world.

For centuries the trade in spices had mostly run through the Mamluk sultanate, the sea route being the only safe passage from India via Cairo and Alexandria. Europeans had long resented the virtual monopoly the Mamluks shared with the Venetians, and by the fifteenth century the search was on for an alternative route to India that bypassed the Mamluk sultanate and its excessive tolls, but at that time nobody knew of sea routes too far beyond Europe. Columbus originally set out from Spain to find the westward route to the Indies.

The Portuguese searched southwards. Gradually exploring down the coast of Africa they discovered by 1486 that the continent had a southern limit, and that another ocean lay beyond. When Vasco da Gama set out in 1497, reaching India the next year, he began a traffic of Portuguese ships to the Indian Ocean eager for spices. This would spell catastrophe for the Mamluks and for Muslim trading, for as soon as the interlopers had established their bases in India they set about not only breaking the Veneto-Mamluk monopoly but driving Muslim shipping out of the Indian Ocean. Soon their governor, Francesco de Almeida, was ordering the sinking of all ships bound for Egypt.

The Yemenis and the Gujaratis appealed to the Mamluk sultan for help. Qansuh ordered a naval expedition, though his fleet was hardly prepared for such a venture. His mamluks flatly refused to go to sea; they would not contemplate doing battle without their horses. When the fifty ships set sail in 1505 their crews were Egyptians, Syrians and Moroccans, under the command of the amir Husain, a Kurd. Husain's efforts were at first successful. In January 1508 a combined Egyptian and Gujarati fleet destroyed a Portuguese squadron off Chaul. But this success was reversed the following year when Almeida attacked them with a large force near Diu. Poorly equipped by European standards, the Muslim fleet was decimated and they never resisted the Portuguese again.

Also in 1509, Almeida's successor, Afonso de Albuquerque, brought the fight to the mouth of the Red Sea. By 1513 the Europeans had taken Karaman Island there and menaced the Sudanese coast, wilfully destroying pilgrim ships to Jeddah, and leaving Muslim pilgrims to drown. Albuquerque had grandiose plans, such as diverting the course of the Nile, but his brief also involved dominating trade in the Indian Ocean and struggling against Islam, and he was making headway in both. He sought to capture Jeddah and struck out for Suez on this campaign but eventually withdrew without any gains. The damage was nonetheless serious; the Mamluks were the protectors of the Pilgrimage, and this failure was a blow to their standing in the Islamic world. The Eastern trade in spices and other precious commodities was also disrupted.

But there was little they could do to stop the Portuguese sailing into the Red Sea. Qansuh was said to have assembled a large land army at Suez to meet any attempted landing in 1516; he did not know that Albuquerque had fallen from grace and died soon afterwards. The Portuguese eventually abandoned their Red Sea campaign, but they continued to dominate the Indian Ocean.

The Mamluks had gained a foothold in the Yemen coastal region in 1515, their last ever territorial gain. There was little that Qansuh could have done; naval warfare was by no means the forte of the Mamluks. He sent an ultimatum to the Pope that he would destroy the Holy Sepulchre if the Portuguese attacks did not stop, but this had no effect. He ordered the building of a new fleet to strike back, but by the time it was ready to sail Qansuh was dead and the Mamluk sultanate had ceased to exist.

By 1514, trade with Europe was practically non-existent. No Frankish ship had docked in Alexandria for some years. In its last days the Mamluk sultanate came close to bankruptcy, the loss of the spice revenue the latest of many financial disasters. Almost as damaging was the loss of prestige. As the traditional protector of Islamic peoples, the Mamluks had failed and the Portuguese were threatening the Holy Cities. At one point the Sharif of the Hijaz suggested an appeal for aid to the Ottoman sultan. This Qansuh blocked, but it was ominous that he was now looking to Constantinople for protection.

The Ottoman Turks had long given the Mamluks concern, and now their fears were confirmed. Expansion into eastern Anatolia resulting from campaigns against Cilicia had brought the Mamluks into contact with new enemies there and for almost a century various Turcoman princes had fought the Mamluks. Early in Qansuh's reign the Safavids, a Shi'ite dynasty based in Iran, had been the principal enemy, and for a time Shah Ismail conducted his energies eastwards at the expense of the diminishing Timurid state. By 1514, both Mamluks and Safavids were threatened.

The Ottoman sultanate had appeared in western Anatolia, on the borders of the Christian Byzantine empire, but their expansion eastwards brought tension with the Mamluks concerning control of the region. In 1291 the Turcoman tribes of western Anatolia withdrew their homage from the declining Seljuk sultanate of Caesarea. One Turcoman chieftain named Osman, the only one whose territory now bordered Christendom, soon found greater human resources at his disposal than he could normally hope for. When the chaos of the collapsing Seljuk sultanate, and later of the Mongol Ilkhanate, caused many to flee west, Osman offered to all comers the opportunity of gaining lands by new conquest. Renewing the drive into Christian territory, he expanded his petty domain many times over.

Osman was succeeded by a line of aggressive warlords. His son Orhan expanded further by absorbing Muslim neighbours, gaining territory on the western side of the Dardanelles, and as the first of his line to assume the title of sultan. By 1400 all of western Anatolia and most of the Balkans had been absorbed into the domain of the 'Osmanli' or 'Ottoman' sultans. Tamerlane's defeat of Sultan Bayazid at Ankara in 1402 halted Ottoman plans for conquest, and many eastern territories regained independence, but recovery began soon after. In 1453 Sultan Mehmed 'the Conqueror' finally took Constantinople, ending Byzantium's thousand-year empire.

Although there can in theory be one sultan to rule over all Islam, relations between the Mamluk and Ottoman sultans remained quite amicable in this early period. The Ottoman acknowledged the Mamluk as the superior of the two, at least at this stage, but as the Ottoman sultan was engaged in bringing new territory in the Balkans into the sphere of Islam, he could claim pre-eminence and with it the right to lead the Hajj and to drape the Kaaba. Ottoman ambitions in eastern Anatolia began tensions between the two; as early as 1399 the Ottomans had seized the town of Malatia in Mamluk Cilicia and after 1453 Mehmed resumed his push to the east.

In the 1460s Mehmed came into contact with Uzun Hasan of the White Sheep and fought several campaigns in eastern Anatolia. At one point the Ottomans again invaded Mamluk Cilicia by occupying Tarsus and Adana, but a Mamluk army quickly appeared and drove them out. In 1468 the Ottomans overran and annexed the amirate of Qaraman, a Mamluk vassal state, bringing them to a common frontier with the Mamluks. From then on the Ottomans continually accused the Mamluks of harassing pilgrims and caravans and inciting Turcoman tribes against them. But the Mamluks also had Uzun Hasan for an enemy. Early in his reign Qait Bey entered into an alliance with the Ottoman sultan against the White Sheep, but this co-operation ended in 1471 when Uzun Hasan finally ceased to threaten Ottoman territory.

When Mehmed died in 1481 there was a brief civil war between his two sons. Bayazid II emerged victorious and his defeated brother Jem took refuge in Syria. Qait Bey not only received Jem into his protection, refusing to give him up, but gave him military aid in his unsuccessful attempt to overthrow Bayazid a year later.

A few years later Ottoman interference in the Dulqadir amirate, another Mamluk client state, brought the two empires into a war. The amirate, situated on the convergence between the Ottoman, Mamluk and White Sheep empires and dominating the Upper Euphrates, had previously been a source of trouble to the Mamluks when its ruler, Shah Suwar, raided Syria. After Shah Suwar's execution in 1472 his brother Budak had been installed as Qait Bey's puppet. But in 1480 Budak was ousted by another brother, Ala-ad-Dawla, Bayazid's nephew by marriage. Ala-ad-Dawla raided Mamluk territory several times and incited the Ottoman governor of Caesarea to do the same. Qait Bey retaliated, attempting to restore Budak, and Ala-ad-Dawla appealed for help to Bayazid.

In 1488 the Mamluk and Ottoman sultanates fought a war, which lasted until 1491 and consisted of six campaigns that were little more than skirmishes. The Mamluks won the initial encounters, driving the invaders from Cilicia, but they did not follow up their successes and subsequent campaigns proved inconclusive. Ala-ad-Dawla and Budak both changed sides during the war. Finally both sultans made peace, agreeing to observe the situation as it was before: the Mamluks kept the plain of Cilicia, the Ottomans the passes of the Taurus Mountains, and Ala-ad-Dawla remained in Albistan under Mamluk suzerainty.

Relations remained calmer for some time afterwards while Bayazid became more occupied with European affairs, thinking it prudent to follow more conciliatory policies towards Cairo. There was still tension in the border regions, and over Ottoman claims to lead the Pilgrimage, but there were also instances of friendly co-operation, all the way up to the final confrontation. In 1511 the knights of St John captured a flotilla of Mamluk-commissioned ships on the way from Cilicia to Egypt laden with materials for building ships to fight the Portuguese. On hearing of this Bayazid sent vast supplies of timber, guns and other materials to make good the loss, declining to accept any payment. The Mamluk naval expedition against the Portuguese in 1515 had an Ottoman commander.

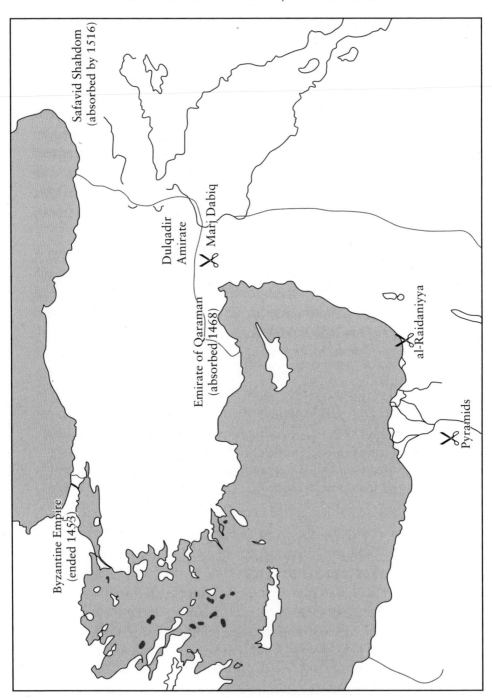

Safavid Shahdom
(absorbed by 1516)

Dulqadir
Amirate

Marj Dabiq

al-Raidaniyya

Emirate of Qaraman
(absorbed 1468)

Pyramids

Byzantine Empire
(ended 1453)

The Advance of the Ottoman empire by 1517.

But during these easy times and after the inconclusive war with the Mamluks, Bayazid sought to improve the Ottoman army. This was composed of several elements, including the *Sipahis*, or feudal cavalry, and the *Azeban*, enlisted irregulars. The elite of this army was the corps of *Janissaries*, trained slave infantry soldiers; this latter was an institution not unlike that of the Mamluks. Bayazid added to these a corps of musketeers, which began the Ottoman love affair with firearms.

From 1501 there was a new threat to the Ottoman empire when Shah Ismail founded the Safavid state in Iraq and Iran and encouraged the spread of the heterodox religious views of Twelver Shi'ism in the region. Many Ottoman subjects, converts to this doctrine, became known as the *kizilbash* for the red hats they wore, and when some of them revolted openly against the Ottomans in support of Shah Ismail from 1514 there was war with the Safavids who supported them. Bayazid was deposed at this time in favour of his son Selim I ('the Grim'), who resolved to destroy the Safavid threat.

The Mamluks, equally uneasy over the spread of kizilbash propaganda, gave Selim their support. In practice Qansuh al-Ghuri did little apart from ordering the governor of Aleppo to resist the kizilbash spreading into Mamluk territory. In 1513 Qansuh made an alliance with Selim, which effectively meant refraining from hostilities while the Ottoman army dealt with the Safavids.

Selim then set out on campaign in eastern Anatolia, first slaughtering thousands of kizilbash and then invading Safavid territory. He crushed Shah Ismail's army at Chaldiran in August 1514, taking Tabriz a month later. The Ottoman army withdrew soon afterwards, having run out of supplies.

Selim had not only temporarily routed the Safavids but had strengthened the Ottoman position in eastern Anatolia. In 1515, on a new campaign, he took Dyarbekir and Mosul in northern Iraq. As Ala-ad-Dawla had hindered the previous campaign, the Ottoman sultan invaded and annexed the Dulqadir amirate, killing its feckless amir during the assault. The Mamluks now had cause to feel unease.

The Ottoman advance having increased that empire's leverage in eastern Anatolia, Qansuh and his amirs in Cairo began to see them as the more serious enemy, well positioned to menace Mamluk Syria. Qansuh then corresponded with Shah Ismail, forming a secret alliance against the Ottomans. He has been criticised for this, as the Mamluk sultanate had so many internal problems and the threat from the Portuguese, but it seemed only a matter of time before open warfare with the Ottomans would begin. Some Mamluk amirs were already in secret correspondence with Selim, and the amir Khair Bey, Mamluk governor of Aleppo, was aiding the Ottomans by diverting caravans into Anatolia while preparing to desert when the opportunity presented itself.

Qansuh al-Ghuri was seventy-five, though he could still ride a horse. He must have known that so much was wrong about his sultanate and its capacity to defend itself. His troops were showing excesses of indiscipline and demanding money before they marched, and Qansuh had difficulty raising anything like enough troops for what would be the most crucial campaign of his reign. Prestige was low, and popular support practically non-existent; Selim could even pose as the saviour of the native peoples from Mamluk tyranny and extortion. It must have been a sad sight when, early in 1516, the elderly sultan collected whatever troops he could and set out for Aleppo at the head of his force, fearful that the Ottomans would pose a serious threat once they had defeated the Safavids. Qansuh had brought the Caliph with him as a morale boost, along with the chief qadis and a pretender to the Ottoman succession, and was glad to see some provincial contingents joining as the army marched. Khair Bey had joined at Aleppo, and Qansuh did not distrust him despite reports of his connivance with Selim. By August he had marched further north, near to Selim's army.

It is likely that Selim had at least considered a campaign against Syria; did he suspect Qansuh of mobilising against him? Perhaps he planned action against the Mamluks sooner or later, given their previous enmity. There were embassies exchanged with sumptuous gifts, but when he heard that the Mamluk army was approaching he decided that it was time to deal with them, if only to protect his flank. When Qansuh's ambassador arrived with a profession of peace Selim treated him with the utmost contempt, ordering his hanging; he then relented, and sent the envoy back, saying, 'Tell your master he will meet me at Marj Dabiq.'

Qansuh did meet him there on 24 August 1516 in full strength. From sunrise to mid-afternoon the two armies fought, in intense heat and with a cloud of dust obscuring their vision. The battle would decide the sultans' dispute, the fate of Syria, and ultimately that of the Mamluk sultanate. The sources tell of the damage that the Ottoman guns did to the Mamluk side. They certainly suffered from Ottoman firepower, which they could not match. But it was in fact more traditional methods of warfare that decided the battle, for the Ottomans had by no means abandoned their cavalry tactics.

The amirs Sudun and Sibay – the former the atabak – led the attack of the right flank with a corps of experienced troopers, and even when military standards were known to have fallen the Mamluks still acquitted themselves remarkably well. Qansuh had brought no cannon to the battle; they would have taken too long to transport, and there were few musketeers. But using the tactics for which they had long been acclaimed, they killed several thousand Turkish soldiers. By mid-morning they had captured seven Ottoman regimental standards, a number of enemy cannon and many musketeers as the Ottoman left wing was beaten back. Ottoman troops began to desert the field and Selim, hearing of the loss of 10,000 troops, was seriously considering either a retreat or surrender to Qansuh.

Ibn Iyas, whose account of the battle is the main source, cites petty jealousies among the Mamluk forces. The qaranis, probably those of Qait Bey, felt that the sultan favoured his own, and some were uneasy over his intentions. A rumour went among them that Qansuh had told his less experienced mamluks to hold their positions rather than attack. If he really had done this, it was probably out of concern that inexperienced troops could be a liability in the potentially decisive charge to come. In any case, the rumour spread to the right flank and many troopers refused to fight on. Some even deserted.

At this point the battle turned against the Mamluks. The Ottomans charged and not only were Sudun and Sibay killed but the Mamluk right flank panicked and broke. Khair Bey, commanding the left flank, chose his moment to give Selim the opening he needed. When he was expected to lead the cavalry charge that would have shattered the Ottoman line, Khair Bey shouted that the battle was lost and took the entire left flank off on a retreat in the direction of Hama. His treason sealed the fate of the defenders. The moment lost, and with the Ottoman army returning to the offensive, Qansuh did all he could to rally the defence but few heeded him; many of his men were already running for Aleppo. Eventually the amir Tanam persuaded the sultan to retreat and take the colours to safety.

As the demoralised Qansuh rode off, he appears to have had a stroke – according to Ibn Iyas he suffered a burst gallbladder – and fell from his horse with blood pouring from his mouth. As the amirs ran to him, the Ottoman force charged and the fighting centred around the fallen sultan. Soon the entire Mamluk army had either fled or been cut down. Qansuh's body was never found.

After Marj Dabiq, the Ottomans virtually had Syria. Khair Bey opened the gates of Aleppo to Selim, the governor of the citadel having fled. Most of the Mamluk provincial governors had fallen in the battle, as had many Syrian amirs. The remains of Qansuh's army gathered at Damascus. They first debated over appointing either Qansuh's son or the senior amir Janbardi al-Ghazali, but as the Ottoman force drew near they all left for Cairo. It would have been a meaningless gesture had they stayed. Selim's army took possession of Syria and then Palestine by October, the provincial governors mostly killed and other Mamluks either fleeing to Cairo or submitting to Selim.

By the end of 1516, with disease in the camp and supplies running low, Selim was wearying of the campaign. He wrote to Cairo offering terms for peace, and there the forty-seventh and final Mamluk sultan, a second Tuman Bey, was obliged to consider the Ottoman demands. Once a mamluk of Qansuh, Tuman had risen to the rank of senior amir and was entrusted with the defence of Cairo when Qansuh marched northwards. Proclaimed sultan on Qansuh's death, Tuman's accession had not been legitimised – the Caliph and three of the four chief qadis were now Selim's prisoners, and most of the sultan's regalia was missing at Marj Dabiq – but someone had to take the position in such circumstances. He showed himself a likely candidate in the short time he was sultan, ruling in a benign fashion. He reversed many of his predecessor's harsh acts and refused to plunder orphanages and other pious foundations, although his policy of pardoning wanted criminals in exchange for enlistment in the defence of Cairo was unpopular.

Selim had offered Tuman Bey the governorship of Cairo under Ottoman suzerainty, with the khutba recited in the name of the Ottoman sultan and coinage struck in Selim's name. Given the circumstances Tuman thought it best to accept, but his amirs insisted that he continue the fight and he was forced to comply. This course of action was hardly viable. Qansuh had left an empty treasury, and for all their belligerence the amirs refused to march on Syria. They might have defended Gaza, but the city was taken before Tuman's force under Janbardi's command could reach it, and they were driven back.

Tuman shrewdly planned to meet the invaders at as-Salihiyya, on the edge of the Sinai Desert, but the amirs instead demanded that he take a position at al-Raidaniyya, just outside of Cairo near the Muqattam Hills. He was in weak position, with his amirs disinclined to follow his commands and even executing the Turkish envoys. Tuman would have understood the gravity of his situation, with Syria lost and the Ottoman army of conquest approaching while the amirs pursued their own ideas of strategy. He was forced to agree to the defence at al-Raidaniyya.

The Ottoman army crossed the Sinai in five days – no mean feat – to reach al-Raidaniyya on 22 January 1517. Tuman had prepared his defence by digging a great trench with a breastwork behind it. On this wall he placed as many cannon as he could find, and raised and deployed a number of musketeers. The Mamluk cavalry would defend and give support to the artillery. This was a departure from centuries of Mamluk tactics, perhaps brought on by unease over the Ottomans' deployment of cannon. The big guns could not be moved or even redirected, and this stationary artillery did not gel with the supporting cavalry methods. An Ottoman party crossing the Muqattam Hills took the defenders at the flank. Tuman himself fought frantically, supposedly battling his way to Selim's tent, but Ottoman numbers prevailed and the Mamluks were driven two miles up the Nile as the Ottomans pushed on to Cairo. Breaking through, they first plundered the city and sought important people for ransom. They hunted down the Mamluks and slaughtered all they could, displaying their heads. The Caliph, still a guest of the Ottomans, endorsed Selim and the Friday prayers were recited in Selim's name.

Tuman, along with some Bedouin allies and whatever troops remained to him, actually succeeded in retaking Cairo for a time, but the Ottomans returned to drive him out and Tuman fled to Giza. Selim offered amnesty, specifically excluding the Mamluks and ordering death for all and those who sheltered them. The Caliph entreated for some, and Janbardi and Qansuh's son were both pardoned, the former given a command to fight the Bedouins.

Tuman Bey returned to the offensive, no doubt in order to reach terms. He did meet with an Ottoman deputation in the Caliph's name and showed willingness to accept the amnesty, but again the other Mamluk amirs destroyed this chance, killing the Turkish representatives and one qadi. Forced to fight on, and aware of Selim's desire for reprisal, he called his troops to assemble at the Pyramids and built a bridge of boats across the Nile. On 30 March the Mamluk and Ottoman armies fought their last battle. After two days of pounding by the Ottoman guns, Tuman escaped to hide in a Bedouin village in the Delta, and there he was betrayed and captured. After the murder of the envoys, Selim, who had already executed fifty-seven captive Mamluks, was determined to visit revenge on Tuman, despite his denial of complicity.

Selim had the last Mamluk sultan hanged outside the Zuwaila Gate like a common criminal on 13 April 1517. Tuman died valiantly, the rope breaking twice before his end came, and with him ended the Mamluk sultanate. It ended as it had begun, by military confrontation with its invader. Over two centuries the prestige of the Islamic dynasty that had ended the Mongol advance and destroyed the Frankish colonisation of Syria had accompanied this regime, and perhaps it was little more than a long-redundant reputation, the Mamluks of Qansuh al-Ghuri failing to live up to the standards set by the Bahris in the thirteenth century. Yet there are many qualifying factors, and the Mamluks might easily have won.

After the days of Baibars, Qalawun and an-Nasir Muhammad, when the state was well run, well defended and politically stable, the Mamluk story had been one of economic reverse and political instability. The Mamluks were not to blame for plague and depopulation, but the predatory nature of the one-generation interlopers and their accepted procedure of accession by usurpation did not encourage stable government. The gradual erosion of the military system that made them formidable warriors produced a less effective military force, and its shortcomings were remarked upon during the fifteenth century. Economic decline meant that fewer military resources could be sustained.

One could see in the later period a decaying state with unproductive institutions and towns in disrepair. It became difficult to raise troops in large numbers, though this was not such a pressing issue after 1315, when apart from the Timurid and Ottoman invasions only a smaller force was needed for campaigning. The Mamluk sultanate might have been defeated on the battlefield, but the institutional rot contributed to that loss, or perhaps even caused it. They could have won at Marj Dabiq – that morning it looked as if they would – but poor attitudes, jealousies and even treacherous intriguing with the enemy turned the battle. Khair Bey was more interested in his own governorship than the defence of Syria, and Tuman Bey found his leadership shackled by insubordinate amirs. It looks to have been a widespread lack of collective responsibility that lost the war.

Poor government had run down the Mamluk sultanate. The destruction of the regime was the only way by which Egypt and Syria could recover.

13

IN ECLIPSE

The Mamluk sultanate had come to a blood-drenched end in 1517, but this was by no means the end of the Mamluk institution. The Mamluks themselves would soon return to a state of power and privilege, and they would remain there for three more centuries. They remained a vital force in the region, at times even coming close to regaining the sovereignty of Egypt.

Selim the Grim remained in Egypt for five months after Tuman Bey's execution. He continued to suppress the remaining pockets of Mamluk resistance, executing more than 800 Mamluks and receiving the submission of all others remaining. During this time he divided the former Mamluk territories into three large provinces, or *beylerbeylerliks*, centred on Aleppo, Damascus and Cairo. There were later created separate provinces of Tarabulus and the Lebanon. Aleppo, the most important for commercial and strategic reasons, now had an Ottoman governor. Damascus ranked next, especially in relation to Selim's new role as guardian of the Pilgrimage, and for its governor he appointed the Mamluk amir Janbardi al-Ghazali.

As an Ottoman province, Egypt was primarily expected to supply tribute to the sultan. Its governor was that other Mamluk renegade, Khair Bey. Selim called him Kha'in Bey ('Prince of Traitors') ever after, for he had betrayed his previous sultan. As governor Khair Bey behaved exactly like a Mamluk sultan: he took up residence in the Citadel, received the four chief qadis on the first day of the month, and presided over public ceremonies, adopting the same protocols as had the Mamluk rulers.

When Selim returned to Constantinople he took the Caliph al-Mutawakkil III with him, but was soon so enraged by the Caliph's drunkenness that he had him imprisoned. Three years later, Selim's successor released al-Mutawakkil and allowed him to return to Cairo with a small pension once he had renounced the Caliphate. Much later, the Ottoman sultans included the title of Caliph among their many epithets.

It was probably on Khair Bey's urging that the Mamluks soon had some of their former powers restored, and came into the Ottoman sultan's service. Selim gave them back their lands, and even had an impetuous wazir beheaded when he suggested that Selim had treated them too leniently. Soon after Selim's departure the Mamluks were allowed to ride on horseback and bear arms, and they were later assimilated into the Ottoman army. In a familiar twist, now that the regiment of Janissaries stationed in Egypt was becoming difficult to control, terrorising the public and deserting in large numbers, the Ottomans commissioned the Mamluks to keep order and pursue fugitives. Selim also thought it prudent to enlist the Mamluks' services rather than leave them to become a focus for discontent.

These new Ottoman provinces remained quiet at first, and this eased the transition. But when Selim the Grim died in 1520 the standard of revolt was once again raised in Damascus, this time by Janbardi al-Ghazali against the new Ottoman sultan. Janbardi wrested the citadel of Damascus from its Ottoman commander and marched on Aleppo. He had the qadis recognize him as 'Sultan of the Two Holy Sanctuaries', a similar title to one held by the Mamluk sultans, which Selim had since assumed. As a sovereign ruler Janbardi raised a militia to defend his capital. But there was no Mamluk resurgence. Khair Bey condemned the rebellion, reaffirmed his allegiance to the Ottoman sultan and did all he could to prevent Mamluks in Egypt from joining with Janbardi. He also sent an army to Gaza, and its troops toppled and slew the governor Janbardi had appointed. By the end of 1520, Janbardi had abandoned the siege of Aleppo and retreated to Damascus. An Ottoman army followed him.

Janbardi was killed in the ensuing battle on 5 February 1521, and the city was devastated. An Ottoman governor arrived soon after to take charge of the province. Khair Bey continued as governor of Egypt, but when he died in October 1522 another Ottoman official, Mustafa Pasha, filled his place. Two Mamluk amirs, Inal and Janim as-Sayfi, both khashifs, led a revolt against Mustafa soon after his arrival. After offering terms to the rebels, and after Inal beheaded his envoy, Mustafa crushed the revolt, killing Janim in battle and forcing Inal to flee.

Ottoman rule firmly established, it was again overthrown in August 1523 by Mustafa's successor, Ahmad Pasha, called al-Kha'in ('the Traitor'). A Circassian in Ottoman service, Ahmad gained the support of the Mamluks, partially through their racial affinity, but then attempted to resurrect the Mamluk sultanate. He had a member of the Abbasid family proclaimed Caliph in order to have his own reign legitimised. He also had his name struck on coins and recited in the *khutba*. Ahmad's reign lasted six months. The peasants refused to pay taxes and the Janissaries stayed loyal to Constantinople, holding the Citadel until overcome by force. In March 1524 a counter-coup supported by both Ottoman and Mamluk elements unseated Ahmad, his own support having faded, and put him to death. His successor Ibrahim Pasha restored the sultan's authority and reorganised many institutions to suit Ottoman rule of Egypt.

The new Ottoman sultan, Suleiman I 'the Magnificent' (although the Turks themselves call him 'the Lawgiver'), became the most prestigious of all, and in his reign the Ottoman sultanate reached its zenith while he expanded his domains into Iraq, the Ukraine and central Europe. In this reign little is recorded of Egypt and the province seems to have been comparatively quiet in this time. One of Qansuh al-Ghuri's relatives, Ozdemir, played a part in Ottoman expansion. Ozdemir was governor of the part of the Yemen that the Mamluks had captured in 1515, now incorporated into the Ottoman state with the rest of the Mamluk possessions. In the 1550s Ozdemir led expeditions in Suleiman's name onto the Nubian and Abyssinian coastlines. He gained some territory on the coast and its hinterland, but by his continual absences Ozdemir lost most of his Yemeni territory, and his sons had to regain it for the sultan.

When Suleiman died in 1566 Ottoman fortunes reversed dramatically. A palace coup placed Selim II ('the Sot') on the throne, ousting a more capable brother. As the epithet suggests, Selim was a drunken degenerate, nor was he the last unsuitable sultan, for few of his descendants showed much acumen. Now the tide turned everywhere against the Ottoman sultanate. The Ottoman defeat at the naval Battle of Lepanto in 1571 was followed by the sultan's enemies regaining ground. Inflation, inadequate administration causing inefficiency and corruption, insubordinate governors, brigandage and many other ills also caused further reverses. The Ottoman sultanate only came to an end after the First World War, but after 1566 it had gone the way of the Mamluk sultanate into a long and progressive decay.

The effects of Ottoman decline soon became obvious in Egypt. Inflation ate into the fixed salaries of the Ottoman officials and soldiers stationed there while corruption, maladministration and indiscipline were common from that time on. The Janissaries, once the sultans' crack troops, had been recruited from Christian slaves and were forbidden to marry, but such a regime had ceased and the Janissaries had married native Egyptians and had sons admitted into the corps. The Janissaries may have continued as a powerful force but were mainly composed of second- and third-generation Egyptians with little reason for loyalty to the sultan alone. In 1586 the Janissaries mutinied for higher pay, for the first of several times. The Sipahis as free men would also be difficult to control, and they too revolted. The Ottoman governors could soon rely only on their personal bodyguards and the corps of pages, both small in number. In such a weak position the governors had little real authority, and could only govern by playing factions off against each other.

It was at this time that the Mamluks reappeared on the stage in a new form: as *beys*. Although the beys included some Ottoman courtiers and military officers, and even a few Bedouin chiefs, they were essentially a continuation of the body of Mamluk amirs. Most were Circassians and many Bosnians were included, mostly former slaves recruited under the mamluk system. The origins of the beylicate in Egypt are obscure; it is not mentioned in the administrative reforms of Ibrahim Pasha but must have been formed soon after. The title of bey, similar to that of amir, was a rank rather than an office and entitled its holder to an annual salary rather than a fief. The beys soon became governors of sub-provinces and khashifs, in a format reminiscent of Mamluk governance. The Porte, the government at Constantinople, continued to appoint the key officials: the viceroy, the *defterdar* (chief financial administrator) and the chief qadi, always a Hanafite once the four-tier system was abolished. The growing presence of the Mamluks can be seen in many of the other offices from the late sixteenth century onwards. There was an addition to the Sipahis of a third corps, known as the *Cherikase* ('the Circassians'), recruited from the Mamluks. In 1604 the Sipahis, the Cherikase included, spearheaded a revolt in which the Ottoman governor was slain. They had much support as poor economic conditions, famine and drought had created disaffection.

The new viceroy, Muhammad Pasha, known as *Kul Kiran* ('breaker of the Mamluks') conducted severe reprisals for the revolt, including the execution of the ringleaders and banishment of several beys for complicity. He ordered the suspension of the *tulba*, an unofficial tax levied by the Sipahis and the Mamluks, which caused a new revolt in 1609. Although most of the beylicate remained loyal, many Mamluks joined the rebellion. There was even an attempt at restoring the Mamluk sultanate before Muhammad's troops again ended the revolt. Muhammad Pasha was able to maintain control over the beylicate, but after his departure four years later the beys reasserted themselves. Soon they acquired rights over various offices, mostly military, and later they established them. The Mamluk military class regained some of the control it had previously had by holding such offices and securing recognised rights to them.

Two offices were significant inclusions: that of *Amir-al-Khazna*, who took responsibility for delivering the annual tribute to Constantinople, and that of *Amir-al-Hajj*, which led and protected the Pilgrimage. The latter office, which echoed a similar placing of the Mamluk period, was held by the most powerful bey. A single bey governed the whole of Upper Egypt as an enlarged sub-province with the title 'Governor of the South'; Upper Egypt was a stronghold for the Mamluks for the next two centuries. The beys also acquired the office of defterdar. From this time they could exert some influence on the Ottoman governorate. When the viceregal office was vacant they could appoint a *qa'im maqam*, or acting governor pending a replacement Pasha's arrival. After 1604 the qa'im maqam was always a bey. The beys used this device to depose the governor in 1631. Musa Pasha had had his enemy Qaytas Bey assassinated, and the beylicate rose and removed him from the governorship, appointing a qa'im maqam. The Porte accepted this action, but sent a replacement. This act made it possible for the beys to control the Pashas.

At this time two factions dominated the beylicate; the Faqariyya and the Qasimiyya. The Faqariyya leader Ridwan Bey al-Faqari was the most powerful man in Egypt. He claimed descent from Barsbai, Barquq and even the Quraishi tribe, tantamount to claiming legitimacy as a Mamluk sultan. But he never challenged the rule of the Ottoman sultan, contenting himself with the title of Amir-al-Hajj and rule over Egypt in all but name. After Ridwan's death in 1656 the Faqariyya lost control. Imprudent actions by its new leadership brought a dispute with the Pasha, and when the Faqariyya rose in arms the Ottoman crushed them with Qasimiyya support. The Faqariyya leaders were executed, and the faction's influence was destroyed. The Qasimiyya, led by Ahmad Bey the Bosniak, took its place, despite the Faqariyya holding the governorship of Upper Egypt. But the Qasimiyya did not maintain supremacy. Ahmad had quickly become so powerful as to rouse the governor's unease, and he had the bey murdered in 1662. The beys were so divided that they were unable to rise in reprisal. The Qasimiyya soon lost any influence it had. The entire beylicate was beaten back in its aspirations as a result, losing influence for a time.

A Janissary officer, Kujuk Muhammad, now took the lead, but other Janissaries dissented, and one had a musketeer assassinate Kujuk in 1694. The Janissaries continued as a rebellious element until the Great Insurrection of 1711. In this the beys took sides, the Faqariyya supporting the Janissaries and the Qasimiyya the Azeban. These alliances continued for some time throughout the century. The revolt ended with the Qasimiyya in power again, but soon the victorious Qasimiyya were divided. In 1724 two Qasimiyya households fought each other, and the Faqariyya used this to oust their rivals. Soon the Faqariyya split into two, fighting their own civil war. From this fragmentation other factions appeared, fought each other, gained supremacy and fell throughout the eighteenth century, often with the support of the other military groupings.

The Mamluks were not the only powerful grouping in Ottoman Egypt, but they were gradually regaining ground. In accordance with Ottoman law, they now took Arabic names. They lived in large, fortified houses in Cairo, those of the wealthy beys around the lake of Uzbekiah where they were surrounded by splendour: sumptuous furnishings, Arab horses, pistols with gold inlay and ornamental weapons. They wore brightly coloured clothing made of the most expensive materials, and expected a new outfit every Ramadan. Their wives, similarly clothed in the richest of raiments, also boasted impressive arrays of jewellery.

The Mamluk was described then as the world's most expensive soldier. Indeed, the fellahin still paid for their extravagances as the Mamluks continued to draw more and more from the peasants, often demanding they sell their livestock if necessary. Eighteenth-century European travellers often gave accounts of the wretched condition of most native Egyptians and the greedy behaviour of their Mamluk masters. Plague, maladministration, corruption and the Mamluks all wore down the province's social and economic well-being, while increasingly rebellious Bedouins encroached upon settled lands. The population was still declining.

The Mamluks did little to earn their huge incomes; in present-day Italy an extremely lazy person is described as a *Mammalucco*. Mamluks did fight in some of the Ottoman sultan's wars, usually under the command of Mamluk beys, but their chief concern was still the struggle for the *ra'isa*, political ascendancy in Egypt. From the early eighteenth century the most powerful bey held the title of *Shaikh-al-Balad*, or Lord of the Land. The beys still raised private armies from the slave markets as they had always done. The Ottoman governors were mostly ineffective; only the Janissaries could check the Mamluks' bid to regain power, and not always even then.

Syria was no longer within the Mamluks' ambitions, apart from one brief period late in the century. In Baghdad at this time the Ottoman governor created a mamluk system, raising into military and administrative positions ex-slaves who eventually succeeded him. There was no link with the Mamluks of Egypt, apart from the similarity of the recruiting systems. This practice survived in Baghdad until comparatively recent times.

In 1790 the new Shaikh-al-Balad was a colourful character named Ali Bey, popularly known as *Bulut kapan* ('Cloud Catcher') for his grandiose ambitions. Once he had installed some of his 6,000 mamluks in positions of authority he banished some of his former supporters, including his former patron Abd-ar-Rahman Kahiya, head of the Qazdughiyya faction, and Salih Bey, the last significant Qasimiyya bey. In 1769 he brought the Egyptian customs service under Mamluk control and it did not take long for the Mamluks to disrupt it completely with their demands for money. By 1769 Ali had deposed the Pasha, making himself qa'im maqam, clearly as a prelude to establishing himself as an independent ruler. He spoke of the time when Egypt was ruled by Mamluks like himself. He also assumed the title of *Aziz Misr* ('Mighty One of Egypt'), a title the Ottomans had once associated with the Mamluk sultans.

But Ali was slow to break with Constantinople. Perhaps for all his bluster, he knew it could be a mistake to do so prematurely. In 1770 he sent an army to the Hijaz, ostensibly on the Ottoman sultan's behalf, to intervene in a dynastic dispute, but he afterwards installed a Mamluk as governor who reported to him rather than the sultan. Ali was also intriguing with the Tsar of Russia, then at war with the sultan, seeking independence through such means. Next Ali invaded Syria. The Russian navy had recently sunk the Ottoman fleet in a war, and this made it far easier. In the summer of 1771 Ali captured Damascus. He was well on the way to recreating the Mamluk sultanate.

But dissent between the beys and vested interests denied Ali the support he needed for such a scheme. As he was close to regaining Syria, a mamluk of his own called Muhammad Bey, also known as Abu-l-Dhahab, began a rebellion against him by evacuating Damascus without apparent reason. This revolt continued until May 1773, when Ali and his former protege fought it out in the Delta. Ali was captured and died a week later, probably poisoned.

Abu-l-Dhahab, now in control in Egypt, professed loyalty to the sultan, and was invested governor as a reward, or possibly as an expedient. In 1775 he invaded Palestine, professing to suppress a revolt, and died on the campaign. Whether Abu-l-Dhahab wished to complete Ali's plan for a resurrected independent

Mamluk sultanate is uncertain, but this was the last time the Mamluks could have been independent rulers over both Egypt and Syria again, and their lack of unity and self-interest put an end to it. It does show that the Mamluk state was still looked upon as a desirable bygone era long afterwards, while the Ottoman empire had already lost its allure.

The deaths of Ali Bey and Abu-l-Dhahab left a vacuum in which Qazdughli factions fought for nearly ten years. Two of Abu-l-Dhahab's mamluks, Ibrahim Bey and Murad Bey, finally emerged after ousting Ismail Bey, another Qazdughli, in the early 1780s. They then quarrelled over the ra'isa, but agreed to share it: Ibrahim would be Shaikh-al-Balad while Murad took the office of Amir-al-Hajj. As Ibrahim grew older he tended to leave the active role to Murad. The two exercised strong control over the Pasha, dismissing him when he invoked their displeasure. A ceremony emerged for the occasion. Echoing the days of the Abbasid puppet Caliphs in the Mamluk period, a herald in a black robe would arrive at the Citadel on a donkey, present himself to the Ottoman viceroy, pronounce the ritual address *Inzil ya Pasha* ('Descend, O Pasha'), and hand him a letter of dismissal from Ibrahim and Murad.

The Porte did not concern itself much with who ruled Egypt, but when the two beys decided to end the tribute to Constantinople it was a different matter. In July 1786 an Ottoman army landed at Rosetta and marched on Cairo. Ismail Bey was restored. Ibrahim and Murad still held Upper Egypt, despite attempts to dislodge them. Nor could the Ottoman commander come to terms with them. A new war the sultan was fighting with Russia caused the withdrawal of his troops from Egypt, leaving Ismail with a small force. Ibrahim and Murad had regained full control in Cairo by 1790, after Ismail's death.

European accounts of Egypt in the closing years of the eighteenth century show the country sinking even further into economic chaos, mostly through misgovernment. It became increasingly difficult to carry on commerce, making Cairo the most precarious trading centre in the eastern Mediterranean, while the Mamluks kept increasing duties and prices as law and order deteriorated. In 1795 the British Consul withdrew from Egypt, concluding that normal commercial dealings were impossible under such conditions. Shortly before this the French philosopher Volney had visited Egypt, his own account telling of the wretched condition of the Egyptians and of their predatory Mamluk overlords. Volney suggested that only through a European intervention could this deplorable situation be improved.

Had no intervention come, the Mamluks would probably have continued in the same way. They had in part regained the supremacy the Ottomans had taken from them, but not decisively so. Whether they could have restored the Mamluk sultanate is a matter for debate; the Mamluk corps showed little unity and the Ottomans were not so weakened that Egypt could break away easily. There was little will for independence after Ali Bey. Meanwhile they ruled over the Egyptians as predators, demanding more all the time and running down each source of wealth as they did. It is ironic that as a French intervention in the Delta had set in motion the rise of the Mamluks, another would eventually bring about their end. They were not crusaders that disembarked near Alexandria on 1 July 1798, but soldiers of the French Republic, under the able young commander Napoleon Bonaparte.

At twenty-eight Bonaparte was still seeking his destiny. Not yet the Napoleon of popular acclaim, but now commander of the Mediterranean theatre of the Revolutionary War, he was already planning to overthrow the Directory in Paris. Citizen General Bonaparte invaded Egypt on his own orders. His reasons were many: to menace British interests in India, to begin conquering all Asia, to win prestige for himself as a prelude to his coup in Paris, and to satisfy a personal interest in Egypt. Besides his 35,000 troops he brought 167 scholars, who would research every aspect of the land past and present. The French first took Alexandria, and as they advanced up the Rosetta branch of the Delta, Ibrahim and Murad at first saw no cause for alarm; they considered an army of foot soldiers inferior. Murad set out with a small force, confident of an easy victory.

Bonaparte already knew plenty about the Mamluks. He had studied his friend Volney's account prior to the expedition, particularly where the philosopher had described Mamluk military prowess as 'mere brigandage'. In the event the Mamluks met a modern European army for the first time, while their own military methods remained unchanged since the thirteenth century. They may have added some firearms to their arsenal, but the weapons the French captured were mostly ornamental spears, bows, axes and swords.

When on 14 July Murad met the French near Shubra Kit, he charged with confidence. The French soldiers then formed into squares and their gunfire buffeted the Muslims between them. There were many casualties. Murad ordered a second attack to break their formation, and lost more. He then ordered a withdrawal, deciding to hit the French with the main body of his army.

Eighty miles south, at Imbaba near the Giza Pyramids, Murad and Ibrahim together planned a more concerted defence. They raised all the troops they could – Janissaries, fellahin and over 12,000 Mamluk troops – and outnumbered the French three to one. On 21 July they did show a more concerted effort than they had for a long time, but their strategy for defence was a pathetic imitation of that Tuman Bey had used in 1517. Why they resorted to this is unknown, but the fight at Shubra Kit might have told them that light cavalry did not do so well against well-coordinated infantry armed with firepower. Behind a ditch they had placed a breastwork, on which forty cannon were mounted, and the Mamluk cavalry were deployed to support this cannon defence. They do not seem to have learned from al-Raidaniyya, the last time the Mamluks had fought a pitched battle to defend Egypt three centuries before. Again the guns were not easy to move or even turn, and once Bonaparte had lured the Mamluk cavalry out of their range their entire strategy was working against them.

Commencing what is known in Napoleonic legend as the Battle of the Pyramids, Murad led the charge. The French, again in squares, held their fire until the enemy had almost reached them. Then the Muslim formation was shattered, the gunfire again herding them from square to square. Murad was forced to withdraw to behind the Great Pyramid, pursued by General Desaix's cavalry, who quickly outflanked the breastwork once his troops arrived. Within an hour it was all decided. The French were storming the line of defence, and the enemy troops either fleeing or falling. Many tried to swim the Nile, but some were shot doing so. Ibrahim, waiting on the far bank with the reserves, saw he could do nothing and retreated eastwards while Murad took the remains of his army to Upper Egypt. An army of medieval Islam had encountered one of European colonialism, and the result was predictable. The French marched unopposed into Cairo.

Bonaparte, styling himself *Sultan Kabir* ('Great Sultan'), immediately set about creating a government designed as a hybrid of Islamic and French Republican influences. He issued propaganda with the use of the printing press he established – the first seen in the Islamic world – which spoke of his love for the Egyptian people. He had come, he said, to set them free from the Circassian and Georgian slaves who had long oppressed them. He sought the support of the ulema, telling the sheikhs at al-Azhar that the French soldiers were true Muslims and would gladly convert if the tenets concerning alcohol and circumcision were dispensed with. Dressed as a Grand Sheikh, Bonaparte participated in religious festivals and led the Muslims in prayer. The French savants soon embarked on their monumental survey of the land.

Within a week of his victory at Imbaba, Bonaparte's fortunes reversed dramatically. Horatio Nelson, whose British fleet had been looking for Bonaparte all over the Mediterranean, finally came upon the French fleet at Aboukir Bay and destroyed it, leaving the French army stranded in a hostile country with no supply line from France. At this time too the Porte was showing its concern over his invasion of Ottoman territory. Bonaparte's campaign to win over the Egyptians failed completely. The ulema remained unconvinced and many Muslims were scandalized by the drunken and licentious behaviour of his soldiers. The Revolutionary ideals of Liberté, Égalité and Fraternité were completely alien to the Muslim mind at this time. The command to the Egyptians to wear the tricolor cockade in their turbans was not well received. Much worse was the effect of the new Grand Sultan's taxes and his methods of raising revenue.

Bonaparte confiscated the property of the Mamluks to raise funds. Either in exile in Upper Egypt or reduced to beggary, they lived on the charity of the Egyptians. They had been harsh masters, but they were still Muslims, and their wives' generosity was not forgotten. The Mamluks still held Upper Egypt, which Murad used as a base for raids. Bonaparte offered to recognise them as rulers of the Upper Nile in return for peace, but they refused to listen. In October the French suppressed a popular uprising with noted savagery. His troops even defiled al-Azhar when they executed two sheikhs there, marking the end of any attempts to gain support from the Egyptians. Soon afterwards the sultan declared war on the French.

Bonaparte remained ambitious. Entertaining a grand design of conquering the Ottoman empire, he took an expeditionary force into Syria in February 1799. Sir Sidney Smith had arrived there before him aboard the HMS *Tiger*, and at Acre the French force was halted by one Ahmad Pasha, known as *al-Jazzar* ('the Butcher'), a former mamluk of Ali Bey, who was in fact a butcher by trade and now Ottoman governor of Sidon. Al-Jazzar, with support from the British, held Acre against the French for two months until, finally depleted by disease and inconsequential fighting, the would-be invaders withdrew to Egypt. Their general lamented that he had missed his destiny in 'that miserable hole'.

A month later the sultan's troops, including an Albanian contingent, landed at Aboukir Bay, again with Sir Sidney's support, but Bonaparte repulsed this invasion, capturing the Turkish commander. After the battle the French general learned, from outdated newspapers Sir Sidney had sent to him, that the political situation in Paris was becoming serious. The time was now opportune, he concluded, to wrest control from the Directory, even if it meant abandoning his army in Egypt.

On 22 August 1799, Napoleon slipped away to sail for France with some of his close companions. He took with him a Mamluk named Rustam who acted as his bodyguard for ten years. On reaching Paris he soon mounted his coup, establishing a dictatorship. He had left a letter informing his colleague General Kléber that he was now in command, and although displeased by this Kléber carried on. He may have taken heart on hearing that Napoleon was in control of the government in Paris a few months later, but no supplies or reinforcements arrived. It was difficult enough to ensure the army's survival while there were still Ottoman troops in Egypt and a likely new invasion.

In June 1800, Kléber was assassinated. General Menou, a French convert to Islam, took his place but did little better. He was soon confronted by a joint invasion of Turks at Rosetta and a British expeditionary force under Sir Ralph Abercromby at Aboukir Bay, and still nothing came from France. The two European armies fought sporadically for fifteen months, with little result either way. Napoleon then agreed to the Peace of Amiens with Britain in 1802, which involved a joint evacuation from Egypt. Before they left, the British tried to create a state of affairs which would prevent the French returning.

The Mamluks had since reappeared in the picture. Ibrahim Bey still lived, but was no longer Shaikh-al-Balad. Murad Bey had died of plague in 1801, and two of his mamluks, Uthman Bey al-Bardisi and Muhammad Bey al-Alfi, disputed the ra'isa between them in typical fashion. Other Mamluks petitioned for the return of their property. The British favoured the restoration of the beylicate. They considered the Mamluks to be courageous, loyal and possessing other fine qualities, although it is not known how they arrived at this assessment; they had obviously not had too much contact with them. They did decide that neither the Mamluks nor the Turks on their own would be strong enough to effectively resist the French, however. During the brief period before the evacuation General Hutchinson laboured for reconciliation between the Mamluks and the Ottomans, but the Turks repudiated a previous agreement to restore the Mamluks' property and called for their expulsion from Egypt. When the British finally withdrew in 1803, in accordance with the Treaty of Amiens, no settlement had been reached.

Al-Alfi had been known to intrigue with the French, but the British now favoured him as a possible ruler of Egypt. They left weapons and ammunition with the Mamluks, and a British agent in Cairo to support Mamluk interests. They even took al-Alfi with them to plead his cause in London. But the Mamluks' defeat of 1798 had been more serious a blow than they realised, and the departure of the Europeans left many elements to fight with when seeking to regain ground: the Ottomans, the Janissaries and the Albanians in particular. The Mamluks were only one group now.

The Ottoman conquest of 1517 had not destroyed the Mamluks. They had remained as a military feudal class for three centuries. At times they came close to regaining control and sovereignty together, but they were either unwilling or unable to find decisive leadership and break with Constantinople. Meanwhile, they used every method at hand to drain more and more money from the native population. They might have continued to do so had the French not invaded.

The European invasions had left the region wide open to anyone who could restore order by force. In the struggle for supremacy after the European armies departed, the Mamluks would not succeed.

14

FINAL DAYS

Given the pattern of events from 1517, it was expected that the departure of the European armies would signal the return of the Mamluks to the wealth and political power they had always known. This time was different, and a new player was the Mamluks' undoing.

The Mamluks still had a hold through their fiefs on the revenues of the land, of which they often withheld payment from the central government. They could also control the grain supply, even refusing distribution should they so desire. Between them the Mamluks still held all Upper Egypt to the exclusion of any other authority. In 1802 the Porte had forbidden the importing of boys to Egypt, but it is certain from subsequent events that the mamluk system continued for some time longer. There were still about 1,200 Mamluks left in 1803.

The British were keen on a Mamluk restoration, and when Muhammad Bey al-Alfi returned to Egypt after the evacuation the British favoured him as their candidate. There was now a limited company floated in London to advance his interests and al-Alfi was planning to create an independent Egypt with himself as sultan. Other beys also thought themselves likely contenders, although only Uthman Bey al-Bardisi, al-Alfi's former khushdashin, proved a serious challenger.

But it was no longer only the Mamluks who fought for the ra'isa. The Ottoman sultan Selim III, on a programme of reforming his empire, had installed Khusrev Pasha in the Cairo Citadel with a directive to purge the province of the Mamluks. The Janissaries were another powerful body to condend with, while of the Ottoman army in Egypt the 6,000 Albanian troops that had landed with the British formed the majority. Their commander, Tahir Pasha, was preparing his own bid for control of Egypt, and his army was large enough to advance such a claim. The French preferred the Albanians to control Egypt but could do little to help them.

The eventual victor, and destroyer of the Mamluks, was Muhammad Ali, a young Macedonian who came to Egypt in 1801 as a junior officer in the Albanian contingent. Since then he had risen to become Tahir's second-in-command and awaited his own opportunity. In 1804 Tahir made his move. Khusrev Pasha proved both a poor administrator and a harsh one, and made the mistake of not paying his troops for five months. The Albanians rose, drove Khusrev out of Cairo and hailed Tahir as qa'im maqam. The Porte confirmed Tahir as the new Pasha. Three weeks later he was assassinated by two Janissaries.

When two unpopular Ottoman viceroys succeeded Tahir, Muhammad Ali, now in command of the Albanians, allied with al-Bardisi. He also built a following among the Egyptians, in particular the shaikhs of al-Azhar and the merchants. The ulema had emerged as a powerful force from the first invasion, and the merchants had traditionally allied with the Mamluks. Otherwise Muhammad Ali became a popular hero, taking the Egyptians' side against their many oppressors. He forbade rioting and looting, thus becoming their protector and restorer of order. He later quarrelled with al-Bardisi over the Mamluks' unofficial taxes.

The Albanians eventually drove al-Bardisi and his followers away, and the Mamluks were thus expelled from Cairo.

Muhammad Ali was proclaimed governor by the Cairenes, and drove out the latest Pasha, Khurshid. By 1805 Ali was securely in command, after which Constantinople formally endorsed him as viceroy and quickly came to rely on him to combat the fundamentalist Wahhabi insurgents in the Hijaz. Muhammad Ali Pasha ruled over Egypt until 1848, the year before his death. At one time, somewhat in Mamluk tradition, he extended his authority over all Syria, and it was his intention then to conquer the entire Ottoman empire. In 1841 the European powers forced him to give up all but Egypt, but he succeeded in turning this province into a hereditary pashalik, virtually independent from Constantinople. He began Egypt's transition into the modern age, setting up home industries, railways, state education, a navy and a modern-style army. His descendants ruled Egypt until the July Revolution of 1952.

In 1805, however, it was not expected that the new Pasha would last long. His writ did not run far south of Cairo and at times he could not keep order in the Delta. The Mamluks, with their Bedouin allies and the mercenaries they now employed, held Upper Egypt in defiance of Muhammad Ali and at times raided Lower Egypt.

But no alternative body in government could be tolerated in such a modernised state. Still leading this resistance were al-Alfi and al-Bardisi. Al-Alfi, the Pasha's most serious rival, was expected to eventually supplant him as the most able. In addition to the beys other disruptive influences made Egypt almost ungovernable, including the Janissaries, the Bedouins and the *Delhis*, irregulars and religious fanatics imported from Syria by the last governor to serve his own purposes, among several marauders and brigands. The Mamluks were still the most serious threat to Muhammad Ali. He did not need to break the Janissaries until 1826, and the others were dealt with more easily. The Pasha's eldest son, Ibrahim, led several expeditions into Upper Egypt but did not succeed in dislodging the Mamluks. Confiscations of Mamluk property and offices in Lower Egypt went on, attempting to wear down the hold of the Mamluks on the country and on its revenues.

Late in 1806, al-Bardisi suddenly died, allegedly poisoned by al-Alfi. In January 1807 al-Alfi followed him, probably dying of cholera. This pleased Muhammad Ali, and he remarked that the rest of the beys did not matter. This was far from true, but after al-Alfi the Mamluks produced no leaders who could effectively challenge the Pasha, and his death ended the last chance of a Mamluk restoration.

Shortly after al-Alfi's death, Muhammad Ali was forced to soften his aggressive policy towards the Mamluks. The Albanian troops, his own means of effective control, were becoming mutinous and unreliable. There was also a new invasion from Europe and he appeared to attempt reconciliation. As the Napoleonic Wars continued in Europe, yet another permutation in its shifting alignments put Britain at war with the Turks. The British found it expedient to invade Egypt again in March 1807, occupying Alexandria as a base for naval operations. General Mackenzie-Fraser progressed towards Rosetta with only a small force, and they expected the Mamluks to rally to their banner. There had been agreements with Alfi Bey that he would gain control in Cairo on such an invasion, but the bey's death had altered this strategy and the invaders were dismayed to see many Mamluks riding with the Pasha's forces. The conciliatory policy and their demonstrating that they hated Europeans more than they did Muhammad Ali lost them this chance. The invasion soon became a sordid defeat for the British; after retreat at al-Hammad, the British forces were besieged at Alexandria and withdrew from Egypt in September.

Despite the clash with the French in Egypt, many Mamluks took service in the French empire. It appears that Napoleon thought highly of his Muslim opponents and considered incorporating them into his own military forces. By his own account he bought 2,000 mamluks from merchants in Cairo. It is unlikely that he took these with him when he absconded to France – he left his regular army behind – but he maintained his interest. This force probably aided General Kléber against the Turks and British. In 1801 he ordered the raising of a small force of Mamluk irregulars that were invited to Marseilles for the purpose, and although the planned numbers were reduced, this unit was attached to the Chasseurs-à-Cheval of the Imperial Guard. Not all of these were mamluks recruited in Egypt, but they used the same military methods. The 'Mamelouks' became a prominent feature of the Napoleonic campaigns, in their red baggy trousers and turbans, armed with a brace of pistols, a scimitar and a dagger. They were commended for their contribution to the victory at Austerlitz in 1805 and were famed for their activities in Spain in 1808, particularly as Goya's picture on Dos de Mayo commemorates.

At the end of the Napoleonic era, the Mamelouk regiment was disbanded and felt the backlash against Bonapartist institutions when eighteen Mamluks were massacred in reprisal while waiting in Marseilles to return to Egypt. Not even Rustam would follow the Emperor to St Helena, instead living out his retirement in France. After the 1830 revolution, the remaining Mamluks served in the French Foreign Legion.

For a few years after the British invasion the Mamluks lived at peace with Muhammad Ali. Many of them now sided with the Pasha, including Shahin Bey, the leading Mamluk since the death of al-Alfi. There were still about 800 Mamluks, many of whom still owned enslaved trainees despite the Porte's prohibition. Nevertheless, the detente would not last forever. He wanted to appropriate the revenues they controlled and mostly withheld. Rather than resuming his policy of suppression by force, which had produced little success before, Muhammad Ali resorted to an act of supreme treachery.

Early in 1811, he invited all the Mamluks to a banquet in the citadel of Cairo. The Pasha's favourite son, Tusun, was to command an expeditionary force against the Wahhabis in Arabia, and the feast was held on the occasion of his investment with a robe of honour. Old Ibrahim Bey, the former Shaikh-al-Balad, declined the invitation and tried to dissuade his fellows from attending as he sensed a trap, but most were so pleased at the prospect of returning to Cairo that they did not heed him.

Accounts vary on the exact details of the events of Friday 1 March 1811. It was said that almost 500 Mamluks attended: Shahin Bey, twenty-five other beys, sixty khashifs and the rest lesser Mamluks. They were reassuringly well received by Muhammad Ali in the audience chamber of the Citadel with lavish hospitality. Before the banquet, there was to be a procession through the streets of Cairo and the Mamluks were granted the place of honour in the procession, with an escort before and after. As the procession rode out, it was to emerge from the Bab al-Azab, a gate at the lower level of the Citadel.

On the way to this gate the Mamluks followed the others down a narrow passage cut into the rock of the Citadel. At an arranged point the Pasha's escort halted, and gates were closed on the Mamluks, trapping them in the passage. Albanian sharpshooters posted on the walls above then opened fire, as did other troops in the passage. Within fifteen minutes all Mamluks present had been killed, apart from the few who escaped over the walls into the harem, and these were pursued and cut down by the guards.

There is a story that is mostly dismissed by historians as apocryphal but more recently considered as true. Hasan Bey, al-Alfi's younger brother, is said to have escaped by riding his horse up a ramp and jumping it over the wall. He fell 50 feet, landing on the tent of an Albanian amir. His horse was killed by the impact, but Hasan ran on to raise the alarm. It was too late. The Pasha's troops quickly spread into the city, slaughtering the remaining Mamluks and their followers. A few days later Ibrahim Pasha led an army towards Upper Egypt, and over the following years he would destroy the remaining strongholds of Mamluk

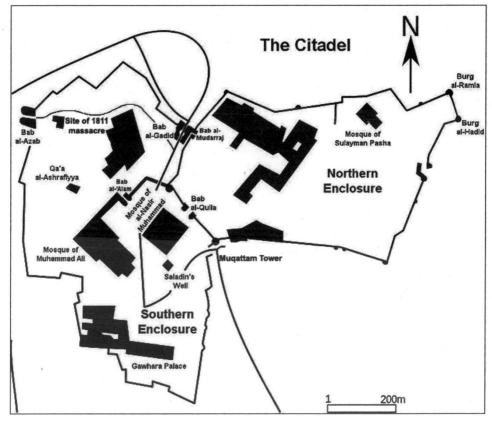

The Cairo Citadel. The layout of the unnamed buildings is speculative.

resistance. A few Mamluks escaped into the Sudan, carved out territory and lived on, replacing their numbers with Africans by the traditional system.

The massacre of 1811 ended six centuries of the Mamluks as a political and military force. Few mourned their passing – they had long been an unwanted anachronism.

Although most narratives on the Mamluks end with the 1811 massacre, the Mamluk institution survived a little longer. A few who sided with Muhammad Ali stayed on in Cairo. There were also some 2,000 boys who became the Pasha's property when he confiscated the Mamluks' belongings. He first used them as a personal bodyguard and later made them officer cadets.

Some other Mamluks may have joined Muhammad Ali when he campaigned in the Sudan in the 1820s.

The mamluk system continued for as long as there was slavery in Egypt. It was still an effective method of building loyal followings. It appears that the Ottoman prohibition did not stop people raising mamluks in the long-established way, either. Edward Lane, an English orientalist writing late in Muhammad Ali's reign, said that only Turks living in Egypt could afford to keep mamluks. There must have been others, as many people kept slaves, and mamluks are still mentioned in the sources.

As before, inheritance often passed from master to ex-slave. A wealthy man's mamluk might practically take his place on his death, marrying his widow and raising his children, but could not inherit any position of authority. Some mamluks would go into the army, but their chances of advancement depended on their own prowess rather than their former masters' patronage. The army had many mamluks, but they were no longer as conspicuous.

There was also a curious echo of previous times in July 1854, when Abbas Pasha, grandson of Muhammad Ali, was murdered by his own mamluks. Two versions of this event exist. In the first the two concerned, Umar Wasfi and Shahin Husein, were punished for taunting the Pasha's favourite mamluk, Khalil Dervish Bey, and allowed assassins into the bedchamber while on guard, even preventing Abbas from escaping. The other story says that Umar and Shahin were agents of Abbas' aunt and, in order to get close enough to kill him, sold themselves into his service. This shows the continuing practice of using mamluks in intimate service, and how volatile this institution could still be.

There were Circassians in the slave markets of Cairo again in the mid-to-late nineteenth century. The Tsars of Russia were conducting campaigns to subdue the Caucasus, and many were enslaved as an indirect consequence. The Khedive Ismail, also of Muhammad Ali's line, bought many Circassian slaves. But the institution of slavery itself came under attack in the 1870s.

British and French influence had been increasing in Egypt since the Suez Canal opened, especially when the British took over control of Egypt's finances as a result of the Khedive's extravagance. In 1877 some Egyptians began campaigning for the abolition of slavery, although it took until 1895 before they succeeded completely. The slave trade soon ended, although there were still many mamluks when supplies dried up. The British occupation put an end to the mamluk system.

In 1881 Urabi Pasha, the Egyptian nationalist leader who had been appointed minister for war in response to anti-European sentiment, ordered that all Mamluks be expelled from the army. His reasons are not clear, but it may have been to do with historical connotations for they were no longer a definite grouping. This was the last-ever mention of Mamluks in any official capacity. The order was never carried out, for the following year the British once again invaded Egypt, this time to stay. As a feature of the occupation the Egyptian army was disbanded, the Mamluks in it losing what little they had retained after 1811. Now unable to perpetuate themselves, this military class was reduced to a last generation, deprived of their means, left to die out.

What became of the last Mamluks? This Sir Edwin Muir, who wrote the first English study of the Mamluk dynasty, felt the need to discover. In 1895 he wrote to his informant Yacub Artin Pasha in Cairo and was told of their loss of livelihood after the army was disbanded. He was also told that 'a great number of the Mamelukes, however, are still living, and have posts in the public service'.

Such positions probably included those of provincial officials, tax collectors and policemen – quasi-military posts Mamluks had traditionally held other than service in the army. Living in virtual obscurity, many of the last Mamluks at least had employment under British occupation. It is reasonable to assume that there were men living early in the twentieth century who had once been mamluks, perhaps even in independent Egypt after 1922.

What exactly did the Mamluks achieve? What was their distinctive character? Did they merit better coverage in historical writing than they received? It would stretch a point to present the Mamluk sultanate as a stabilising and well-ordered influence, but without them the region would have been reduced to a wilderness from which it would not have recovered for ages.

There is a distinction, although not always a clear one, between the mamluk system as a method of promoting loyalties and raising followings, and the Mamluk class who rose to rule Egypt and Syria. Concerning the former, it could be said that the mamluk system was in existence long before the Mamluks came to power and continued a while afterwards, only ending with slavery in Egypt itself.

The true value of this system has been questioned, and it certainly had its limitations. Loyalties between fellow mamluks may have been a stabilising influence but could be forgotten very easily where personal ambition was involved. Mamluk loyalty towards their patrons generally held true, and while there are instances of this trust being violated such cases were viewed with shock. Gratitude on being freed alone cannot be expected to ensure lifelong devotion; a freed mamluk would still rely upon his patron for material support and further advancement, and otherwise he had no other means. Mamluks were often greedy and self-seeking, and there was always an element of self-interest. Nevertheless, the system continued because it worked. It lasted for a thousand years, and its transgressors did not discredit the practice as a whole. Compared to dynasties in which family loyalties formed the basis for relationships, the mamluk system proved more stable.

This book has been chiefly concerned with one continuous line of mamluks, perpetuating itself from those bought by as-Salih Ayyub to the last generation murdered by Muhammad Ali's soldiers in 1811. For 267 years, this homogenous grouping ruled over Egypt and Syria and controlled Egypt intermittently for long after under the Ottomans.

The Islamic world in the period between the Crusades and the Ottoman explosion has been given scant attention. Medieval Islam had much to contribute to the world but suffered a serious blow when the Mongols turned Iran and Iraq into a wilderness and reduced Baghdad to rubble. The Ottoman impact on Europe was different in its character, bringing an aggressive and less substantial version of Islam into comparatively modern times.

To the Mamluks' major credit was their achievement in halting the westward expansion of the Mongols. To look at Islamic civilisation and its artistic, scientific and architectural advances, and to see all these in Iraq and Iran destroyed and its people slaughtered can only prompt the conclusion that the Mongols at that time were a destructive force that did harm to humanity. The Mamluks' victory in 1260 owed much to reduced Mongol numbers; when Hulagu withdrew most of his forces while he raced to Karakorum he missed a crucial window and allowed the Mamluks to defeat his remainder. Ain Jalut proclaimed the Mamluks as the victors and protectors over Islam, and the Mamluk defence of Syria kept the Mongols beyond the Euphrates until the Ilkhanate collapsed three generations later. In contrast with the virtual wasteland that Iran and Iraq had become, Islamic society flourished under the Mamluks. The civilisation had lost most of its creative drive by the thirteenth century, but its level of learning was maintained, and could at least continue until further advances in knowledge and the arts could be made. It is the West's loss that Ibn Khaldun's philosophy was not discovered until comparatively recently, for the discipline of history could have advanced much earlier.

When Baibars and his successors destroyed the Frankish states they put an end to the eroded remnants of the European settlements created in the previous century. There was little left of them, but they were a danger as a landing place for new crusades and possible Frankish alliances with the Mongols, and this hastened their demise. There was no lack of crusading zeal in Europe (even if it did not always turn into actual crusades), but

Mamluk vigilance made sure that no crusaders settled in Syria again. The Mamluks can be commended for frustrating further European aggression.

The decline in prestige coincides with the end of the Mongol threat. With their principal role gone, the Mamluks had outlived their purpose. A Mamluk's humble origins as a child in inhospitable regions and then as the personal slave of someone else may have produced able and ambitious warriors, but it perhaps also taught them many negative traits. The typical behaviour of Mamluks shows a greedy, cruel, treacherous and self-centred disposition. It is to their discredit that they were at times only marginally better rulers than the Mongols, that their behaviour caused the native populations such suffering and that their ambitions continually disrupted government. But the same could be said of many contemporary rulers. Atrocities in the Mongol empire were often much worse and more senseless. Public executions and carnage were commonplace in Europe, and treachery is universal. The Mamluks succeeded in playing these terrible games much better than anyone else, and individuals often reached the top by becoming the most successful players.

Not all Mamluks behaved in the same manner. Some gave generously, as fervent Muslims, for the good of the poor. Many were popular for this, even though they might act as ruthlessly as their fellows in the sphere of politics. Possibly the best way to remember the Mamluks is in these pious works, and the resulting buildings. Like many oppressive tyrants this world has known, from Ramesses II to Hitler, the Mamluks left some of the world's most impressive buildings. There is much of beauty left from the Mamluk sultanate, and it was their wealth that financed it. Even now it is difficult to visit the medieval quarter of Cairo without encountering such fascinating works of architecture, which are an indisputable part of the Islamic landscape. It is also difficult to imagine the Muslim world without al-Azhar, an important centre of religious learning. Although instituted as a Sunni religious centre by Saladin, Baibars and his successors raised it from dilapidation and saw it flourish.

From a promising beginning in 1260. The Mamluks reached their zenith under an-Nasir Muhammad but their story afterward was far from encouraging. It is remarkable that the Mamluk corps lasted so long, and even in the nineteenth century they were still in action, having long outlasted their *raison d'etre*. The world may have been a better place for the departure of the Mamluks, but they left something of value.

Appendix 1

EXPLANATORY NOTES

Writing conventions used in this book may not always coincide with those used in others of this kind. The intention has always been to present the material in a format that is as easy to read as possible, and the book is written with those in mind who may not be knowledgeable in Islamic history.

However, in order to correlate this book with others, the following explanations are given.

I: Concerning Chronology

All dates given in the text are based on the 'Common' dating used in the West, i.e. the Christian chronology and calendar. Muslim dating is calculated from the Hijra, or Emigration of the Prophet from Mecca to Medina in AD 622. Accordingly, the year AD 1250 is also given as 648 AH or 648 Hijra.

In addition, the Islamic year begins with the Hajj, or Pilgrimage, and is based on lunar months as given below:

1. Muharram
2. Safar

3. Rabi I
4. Rabi II
5. Jumada I
6. Jumada II
7. Rajab
8. Sha'ban
9. Ramadan
10. Shawwal
11. Dhu'l Qadr
12. Dhu'l Hijja

As the lunar calendar has 354 days in one year, the months begin at different times each year, and the festivals of the Hajj, Ramadan and Eid alter accordingly.

In Appendix II regnal dates in both chronologies are given, with the customary formula AH/AD (e.g. 648/1250, or 922/1517).

II: Concerning Transliteration
There are sounds in Arabic, Mongolian and Turkish that have no written equivalent in English, and all three were written at the time in different scripts.

Some books have used distinctive symbols to indicate these sounds. This book makes no attempt to illustrate the phonetics of these languages, but gives names as they are easiest to read. The reader should be aware that spelling of some names may be very different in other books.

No umlauts or unusual accents have been used in this book. The only concession to Arabic transliteration has been the glottal stop (') where needed. Even then, the traditional spelling of the name Qalawun (correctly spelled Qala'un) has been kept.

The following may be borne in mind:

In Arabic names the 'o' and 'u' represent the same sound, which is somewhere between the two.

The 'z' in 'Zahiri' and the 'd' in 'qadi' are the same sound, a pharyngeal fricative.

The 'h' in 'Muhammad' is a glottal fricative. Similarly, the 'q' sound is a uvular plosive.

In both Turkish and Mongolian vowels are similar to the German umlauted ones. They are often shown with umlauts, although not in this book.

The names given in this book are shown with their approximate pronunciation, in order to make the text more readable.

III: Concerning Names

Nomenclature can be confusing in Islamic history. Many could have a long, detailed name, and be referred to by a part of it. In some books, especially those written by Muslim authors, names could be different from those given here.

The people mentioned in the book are named as they would be best known to Western readers. The man we know as 'Saladin' could be referred to by Muslim writers as an-Nasir, as Salah-ad-Din or as Sultan Yusuf, or a combination of these elements. The book also speaks of 'Tamerlane' and not Timur-i-Lank. Discrepancies in spelling have already been discussed.

Although there were several Mamluk sultans of that name, an-Nasir Muhammad is the name given exclusively to the Qalawunid sultan who reigned between 1296 and 1341.

Below are some notes by which names can be understood.

i) Mamluk and Ayyubid sultans and various lesser princes took throne names. These described their natures as kings. Their titles began with *al-Malik-al-* and were followed by a traditional description. Thus *al-Malik-al-Ashraf* means 'the Noble King', *al-Malik-an-Nasir* 'the Victorious King', and so on.

ii) Members of the military class held an additional title, always a compound of 'of the Faith' (*ad-Din*). Salah-ad-Din is therefore 'Rectitude of the Faith', Sayf-ad-Din 'Sword of the Faith', and Rukn-ad-Din 'Pillar of the Faith'. As with throne names, such titles were often linked with particular personal names. An-Nasir went with Muhammad with all four sultans of that name, and both Sultan Baibars took Rukn-ad-Din among their titles.

iii) Those of Egyptian origin, the awlad-an-nas and the Mamluks after the Ottoman conquest had personal names traditional to Islam, such as Muhammad, Ali, Khalid and Ahmad.

The Mamluks, even in the Circassian period, had names of Turkish origin. These were either given or original names. Many were combinations of names of animals and other elements, such as colours and metals. No explanation has been found for this form of nomenclature. Thus Timurbugha means 'Iron Bull', Qutlubugha 'Lucky Bull', Aqtai 'White Colt', Qarasunqur 'Black Eagle', Baibars 'Lord Panther' and Barsbai reverses the same two elements.

The etymology of Qalawun has been given in chapter 4.

African slaves usually had names like Gawhar ('Jewel') or Miska ('Musk').

iv) It was common in Islam to refer to a man as the son of someone (patronymics). Hence the title *ibn*. Many of the awlad-an-nas were referred to in this way, such as Ibn Taghri Birdi. The full title of Ibn Iyas was Muhammad ibn Muhammad ibn Iyas. Similar to this was the title *umm*, or mother of, by which many women were known, such as Shajar-ad-Durr as Umm-Khalil. Mamluks did not usually have patronymics, as their fathers were not known in Egypt.

v) As there was often more than one Mamluk of the same name at any one time they were often known by a name of relationship (cognomen), usually as their master's mamluks. The mamluks of sultans, as has been shown in the narrative, took a cognomen based on the sultan's throne name. Thus in the early period the Salihis or Bahris, Zahiris and Mansuris were the mamluks of as-Salih Ayyub, az-Zahir Baibars and al-Mansur Qalawun respectively.

Other cognomens also appear. *Al-Khassiki, al-Jashnaki*r and so on show their former position in the sultan's service. The first Baibars inherited the title *al-Bunduqdari* from his first owner, and Aibak was often known as *at-Turkmanni* as his first owner was a Turcoman.

Appendix 2

THE RULING DYNASTIES

The Mamluks

The Bahri Sultans

648/1250 Al-Malikat-al-Muslimin Walidat al-Mansur, Umm-Khalil (Shajar ad-Durr)

648/1250 al-Mu'izz Izz-ad-Din Aibak as-Salihi at-Turkmanni al-Ashraf Musa ibn Ayyub (co-ruler until 1254)

655/1257 al-Mansur Nur-as-Din Ali ibn Aibak

657/1259 al-Muzaffar Sayf-ad-Din Qutuz

658/1260 az-Zahir Rukn-ad-Din Baibars I al-Bunduqdari

676/1277 as-Said Nasir-ad-Din Baraka Khan ibn Baibars

678/1280 al-Adil Badr-ad-Din Salamish ibn Baibars

678/1280 al-Mansur Sayf-ad-Din Qalawun al-Alfi as-Salihi al-Alai

689/1290 al-Ashraf Salah-ad-Din Khalil ibn Qalawun

693/1294 an-Nasir Nasir-ad-Din Muhammad I ibn Qalawun (first reign)

694/1295 al-Adil Zain-ad-Din Kitbogha al-Mansuri

696/1295 al-Mansur Husam-ad-Din Lajin al-Mansuri

698/1299 an-Nasir Nasir-ad-Din Muhammad I ibn Qalawun (second reign)

708/1309 al-Muzaffar Rukn-ad-Din Baibars II al-Jashnakir

709/1309 an-Nasir Nasir-ad-Din Muhammad I ibn Qalawun (third reign)

741/1340 al-Mansur Sayf-ad-Din Abu Bakr ibn an-Nasir

742/1341 al-Ashraf Ala-ad-Din Kujuk ibn an-Nasir

743/1342 an-Nasir Shir-ad-Din Ahmad ibn an-Nasir

743/1342 as-Salih Imad-ad-Din Ismail ibn an-Nasir

746/1345 al-Kamil Sayf-ad-Din Shaban I ibn an-Nasir

747/1347 al-Muzaffar Sayf-ad-Din Hajji I ibn an-Nasir

747/1347 an-Nasir Nasir-ad-Din Hasan ibn an-Nasir (first reign)

752/1351 as-Salih Salih-ad-Din Salih ibn an-Nasir

755/1354 an-Nasir Nasir-ad-Din Hasan ibn an-Nasir (second reign)

762/1361 al-Mansur Salah-ad-Din Muhammad II ibn Hajji

764/1363 al-Ashraf Nasir-ad-Din Shaban II ibn Husain

778/1376 al-Mansur Ala-ad-Din Ali ibn Shaban

781/1382 as-Salah Salah-ad-Din Hajji II ibn Shaban (first reign)

(784/1382 az-Zahir Barquq)

791/1389 al-Mansur Salah-ad-Din Hajji II ibn Shaban (second reign)

Note: Hajji changed his throne-name on becoming sultan a second time.

The Burji Sultans

784/1382 az-Zahir Sayf-ad-Din Barquq al-Yalbughawi (first reign)

(791/1389 al-Mansur Hajji)

792/1390 az-Zahir Sayf-ad-Din Barquq al-Yalbughawi (second reign)

801/1399 an-Nasir Nasir-ad-Din Faraj ibn Barquq (first reign)

808/1405 al-Mansur Izz-ad-Din Abdul Aziz ibn Barquq

808/1405 an-Nasir Nasir-ad-Din Faraj ibn Barquq (second reign)
815/1412 al-Adid al Musta'in billah (The Caliph)
815/1412 al-Mu'ayyad Sayf-ad-Din Shaikh al-Mahmudi
824/1421 al-Muzaffar Ahmad ibn Shaikh
824/1421 az-Zahir Sayf-ad-Din Tatar az-Zahiri
824/1421 as-Salih Nasir-ad-Din Muhammad III ibn Tatar
825/1422 al-Ashraf Saif-ad-Din Barsbai az-Zahiri
841/1437 al-Aziz Jamal-ad-Din Yusuf ibn Barsbai
842/1438 az-Zahir Saif-ad-Din Jaqmaq az-Zahiri (?)
857/1453 al-Mansur Fahr-ad-Din Uthman ibn Jaqmaq
857/1453 al-Ashraf Sayf-ad-Din Inal al-Alai
865/1461 al-Mu'ayyad Shihab-ad-Din Ahmad ibn Inal
865/1461 az-Zahir Sayf-ad-Din Khushqadam al-Mui'yadi
872/1467 az-Zahir Saif-ad-Din Yalbai al-Mui'yadi
872/1468 az-Zahir Timurbugha az-Zahiri
872/1468 al-Ashraf Saif-ad-Din Qait Bey az-Zahiri
901/1496 an-Nasir Muhammad IV ibn Qait Bey
903/1498 az-Zahir Qansuh ibn Qansuh al-Ashrafi
905/1500 al-Ashraf Janbulat ibn Yashbak al-Ashrafi
906/1501 al-Adil Sayf-ad-Din Tuman Bey I al-Ashrafi
906/1501 al-Ashraf Qansuh al-Ghuri al-Ashrafi
922/1516 al-Ashraf Tuman Bey II al-Ashrafi
The last reign ended 923/1517 with Ottoman conquest.

The Ayyubids
The Ayyubids take their name from Ayyub, governor of Baalbek under Nur-ad-Din and father of Saladin. Only the sultans are given here. For other branches see Bosworth and Zambaur (see Bibliography)

564/1169 an-Nasir Salah-ad-Din Yusuf ibn Ayyub (Saladin)
592/1193 al-Aziz
607/1208 al-Adil I (Saphadin)
617/1218 al-Kamil
635/1236 al-Adil II

637/1240 as-Salih Ayyub
647/1249 al-Muazzam Turan Shah
(648/1250 Shajar-ad-Durr
648/1250 al-Muizz Aibak co ruler with Musa)
648/1250 al-Ashraf Musa (deposed 1252)

The Abbasids

The Abbasids were the descendants of Abu-al-Abbas, uncle of the Prophet Muhammad, and of the Quraish tribe. In 127/749 the first Abbasid Caliph as-Saffah ascended after a military coup. He had thirty-four successors, living in and in the region of Baghdad. In 656/1258 the last of these, al-Musta'sim, was killed by Hulagu during the Mongol destruction of Baghdad. In 659/1261 the Mamluk sultan Baibars I installed al-Mustansir as Caliph in Cairo. There follows the sequence of shadow-Caliphs sponsored by the Mamluks.

659/1261 al-Mustansir
660/1261 al-Hakim I
701/1302 al-Mustakfi I
740/1340 al-Wathiq I
741/1341 al-Hakim II
753/1352 al-Mu'tadid I
763/1362 al-Mutawakkil I (first term)
779/1377 al-Mutasim (first term)
779/1377 al-Mutawakkil I (second term)
785/1383 al-Wathiq II
788/1386 al-Mutasim (second term)
791/1389 al-Mutawakkil I (third term)
808/1406 al-Musta'in (sultan 1412)
816/1414 al-Mu'tadid II
843/1441 al-Mustakfi II
855/1451 al-Qa'im
859/1455 al-Mustanjid
884/1479 al-Mutawakkil II

903/1497 al-Mustamsik (first term)
914/1508 al-Mutawakkil III (first term)
922/1516 al-Mustamsik (second term)
923/1517 al-Mutawakkil III (second term. Deposed by Ottoman sultan 926/1520)

The Mongols
The Great Khans (or Khaqans)
Descendants of Yesugay, khan of a Mongol tribe, and father of Temujin.

1206 Temujin, later Genghis Khan
1227 Ogodai
1241 Toregene (regent)
1241 Kuyuk
1249 Ogha Ghaimish (regent)
1251 Mangu
1260 Qubilai

After the death of Qubilai/Kubilai Khan in 1294 no further khaqans recognised throughout the western territories. Qubilai's descendants ruled China as the Yuan dynasty until 1368.

The Ilkhans of Persia
Hulagu was brother of both Mangu and Kubilai. The latter created him Ilkhan in 1260.

1260 Hulagu
1265 Abagha
1282 Tequdar (Sultan Ahmad)
1284 Arghun
1291 Gaykhatu
1295 Baydu
1295 Ghazan
1304 Oljaitu

1317 Abu Sa'id
1335 Arpa
1336 Musa

The Ilkhanate collapsed in the years following death of Abu Sa'id.

The Timurids
The Timurids descended from a lieutenant of Genghis Khan. Tamerlane's father was a governor in Transoxiana. Only the supreme rulers are given.
1370 Timur i Lank (Tamerlane)
1405 Khalil
1409 Shah Rukh
1447 Ulugh Bey
1449 Abd-al-Latif
1450 Abdallah Mirza
1451 Abu Sa'id
1494 Mahmud ibn Abu Sa'id

The Shaybanid conquest ended the line in 1500.

Appendix 3

GLOSSARY OF ARABIC, TURKISH AND MONGOL TERMS

Below are explanations of the Arabic (A), Turkish (T), and Mongol (M) and other unusual terms used in this book. As they come mostly from languages that use different alphabets, their spelling shows approximate pronunciations.

Amir (A) lit. 'prince, commander.' This term could either mean an officer in the Mamluk army, or the lord of a large domain. It very often meant both. See bey.

Atabak (T) lit. 'father-in-law.' The title given to a regent, army commander, deputy to the sultan, or one who is all of these. In the Mamluk period usually the head of the army.

Atabakkiya (A) The body of senior amirs.

Awlad-an-nas (A) lit. 'the sons of the people.' The sons of Mamluks.

Bey (T) lord, commander. Similar to Arabic Amir.

Beylerbeylerlik (T) A large administrative area of the Ottoman empire, such as Egypt after 1517.

Caliph (A, *al-khalifa*, 'the successor'). The titular head of the Muslim community, successor of the Prophet. See Chapter Eight.

Defterdar (T) The chief administrator, after the Ottoman conquest.

Dhimmi (A) A Christian, Jew or Zoroastrian, allowed to live and worship in a land ruled by Muslims, under apecified conditions.

Dirham (A) The smaller unit of currency. Originally twenty dirhams to the dinar, but fluctuated in the later period.

Dinar (A) The unit of currency in the Mamluk sultanate.

Faris (A) A common trooper, an ordinary Mamluk soldier.

Fellahin (A, sing. fellah) The peasants of Egypt.

Frank (A al-Faranji) The term the Muslims used when referring to European Christians.

Funduq (A) A commercial house, comprising both a trade centre and guest-house, often of a particular nation.

Halaqa (A) lit 'ring.' Previously the elite troops of the Ayyubids. Under the Mamluks the auxiliary forces called for specific campaigns.

Han (T) Tribal leader in earlier Turkish society.

Ilkhan (M) lit 'subordinate ruler.' Here, the title of the ruler over Mongol Iraq and Iran, as granted to Hulagu and his successors.

Imam (A)   (Sunni) The leader in prayer at the mosque, OR (Shi'ite) The divinely-inspired leader of all Islam.

Iqta (A) A fief. A land holding from which the Mamluks took their incomes.

Ismai'ili (A) Heterodox belief in Islam, that the descendants of Ali should be Caliph. See Shi'ite.

Itaqa (A) The document which gave a mamluk his freedom.

Iwan (A) A hall. In mosques the central area for prayer.

Jihad (A) The struggle, or Holy War. The drive to conquer new lands so that Islam may spread. Otherwise the war on non-Muslims.

Jizya (A) A poll-tax, levied against non-Muslims.

Julban (A) The mamluks of a reigning sultan, also called Mushtawarat (see qaranis).

Kaaba (A) The central booth draped with black cloth in Mecca. The object of the annual pilgrimage.

Kalauta (T) The triangular-shaped hat commonly worn by the earlier Mamluks.

Khan (T,M) A tribal ruler or despot, OR a traveller's inn; a caravanserai.

Khassikiya (A) The corps of pages. The sultan's intimate household service.

Khushdashin (A) A barrack-comrade. One who had been the mamluk of the same master.

Khutba (A) The recitation of the Friday prayers in the mosque, in the name of the Caliph and then the sultan.

Kiswa (A) The privilege of draping the Kaaba each year with the black and gold cloth. Awarded to Ayyubids and Mamluks.

Kizilbash (T 'red head,' or 'red hats'). A Shi'ite religious movement. See Chapter Twelve.

Kumiz (T) Fermented mare's milk. An alcoholic drink.

Madrasa (A) A form of mosque serving primarily as a religious school.

Mahmal (A) The practice of having the Pilgrimage to Mecca led by an empty litter or howdah, representing the Mamluk sultan.

Mamluk (A, *mamluk*, pl. *mamalik*) lit. 'one who is owned.' In this book a mamluk is taken to mean a freed slave-soldier. The term Mamluk, with a capital letter, refers to the military ruling class of mamluks.

Mawali (A sing Mawla). Freed slaves of the earlier Muslim period. A forerunner of the mamluk system.

Mu'allim (A) Title awarded to one showing noted skill in one military art.

Muhtasib (A) A market inspector. A civilian official in charge of commercial activities.

Mushtawarat (A) The mamluks of reigning sultan. Also called Julban.(see qaranis)

Mu'tazim (A) A tax-farmer. An appointed collector of revenues on behalf of a fief-holder.

Nilometer (A, *al-Miqyas*) The device on Roda Island where the flooding of the Nile is measured each year.

Pasha (T) A senior official of the Ottoman sultanate. Governor of Egypt after the Ottoman conquest.

Qa'im maqam (A) After the Ottoman conquest, the acting governor of Egypt, in the interim of a new pasha appointed from Constantinople.

Qaranis (A) The mamluks of a previous sultan, often dispossessed of their power and influence. (See Mushtawarat, Julban.)

Ra'isa (A) Political supremacy in Egypt after the Ottoman conquest.

Rawk (A) Periodic land survey and redistribution of fiefs. Best known was that carried out by an-Nasir Muhammad.

Ribat (A) A border fortress.

Sabil (A) A public drinking fountain. See Chapter Nine.

Sabil Kuttab (A) As above. A drinking fountain with an upper storey used as an elementary school.

Shaikh (A) lit 'old man.' Can mean the chief of a Bedouin tribe, a scholar in Islamic learning, the head of a Sufi order or can be a personal name, as in the later Mamluk sultan.

Shar'ia (A) The Islamic law code.

Shi'ite (A) lit 'party.' Heterodox persuasion in Islam. Traditionally those who supported claim of Ali and his descendants to the Caliphate after the civil wars in the seventh century. Shi'ites have different religious beliefs to orthodox Muslims. See Sunni.

Sufi (A) lit *Suf* 'wool.' Member of a mystical order in Islam.

Sultan (T) lit 'executive power.' Theoretically the deputy of the Caliph, from Seljuk times, and temporal ruler over all Islam. In practice the most powerful ruler of a large region, and claimant to supremacy.

Sunni (A) The orthodox persuasion of Islam. Traditionally from those who accepted the Umayyad Caliphate after the civil wars in the seventh century. See Shi'ite.

Tibaq (A, sing. Tabaqa) The training schools for the sultan's mamluks.

Ulema (A) The assembly of religious scholars in a Muslim Community. The ulema collectively interpret the teachings of Islam.

Wakf (A) A charitable foundation, instituted to use the income of a piece of land for the benefit of the poor.

Wali (A) A chief of police.

Wazir (A) A Vizier, a senior court official, or chief minister.

Yasa (M) The Mongol oral law-code.

Zar'iraja (A) 'occult science'. A pseudo-medical lore.

BIBLIOGRAPHY

Primary Sources

Ibn Battuta, *Travels* (trans. H. A. R. Gibb, Jerusalem, 1951)

Denon, Vivant, *Travels in Upper and Lower Egypt Vol I* (London, 1803)

Ibn al-Furat, *Tarikh ad-Duwal wa'l Muluk* (trans. U. & M.C. Lyons and J. Riley-Smith as *Ayyubids, Mamlukes and Crusaders*, W. Heffer and Sons, Cambridge, 1971)

Ibn Iyas, Muhammad, *Histoire des Mamlouks Circassians* (2 vols, trans. Gaston Weit, 1945)

Ibn Iyas, Muhammad, *Journal d'un bourgeois du Caire* (2 vols, trans. Gaston Weit, 1955)

Ibn Khaldun, *The Muqaddimah: an Introduction to History* (trans. Franz Rosenthal, Routledge and Kegan Paul, 1967)

Ibn Tagrhi Birdi, *Al-Nujum az-Zahira* (trans. William Popper as *History of Egypt, 1382-1469 AD*, University of California Press, 1954)

Joinville, Jean de, *The Life of Saint Louis* (in Joinville and Villardouin, *Chronicles of the Crusades*, trans. M. R. B. Shaw, Penguin Classics, 1963)

Lane, E. W., *Manners and Customs of the Modern Egyptians* (1836; East-West Publications edn, 1978)

al-Maqrizi, *Kitab as-Suluk li-Ma'rifat Duwal al-Muluk* (trans. M Quatremère as *Histoire des Sultans Mamlouks de l'Igypte*, Paris, 1845)

Secondary Sources: Books

Ashtor, E. A., *Social and Economic History of the Near East in the Middle Ages* (Collins, 1976)

Atiya, Aziz Suryal, *The Crusade in the Later Middle Ages* (Kraus Reprint Co., 1938)

Baring, Evelyn, Earl of Cromer, *Modern Egypt* (MacMillan & Co, 1908)

Borer, Mary Cathcart, *What became of the Mamelukes?* (Wheaton, 1969)

Bosworth, C. E., *The Islamic Dynasties* (Aldine Publishing Co., 1967)

Boxer, C. R., *The Portuguese Seaborne empire 1415-1825* (Hutchinson & Co., 1969)

Briggs, Martin Shaw, *Muhammadan Architecture in Egypt and Palestine* (1924)

Carri, Jean-Marie, *Voyageurs et écrivains francais en Egypte Tome I* (Cairo, 1932)

Darrag, Ahmad, *L'Egypte sous le règne de Barsbay 825-841/1422-1438* (Institut français de Damas, 1961)

Dodge, Bayard, *Al-Azhar: A Millennium of Muslim Learning* (Middle East Institute, 1978)

Dols, Michael, *The Black Death in the Middle East* (Princeton University, 1977)

Dunlop, D. M., *Arab Civilisation to AD 1500* (Longman Group and Libraries du Liban, 1971)

Flower, Raymond, *Napoleon to Nasser: The Story of Modern Egypt* (Compton Press, 1972)

Fortescue, Adrian, *The Lesser Eastern Churches* (1913)

Gabrieli, Francesco, *Storici Arabi delle Crociate* (1957)

Ghorbal, Shafiq, *The Beginnings of the Eastern Question and the rise of Mehemet Ali* (Routledge, 1928)

Gibb, H. A. R., *The Armies of Saladin* (Princeton University, 1962)

Gibb, H. A. R., *Arabic Literature: An Introduction* (Oxford University, 1962)

Glubb, Sir John, *Soldiers of Fortune. The History of the Mamlukes* (Hodder and Stoughton, 1973)

Gaudefroye-Desmombynes, M., *La Syrie a l'époque des Mamlouks d'après les auteurs arabes* (1923)

Hajji, Hayat, *The Internal affairs of Egypt during the third reign of an-Nasir Muhammad ibn Nasser al-Qalawun 709-741/1309-1341* (1978)

Haldane, Duncan, *Mamluk Painting* (Aris and Phillips, 1978)

Hitti, Philip K., *History of Syria* (Macmillan, 1951)

Hitti, Philip K., *A Short History of Lebanon* (Macmillan, 1965)

Hitti, Philip K., *History of the Arabs* (Macmillan, 1970)

Hodgson, Marshal, *The Venture of Islam. Vols II and III* (University of Chicago Press, 1974)

Holt, P. N. A., *Modern History of the Sudan* (Weidenfeld and Nicolson, 1961)

Holt, P. N. A., *Egypt and the Fertile Crescent 1516-1922* (Longmans, 1966)

Holt, P. N. A., *Capital Cities of Arab Islam* (University of Minnesota, 1973)

Holt, P. N. A., *The Age of the Crusades: The Near East from the eleventh century to 1517* (Longmans, 1986)

Daly, M. N., *From the coming of Islam to the present day* (Weidenfeld and Nicolson, 1979)

Inalçik, Halil, *The Ottoman empire* (Weidenfeld and Nicolson, 1973)

Irwin, Robert, *The Middle East in the Middle Ages: The Early Mamluk sultanate 1250-1382* (Croom Helm, 1986)

Kasbaris-Bricourt, Beatrice, *L'Odyssie Mamelouk: l'ombre des armees napoleniennes* (L'Harnattan, 1988)

Khowaiter, Abdul-Aziz, *Baibars the First. His Endeavours and Achievements* (Green Mountain Press, 1979)

Kuehnel, Ernst, *Die Kunst des Islam* (1962)

Lane-Poole, Stanley, *The Mohammedan Dynasties* (1893)

Lane-Poole, Stanley, *A History of Egypt in the Middle Ages* (Vol. 6, Methuen, 1901)

Lewis, Bernard, *The Assassins: A radical sect in Islam* (Weidenfeld and Nicolson, 1962)

Lloyd, Christopher, *The Nile Campaign* (David and Charles, 1973)

Marlow, John, *Anglo-Egyptian Relations 1800–1953* (Cresset Press, 1954)

Mayer, L. A., *Saracenic Heraldry* (1923)

Muir, Sir William, *The Mameluke or Slave Dynasty of Egypt* (1896)

Nadvi, Suleiman, *The Arab Navigation* (1966)

Papadopoulou, Alexandre, *Islam and Muslim Art* (trans R. E. Wolf, Thames and Hudson, 1980)

Popper, William, *Egypt and Syria under the Circassian Sultans* (University of California Press, 1957)

Poliak, A. N., *Feudalism in Egypt, Syria, Palestine and the Lebanon 1280-1900* (Porcupine Press, 1939)

Porter, Venetia, *Mediaeval Syrian Pottery: Raqqa Ware* (Ashmolean, 1981)

Prawdin, Michael, *Tchingis Khan und sein Erbe* (1938)

Rabie, Hassanein, *The Financial System of Egypt AH 564-741/ AD 1169-1341* (Oxford University Press, 1972)

Amitai-Preiss, Reuven, *Mongols and Mamluks: The Mamluk-Ilkhanid War, 1260–1281* (Cambridge University Press, 1995)

Rice, David, *Talbot Islamic Art* (Thames and Hudson, 1975)

Richmond, J. C. B., *Egypt 1798-1952* (Methuen & Co., 1977)

Russell, Dorothea, *Medieval Cairo* (Weidenfeld & Nicolson, 1962)

Stewart, Desmond, *Great Cairo: Mother of the World* (London, 1968)

Vatokiotis P. J., *The History of Egypt from Muhammad Ali to Sadat* (Weidenfeld and Nicolson, 1980)

Waddy, Charis, *Women in Muslim History* (Longmans Group, 1980)

Waterson, James, *The Knights of Islam: The Wars of the Mamluks* (Greenhill Books, 2007)

Wiet, Gaston, *Cairo, City of Art and Commerce* (University of Oklahoma, 1964)

Zambaur, Edward von, *Manuel de Généalogie et de Chronologie pour l'histoire de l'Islam* (1927)

Ziadeh, Nicol, *Urban Life in Syria under the early Mamluks* (American University of Beirut, 1953)

Secondary Sources – Articles

Ayalon, David, 'The Plague and its effects on the Mamluke Army', *Journal of the Royal Asiatic Society* (1946)

Ayalon, David, 'The Circassians in the Mamluk Army', *Journal of the American Oriental Society*, lxix (1949)

Ayalon, David, 'L'esclavage du mamlouk', *Oriental Notes and Studies*, 1 (1951)

Ayalon, David, 'Studies on the Structure of the Mamluk Army', *Bulletin of the School of Oriental and African Studies (BSOAS)*, 15 (1953)

Edbury, P. W., 'The Crusading Policy of King Peter I of Cyprus 1359-1369' in Holt, P. N. (ed.), *The Eastern Mediterranean Lands in the Period of the Crusades* (Aris and Phillips, 1977)

Flemming, B., 'Literary Activities in Mamluk Halls and Barracks' in Rosen-Ayalon, Myriam (ed.), *Studies in memory of Gaston Wiet* (University of Jerusalem, 1977)

Haldane, Duncan, 'Scenes of Everyday Life from Mamluk Miniatures' in Holt, P. N. (ed.), *The Eastern Mediterranean Lands in the Period of the Crusades* (Aris and Phillips, 1977)

Holt, P. N., 'The position and power of the Mamluke Sultan', *BSOAS*, 38 (1953)

Holt, P. N., 'The Structure of Government in the Mamluk sultanate' in Holt, P. N. (ed.), *The Eastern Mediterranean Lands in the Period of the Crusades* (Aris and Phillips, 1977)

Kurz, O., 'Mamluke Heraldry and Interpretation' in Rosen-Ayalon, Myriam (ed.), *Studies in memory of Gaston Wiet* (University of Jerusalem, 1977)

INDEX

Also available from Amberley Publishing

NAPOLEON'S INVASION OF EGYPT

AN EYEWITNESS HISTORY

JONATHAN NORTH

Available from all good bookshops or to order direct
Please call **01453–847–800**
www.amberley-books.com